Everything but the Squeal

Everything but
the Squeal

a year of pigging out
in northern Spain

John Barlow

W F HOWES LTD

This large print edition published in 2009 by
W F Howes Ltd
Unit 4, Rearsby Business Park, Gaddesby Lane,
Rearsby, Leicester LE7 4YH

1 3 5 7 9 10 8 6 4 2

First published in the United Kingdom in 2008
by Farrar, Straus and Giroux Ltd

A CIP catalogue record for this book is available
from the British Library

ISBN 978 1 40744 267 9

Typeset by Palimpsest Book Production Limited,
Grangemouth, Stirlingshire
Printed and bound in Great Britain
by MPG Books Ltd, Bodmin, Cornwall

FSC
Mixed Sources
Product group from well-managed
forests, controlled sources and
recycled wood or fiber
SA-COC-1565
www.fsc.org
© 1996 Forest Stewardship Council

CONTENTS

EVERYTHING BUT THE SQUEAL

January, and we're in Spain. But this is not the Spain most people know. The rain is incessant, it's freezing cold, and the wind sounds like a jet engine playing the bagpipes. We're driving slowly along the side of a broad, sweeping valley that stretches way into the distance, a crazy quilt of lush green pastureland, any greener and it wouldn't seem natural. Above us the steel grey sky is cram-packed with fast-moving rain clouds that spit and snarl down at us as we peer ahead. With that familiar sinking feeling, we realise we've been on this stretch of road before. We don't know where we are, the clock is ticking, and we're hungry.

Then, quite by chance, we find it. Pulling up at the side of the road, we sit for a moment and look out across the valley. Stone-built farms crop up here amid the potent grassy greens, but now, on a rainy lunchtime, there's no one in sight. And lunch is exactly why we're here. I dash out of the car and struggle to erect the stroller. A wheezing blast of wind slaps me hard in the face. *On purpose.* We're in Galicia, and it's time to eat.

3

We scurry across the road toward a large old tavern that stands right on the road's edge. There is no sign, no nameplate. Is it in fact the place we've been looking for? We've lost the directions, so we'll never really know. For a moment the thought depresses me. Yet this sense of doubt, of not knowing *for sure*, is a very Galician state of mind. In any case, it definitely looks *like* the place we thought we were looking for. We go in, already soaked.

Inside is an old rustic bar, probably the centre of local activity: social club, general store, domino school. The walls boast a few stuffed animal heads and one or two hunting rifles, as well as faded sepia photographs of a nearby monastery that we've just driven past twice in a state of mild confusion. A notice board carries snippets of parish news, and pinned there, right in the middle, is a small, computer-printed poster in vivid colours. A bristly face stares out at us: two glossy eyes, pert little snout, a real sweetheart. It's the kind of shot you might see on an animal welfare ad. XABARÍN! the poster announces in big red letters: WILD BOAR!

Boars are not uncommon in the remoter, wooded parts of Galicia, although their numbers are not huge. Perhaps the poster is part of an awareness-raising campaign, I tell myself, a scheme to help the native animal survive the incursion of modernity on its habitat. But I must be getting confused with campaigns to save the

4

Iberian lynx or the brown bears of the Pyrenees. Because as I read on, it becomes clear that the poster is in fact a warning: *Boars in the area!* Apart from the suggestion that you get your shotgun oiled and loaded, there are a number of useful tips on repelling the evil lettuce-munchers before they trample your market garden to bits. Sprinkling the ground with clippings of human hair, it suggests, will convince these extremely unsociable creatures to stay away. I imagine long queues at the village barbershop, the hair of local farmers getting shorter by the week as the siege of the boars intensifies; then their wives surrender to the scissors, followed by the old folk and the children, until the entire village is bald, but boar-free.

We turn to the bar itself. The proprietor dithers, almost avoiding our stare. He is not pleased to see us. Two parents and a sleeping baby in a stroller, all windswept and dishevelled and dripping onto the stone floor. Have we booked? No. He rubs his chin, and says that he'll see what he can do. But it does not look good. A wash of pure negativity overwhelms him. He shakes his head and seems pained and deflated on our behalf.

Galicians enjoy their negatives like no one else. There's nothing vindictive about it, and neither is it the act of refusal itself that they so enjoy. Rather, it's the indulgence in a sort of constitutional pessimism, an ever-present doubt, a looming complication, something that must be resolved.

5

Or not. Sometimes this seeming negativity might even be a sort of strange friendliness. A straightforward 'yes' is just too curt, too bland. A negation, on the other hand, is an invitation to explore the topic further, to muse, to ponder, to seek a solution, or to bemoan the lack of one. Here, in the rain-swept northwestern corner of Spain, 'no' has many shades of meaning. Straightforwardness is simply anathema to the Galician character. Meet a Galician halfway up the stairs, it is said, and he'll be unable to tell you which way he's going: *Well, that depends . . .* , he'll ruminate, dodging the affirmative as if it's a ball of shit flying straight at him. And trying to insist on a straight yes-no answer from a Galician is just asking for trouble. I know; I'm married to one.

The proprietor decides it is necessary for him to go talk with his wife. We really should have booked, he says as he slouches off, shaking his head and tugging on his saggy cardigan.

Making a reservation has never been strictly necessary in Galicia, especially in less formal places. Eating out, like much else, is a relaxed affair. You turn up, and you eat. However, things are changing. Restaurants of all kinds are booming, and this particular one, though by rights it's a *cantina*, a kind of rustic eatery, is full. There's a move in this part of Spain toward a greater appreciation of traditional cuisine. Not that the old dishes have ever gone out of fashion, but the rustic is becoming more and more valued, especially by city folk, a process that perhaps has something to do with a gradual rise in Galician nationalism. Food and nationhood are nowhere more closely related than in this small, soggy bit of the Iberian Peninsula.

The boss returns with his far bossier wife. She has a look of redoubtability to her, extra-thick-set in her kitchen apron, her eyes never showing the least sign of amiability when they flick over you. But it's all part of the act, the mentality of suspicion, that initial where-are-you-from glance, the same as you'll find in rural villages everywhere. Whenever I stop at a bar or a shop in some out-of-the-way place, and the person in question shows not the least sign of appreciating my friendly visitor smile, it kind of hurts. There I am, miles from the nearest cell phone signal, gallantly ignoring the smell of manure . . . and I can never understand why on earth these people do not give a toss that I have arrived, eager to take in their quaint ways, and are not immediately won over by my inanely deferent grin.

The redoubtable one reminds us that we haven't booked, making it sound like an illness that might get a lot worse before it gets better. She and her husband breathe long sighs, as if they're standing above the open grave of our dearly departed lunch. We plead silently with our eyes, knowing that we've done wrong: if this place is full, all the other *cantinas* in the area will be full too. She actually seems to suck in the air, chew on it, then let it

7

out again, shaking her head slowly. Were this Hollywood, I would simply draw a twenty-dollar bill from my wallet and tuck it into the man's palm with a knowing squeeze. But we are in Galicia, and I suspect that a deft bribe would be greeted with a scornful chuckle, but no table.

A reservations list is examined, and opinions are exchanged in low voices. In the stroller, Nico sleeps on, oblivious to the concern that his arrival has caused. I let Susana do the talking. She was born into this culture of pathological *uhm*ing and *ah*ing, and is capable of smothering the most insistently negative person with wave after wave of angelic patience. I have absolutely no doubt that she will get us a table. If you really want to eat somewhere but have no reservation – whether it's got three Michelin stars on the wall or spit and sawdust on the floor – take my wife along; she'll get you in. Considering that I myself am a very, very impatient food writer, I think I chose well.

As negotiations continue, I look around. The room where we are standing is spacious. It has a high ceiling and perhaps nine or ten tables. The bar itself is a long one, running the length of two of the walls. As our fate hangs in the balance, it strikes me that every single table is empty. It is just coming up to three o'clock, prime Spanish lunchtime. There is not one other person here. Yet it is full.

We are finally granted lunching rights, and reminded to book next time. It is only now, with relief and humility making me light-headed, that I detect something on the air. Below the musty-yet-fresh smell of a place where mud-encrusted boots are the accepted footwear (the stuffed animal heads no doubt add a backnote), a familiar aroma is wafting toward us, and it seems to be coming from a curtained doorway in the corner. A familiar smell, sweet and meaty, pungently savoury, a smell that, at its strongest, actually drapes itself across the membranes of your nostrils and *dares* you to inhale: hot hog. It is, in this case, the smell of a specific dish, pot-boiled pork with turnip greens. And we've driven all the way out here to eat it.

We are led through the curtains into an antechamber. To our surprise, we find seven or eight tables there occupied by people happily at lunch. Since becoming a *cantina*, it seems, the owners have fitted out a back room especially for the new class of customer: smarter chairs, curtains that match the tablecloths and napkins (a loud orange and yellow check), the well-scrubbed stone walls adding to the bucolic charm, unlike the old bar through the curtains, where they were just stone walls with a pleasant accumulation of grime. There are several pieces of colourful, primitivist artwork on the wall that may have been painted by the owner's niece. Lighting is not the regulation fluorescent strip, but rustic wooden candelabras with small, tasselled lampshades in orange and yellow, the same fabric as the tablecloths and napkins and curtains. The decor is *coordinated*, and I am beginning to dislike it.

So this is where we will be eating, well away from the bar, the characterful nexus of village life with its whiff of old boots and taxidermy. The bar owners think we're too good to sit in there and have lunch. As outsiders, we must cross the threshold into an unwanted show of modernity and sophistication, exactly what we did not want. And as we traverse the curtained Rubicon, I turn to see a farmer in his boots enter the old, musty place, prop himself up at the bar, and stick a cigarette between his lips. Back on the coordinated side it is clear in an instant that the other diners are not locals.

It's becoming harder and harder to slum it in Galicia. Everywhere is getting tablecloths. But what does one say? *Let me partake of your rude ways, bumpkin* . . . No, you accept what you find. Yet I like village life. I am from England, where much of the rural landscape is composed of neatly manicured, picture-postcard villages awash with gleaming BMWs and well-heeled commuters (the rural poor moved out years ago; no one knows where they went). In the United Kingdom fewer than 2 per cent of the population work on the land, and most of those in some form of intensive agro-production. The situation in the United States is similar. Galicia, by contrast, is a patchwork of small, low-intensity farms that, together with its fisheries

10

and forestry sectors, accounts for nearly half of the region's workforce. It is, in the words of the Galician novelist Manuel Rivas, 'the land of a million cows', real working countryside. Technically, the term *paisano* (peasant) carries no negative connotations here, although as with everything else, it depends on how you say it.

Even if you say it with a big smile, the average *paisano* generally doesn't want to be stuck in the past. It always comes as a surprise to me that those who live and work in the real countryside harbour a healthy ambivalence toward their own way of life. Pretty stone-built cottages? Sod that, they say. Give us a new house, concrete walls, aluminium window frames. As ugly as you like. Just make the damn thing warm and comfortable on the inside. Better still, make it in the city, away from the pigs. At the very least, make it right on a main road. Galicians do not set their ugly new houses back amid a couple of rolling green acres, they set them as close to the traffic as possible. *Feísmo* ('uglyism'), the building of ugly houses in the countryside, is a hot political issue here. Yet if you've spent all your life in a mud-stained village, and your family has for generations before that, sleeping right above the stables (to make use of the rising heat from the animals), kicking pig shit from your shoes as you tuck into a hunk of lard-smeared bread for breakfast, then the intrinsic beauty of the rural way of life must seem like a puzzle, a metropolitan joke.

We steer Nico into the chichi back room and park at an available table. Nearby a couple of men in baggy pullovers are deep into a pot of *caldo*, Galician broth made with pork bones, pork fat, a little meat, potatoes, chickpeas, and *grelos*. The word *grelos*, as is only right and proper for a native Galician plant, is a bit of a mystery, a little imprecise, with no straightforward translation into English. My dictionary says 'turnip tops', but *grelos* are not turnip tops, exactly; some people say 'turnip greens', which comes closer to the truth, while others say 'bitter cabbage' or 'Galician greens', which is just making names up for the fun of it. Everyone agrees that none of these translations is quite right, yet without doubt they are all perfect renderings of a very Galician word.

The broth sits on the table between the men, in a pot big enough for bathing a baby. It's a watery light brown soup with bits of the dark green *grelos* floating on top. It doesn't look very appetising. It looks, indeed, like what might run from an over-flowing drain after a downpour. Yet it tastes tremendous. And it sums up the tastes of Galician cooking, a sort of edible shorthand: the solid, meaty back-taste of bone stock; the rich but not overpowering notes of pork fat and skin; the lumps of potatoes that, if they are local, are relatively waxy and on the sweet side; the fragments of dark green *grelos*, bitter to the taste, without which *caldo* is just savoury swill. Galician food, it is sometimes said, is essentially the sum total of its ingredients:

there are few herbs and spices, no elaborate cooking techniques, and definitely no fancy chefs with their emulsion and their *assiettes*. It's all about what goes in the pot.

Caldo translates as 'stock' or 'juices', and is about as traditional as you can get. You can make it bespoke from the ingredients above, or it can be nothing more than the leftover cooking liquids from pork stew (see below). Either way, its distinctive flavours trigger strong emotions in the otherwise reserved and unflamboyant Galician character.

I met a research scientist down in Madrid recently. He was Galician, living just a few hundred miles south of his birthplace, yet in some ways a world away from the damp, stolid atmosphere that sets Galicia apart from the searingly dry plains of Castile, the sultry south, and all that other flamenco-and-castanet stuff you think of whenever you hear the word *España*. Our exile in Madrid (a city with thousands of restaurants) admitted making regular trips to local markets in search of pork bones and *grelos* for a pot of good old *caldo*. The same no doubt happens wherever Galician émigrés reside, from Buenos Aires to Brisbane. And it is while eating *caldo* that the lonely, far-flung Galician is most likely to suffer from *morriña*, a profound longing for the native land, a feeling that is said to be stronger and more complex than mere homesickness; 'home-yearning', perhaps, although many Galicians insist that there is simply

13

no adequate translation of *morriña*. Which makes it an even better Galician word than *grelos*.

Back in the *cantina's* high-end zone, the jerseyed men ladle helping after helping of *caldo* into their dishes and drink young white country wine that comes not in a bottle but an earthenware jug. Both of these men have beards. They are in their late thirties, and judging by the way their bellies push at their heavy woollen sweaters, they are accustomed to slow, leisurely lunches. They show all the signs of being *funcionarios* – state workers. They look like teachers to me, but they might be postal workers, or from some other state sector. You can tell *funcionarios* a mile off.

Being a state worker is a dream for many Galicians. It's the same right across Spain, historically a country of high unemployment and a shaky economy where the call of a government job – which is guaranteed for life – is strong. The Galician economy has always been among the weakest in Spain, so miserably weak that the tradition of emigration – to richer European countries, to South America, to the USA – has been a common feature of life for a century and a half. Thus, once a person passes the ferociously competitive public exam and becomes a *funcionario* – be it university professor or cleaner in a public building – it is like an invitation to eat and drink merrily forevermore. You see them hunting in packs, twelve, fifteen tenured tax office clerks out on a Tuesday night for wine and tapas; local government officials in town every

14

morning sipping their coffee with all the ease of those who know their jobs are safe forever, no matter how long they take over their *café con leche*. The men in the woollies are schoolteachers, I soon overhear. And they eat and drink like *funcionarios*, like there's no tomorrow, or, if there is, then it's not something *they* need to worry about.

Susana (who, incidentally, is both a Galician and a state worker) reminds me that we are supposed to be here for the purposes of research. It's true. I ought to mention this: over the course of this book I'll be travelling around Galicia, trying to see as much of this idiosyncratic and relatively unknown part of 'green Spain' as I can. In each place, I'll sample a different part of the pig, in a year-long pursuit of pure pork, the fattiest, juiciest, most unashamedly rustic of meats. Pork stands at the very centre of traditional Galician country cooking, a form of cooking that I fell in love with nearly twenty years ago: hearty, no-nonsense, ridiculously satisfying food, from a satisfyingly no-nonsense part of the world. My travels around Galicia will also include a challenge: to eat every part of the pig, in as many different places as possible. And they eat a lot of the pig here. Not much goes to waste. I might end up eating some parts more than once; others I most certainly won't. But by the end of our porco-graphical tour, rest assured that you will have read about everything the tasty animal has to offer. Everything but the squeal.

15

Our thoughts now turn to the menu. Susana comes from a family where choosing from the *carta* is expected to take at least an hour; anything less and you might as well just phone for a cheese pizza and have done with it. Of the family, Susana normally takes the least time to decide, *for she is a vegetarian*, a phrase that almost doesn't have a translation into Galician. She does eat fish, but even being a fish-eating vegetarian here, in the land of meat and potatoes, makes her about the strangest Galician imaginable, the object of pity and blind incomprehension. When she mentions her vegetarianism to other Galicians, especially the older ones, they screw up their faces and ask her whether she eats chicken. And it's not a joke. An allergy? they ask. Does she have an allergy? A stomach problem? What about rabbit? Can she eat rabbit, poor thing?

We briefly consider the *cantina's* menu, just for Susana's benefit. At the table next to us are a couple of young women, both of whom cast endless smiles at our slumbering baby. (Everyone in Spain smiles at babies.) Both of these girls are elegantly dressed and slightly fragile-looking, not quite undernourished, but on the skinny side. I could easily carry one under each arm if the occasion arose. After a little more eavesdropping, it turns out they are doctors at a public hospital (more state workers), so it is possible that they have a more balanced understanding of nutrition than I do. Whatever, they are certainly not

16

suffering from a lack of appetite. They have ordered *cocido*. The massive serving dish arrives, brought by the stern-faced proprietoress. Instinctively I take advantage of her presence and order the same thing, because I have not come all this way for anything else. If you're in a countryside restaurant in Galicia in January and you're not eating *cocido*, then there's something wrong with you. Such as vegetarianism.

The two men who have just slurped down a gallon of broth also order *cocido*. It's a chain reaction, a Galician wave of hand-raising and infectious nodding. At that moment a noisy retired couple bustle in through the curtains, rattling their walking sticks with menace, and actually bark their request for *cocido* across the room, just to make sure no one is left in any doubt. They are, it seems, regulars, and this gives them shouting rights. Not that in Galicia you need to worry about making a row. Just say things in a needlessly loud voice: you'll fit right in.

Cocido means 'cooked'. Like the name, it is simplicity itself. Take a pot the size of an immersion tank, add a few bucketfuls of water, toss in a sackful of potatoes, three or four yards of chorizo sausage, a bucket of chickpeas, plus several animals (chunked). Boil the whole thing up and let it simmer until next week. Then, around Thursday, you add your *grelos*.

In fact, *cocido* is a selection of slow-cooked, pot-boiled meats. Everything that was in the pot is served: whole chorizo sausages, potatoes, chick-peas, *grelos*, a slab of veal (for variety), plus a great deal of pig. The main attraction is *lacón*, the shoulder (foreleg) ham, but then there's belly, hock (ankle), snout, cheek, armpit . . . any piggy oddments that were to hand. A carnivore's Cockaigne on a plate. Traditionally, these would be all the parts of the animal that were preserved in salt when the pig was slaughtered during the onset of winter, and which could be used in stews throughout the winter, when there was nothing much else to eat.

To say *cocido* is unsophisticated is to miss the point. The combination of all the slow-slow cooking, the meat nudging up against bones and skin, the gradually dissolving pork fat, the paprika seeping out from the chorizo, and all of this ballasted by the potatoes and sharpened by the bitter *grelos* – reduced to stringy softness and oozing those meaty juices from the pot – makes *cocido* as satisfying an eating experience as it is possible to imagine. If you don't love it, you're insane. Or Susana, who orders monkfish.

More than the ingredients, though, *cocido* repre-sents absolutely everything I love about Galician food. Because on the one hand, it can be served decorously. In elegant restaurants you would get all this on a plate, in reasonable amounts, finely arranged, and none the worse for that. But here the platter comes charged with somewhere around three pounds of meat, and you can eat absolutely as much as you want. There is nothing at all that Galicians appreciate more than a healthy appetite. A combination of a rural culture that has evolved close to the land, plus a history of poverty and hardship, has produced a people who are animated by food, who adore eating, especially an old dish like cocido, which is often cooked for special occasions during the cold winter months. However, given that pigs are traditionally slaughtered in late November or early December, the run up to Carnival (literally 'meat time') in the early months of the new year is when by tradition this dish is cooked, with the *lacón* as centrepiece, which will have been kept salted since the slaughter and can now be soaked then slow-cooked to perfection. *Cocido* is the perfect way to begin a pork tour of Galicia, and that's why we're here today.

Next to us, the two skinny medics are wolfing it down. We cast furtive glances at the platter between them, which reduces slowly as they make their way through a staggering amount of food. The bearded jersey-wearers are making even greater headway, huddled over their plates, talking only intermittently now, and already halfway down a bottle of Rioja. For a moment I watch them with admiration. They have jobs for life, wine at a good price, and as much *cocido* as they can contrive to push into their straining abdomens. Is there, I ask, a greater form of contentment? For a fleet second I consider taking the *funcionario* exams.

We begin our own meal with fried squid. You can get fried squid rings all over Spain. They are one of the perennial items on menus along the northwest coast, nearly a thousand miles away from Galicia, where each summer millions of holiday makers from Britain, Germany, and the Netherlands feast on heavily battered squid rings that have been in the deep freeze since General Franco was in power (Franco was a Galician, by the way), and cooked in oil that's been in the deep fat fryer so long that your squid appears to have been dipped in a barrel of Brent crude. In Galicia, by contrast, people know about squid. It is here, after all, where much of Spain's seafood is landed. Galicia, it must be said, is not just a meat and potatoes place; its fish and seafood are magnificent. Our squid today is soft, possibly having been soaked in milk, and the creamy taste of the flesh is as beguiling as always.

However, I am eating merely out of greed and habit. I really do not want a starter, and I try not to take another piece, then another . . . By the end of the course I have tried not to take more than half of the considerable pile. You really don't want a starter before *cocido*. It's as if Paul Newman, in the hard-boiled-egg-eating scene in *Cool Hand Luke*, were to kick off with a nice plateful of dough balls and a garlic dip. I sit back, annoyed with myself, and adopt a position that I think will allow the squid to settle.

Nico, still fast asleep, is nine months old and has only just begun to get a taste for carrot mash, although I have high hopes for his meat-eating future. His mother, meanwhile, is having the fish. So only I will be lunching on *cocido* at our table, and I anticipate a smaller serving platter than at other tables. However, if the helping of pig that soon arrives does rest on a more modest serving vessel, then the difference is one of millimetres; I do not think the chef knows that I am facing this task alone. You tend to eat *cocido* in a group, so an individual portion might be rare, perhaps unheard of. Then again, most people are not married to fish-eating vegetarians *who do not even eat chicken*.

The platter of *cocido* is a magnificent sight. It's as if Pablo Picasso and Jackson Pollock polished off a bottle of cooking brandy then decided to rustle up a pork dinner. The platter is set down next to my starkly empty plate. I consider the sheer amount of animal matter before me, and take up cutlery.

A big hunk of boiled veal emerges from one side of the heap like a flying buttress, precariously shoring up a knuckly hock, its soft, stringy meat falling away from the bone. Somewhere underneath, I imagine, is a doorstep-sized wedge of shoulder ham (*lacón*) that will probably still have its skin on, although I can't actually see it yet. In some parts of the world the front leg is also known as the 'picnic shoulder', but what I have before

21

me is no picnic. Two chorizo sausages loll about at the edges of the pile. They are tremendously solid and tightly packed, and might in other circumstances form the substantial centrepiece of a main course. But here they are like the actors who carry the spears in *Julius Caesar*.

Chickpeas cluster around the base of the meat stack. They'll have been sitting in the juices of the pot so long that their buttery softness will have taken on an almost meaty character. I will come to the chickpeas toward the end, turning to them with relief, in the same way that you pop a lettuce leaf into your mouth after a particularly hefty steak; it's not that you want it, but the moment of freshness, the sensation of something light and delicate, makes a welcome change. When you're doing *cocido*, a forkful of meat-suffused chickpeas is the equivalent of salad.

Then there's a mound of large potatoes at one side, and draped over everything, in a style that can only be described as without any style, are the *grelos*, darkest green, still steaming, and giving all the appearance of having had the very last drop of life throttled out of them. Never have turnip greens been boiled so emphatically to death. None of their bitter, cabbagey taste, though, has gone to waste; it's all in the pot, part of the rich juices that have crept in and out of everything a thousand times over the course of the slow cooking.

The chorizos, I can now divulge, have a role somewhat greater than carrying spears. Small, thin slices can be combined with other meats, the fork-held combination then adorned with some potato, plus a stringy crown of *grelos* to cap it off. It is, perhaps, the only time that a chorizo is the lightest element in a meal. Equally, the sausage can add savoir to a mouthful of the less glamorous cuts from the pig, strands of brown meat pulled from the knuckle bone, perhaps, or a bit of wobbly, unidentifiable semifat, that stuff that is pink and sickly sweet and for which I think there is no name. For this latter, *grelos* are also useful. Incidentally, *grelos* combine perfectly with belly pork, and if you ever have doubts as to whether you really ought to be eating fatty old belly pork, try it with turnip greens, or the closest thing you've got, whatever they're called.

I eat fast, and before long I am breathing heavily. Yet my pile of *cocido* remains almost undiminished. More than once in my life I have had to go lie down after eating *cocido*, and on one of those occasions I seriously thought that something had burst inside me.

After a bit of exploration, I spy part of a porker's tail buried deep within the rest. It's the curly tip, like that twist-in-the-tail that children draw when they do a piggy picture. But its skin, a particularly insipid shade of off-white, is mottled and slightly pitted. I decide that today just isn't tail day, and push it under a thick layer of fat and skin recently shorn from the hunk of shoulder ham, as if I'm putting it to sleep beneath a nice thick duvet.

Eventually my hard work begins to show, as I make it down to the last pound of meat. The monkfish on Susana's plate is long gone, and she now stares across the table at me with that expression unique to vegetarians – part distaste, part incomprehension, part subconscious jealousy.

'You don't have to eat it all, you know,' she says, taking a sip of sparkling water, although I can tell that she's just a little bit impressed at the amount I've stomached already.

I pause, run a thumb across my damp forehead, grunt an acknowledgement, then get right back to it. There comes a point – of this I am convinced – when the pleasure of tasting food gives way to a more visceral, almost delirious delight in the physical act of eating, which is more or less the definition of gluttony, according to the Catholic Church. A friend who did the London marathon a couple of years back explained that the full-lunged, energising sensation of jogging is transformed, after about fifteen miles, into an almost primitive, instinctual feeling, the very act of driving your body through the remaining painful miles bringing with it a grim pleasure. She also said that around mile twenty-two she felt as if she'd taken heroin. Well, even Galician *cocido* won't do that for you. Nevertheless, it is your chance to indulge in one of the Seven Cardinal Sins without anyone looking disapprovingly at you. For that reason alone, you really should try stuffing yourself with pork until you almost pass out.

In the spirit of biblical self-discovery, then, I eat on, eventually making it down to the bulbs of meat that have worked free of their moorings long ago to become mere random nodules with no clear origin. By this stage I can almost hear my arteries seizing up in half-throttled throes of anguish. I placate them as best I can with gulps of a cold, slightly acidic Ribeiro white. My knife and fork work is slow and bumbling, and I know that the end must be near. My toil, though, has paid off, and the platter, once piled defiantly with meat, now comes to know defeat: I have won. All that's left: the duvet of *lacón* fat (which you actually have to be born here to savour), some of the strata of that mystifying gelatinous material for which there is no word, the hock bone (clean as a whistle), and the sleeping tail. The *grelos* are long gone, and where the chorizos stood with their spears, only bright juices remain, turning everything a festive scarlet.

I'm done. I can eat no more. Discarding my knife and fork as if they are suddenly too heavy to hold, I sit back and try to minimise the strain of my belly, which is now pushing up into my chest and feels like I've been pumped full of concrete.

Susana observes the platter intensely, examining it as though it has taken on a life of its own.

'The *whole* pig?' she says, emptying the last of the sparkling water into her glass, and smiling just a touch as she takes a sip.

'Everything but the squeal.'

She makes no reply.

WHY PIG?

Traditionally, pork is the staple meat of rural Galicia. It's a good, dependable food source. But dependable is the word. The pig does not evoke a sense of grandeur. It is an everyday sort of animal. And its meat is not generally considered to be glamorous or sexy. Think *sexy* meat and it's a big juicy fillet of beef winking up at you from the plate, next to it a decent bottle of Bordeaux. Think *healthy* meat, if you must, and it's a small portion of free-range chicken breast, served with a *lolla rossa* salad and a tumbler of ice cold Pellegrino. Whatever your criterion, there's always something outgunning pork for the top spot: *aristocratic* meat (venison, swan), *cruel* meat (dog, suckling anything), *underrated* (rabbit), *overrated* (veal), *fashionable* (ostrich), *unfashionable* (horse), *nauseating* (sheep's eyes), *enticingly surreal* (polecat chops).

Commercially speaking, pork is just plain unattractive, with all the marketing dollars going on franchised beef patties and reconstituted chicken scrapings. And when did you last order pork in a restaurant? Probably that time you didn't feel up for a steak, or when there was nothing interesting like pheasant or jugged hare to get you all dribbly; it's the menu's relief pitcher, down there in the bullpen with chicken à la king and the vegetarian option.

Pork is also much maligned for being high-chol and artery-choking, a food for fatties, for porkers; the world's best known pork chop fan is Homer Simpson. Then there's its reputation as carrier of the deadly pathogens, leading home cooks to cremate their pork steaks in the name of food safety. You know the situation: you inch up out of your seat until you're at a bashful crouch-stand, using your upper body weight to power downward with the blade of your knife on the oven-nuked slab of meat, dry and white and as impenetrable as marble.

Despite all this, when we think about the animal itself, something happens to us. Pigs make a connection; they affect us. Consider the toy farmyard of your childhood. Which animal did you imitate the most? Which one did you love, which one made your eyes light up when you saw one on TV, or in the flesh? It's not the cow (lumbering, docile), the sheep (courteous, decent, but generally unimaginative, an accountant of an animal), or the horse (too high-falutin'). It's the pig every time.

The pig was the first animal to be domesticated, some nine or ten thousand years ago, and perhaps over the ensuing millennia we've grown closer to this descendant of the wild boar than we like to think. Just look at how we imitate its oink. Normally, we use onomatopoeia to describe animal sounds. The sound of a buzzing honeybee, for example, is pretty much the same around the world: *bzz* (Finnish), *bzzz* (French), *bzzz* (Hungarian), *boon boon* (Japanese), *zhzh-zh* (Russian). Same with our friend the cow, who goes *ammuu* in Finnish, *meuh* in French, *mau mau* in Japanese, et cetera. When it comes to the pig's nasal snort, you'd think that every culture had its own different subspecies, each with a radically different oink apparatus. Thus: *n_ff* (Finnish), *groin groin* (French), *reuf-reuf* (Hungarian), *boo boo* (Japanese, where pigs apparently sound like bees), *hrgu-hrgu* (Russian), *kwik* (Polish). To cap it all, in Mandarin pigs go *hulu* and in Cantonese they say *god*.

These noises are not onomatopoeia. They're markers of our fondness for a grunty animal so close to us that we see a little of ourselves in him: the almost human-like pink hue to the skin, the penchant for potatoes, the amiable way he's got of going quietly about his business, like a deaf old uncle pottering in the garden, oblivious to those watching him.

In Orwell's *Animal Farm* pigs stand in place for man. The novel is about a pack of Bolshevik pigs that overthrow human rule, only to play out the (very human) tragedy of a fallen utopia. Why not sheep? Why did Orwell choose pigs? Did he see them as a naked analogue of ourselves? Is the

28

drama played out in Orwell's farmyard so powerful and moving precisely because we know how closely the pig resembles us?

Then there's the matter of transformation. In Homer's *Odyssey*, Circe turns the ship's crew into swine after tempting them to eat like, well, like pigs. So, they stuff their faces wildly, then become the very animal we associate with greed. It's as if such a transformation is a natural one, that we are separated from the porcine by the smallest of margins, and surrendering to our deepest, instinctive impulses can turn us instantly into our piglike true selves.

The roll call of pig comparisons with humans is a long and varied one. We call each other greedy pigs, fat pigs, lazy, smelly, and ugly pigs, untidy and dirty pigs. This reputation for being dirty is wholly undeserved, and when it comes to eating its own waste, the pig only does it when there's nothing else to hand. In any case, hens also slurp on their own droppings, yet no one's choking on their McNuggets or devising cruel metaphors. When they're starving, pigs will occasionally eat each other, but so do we when our airplanes crash in inhospitable places. As for rolling in their mess, pigs have no sweat glands, so their auto-scat is a very efficient form of temperature regulation. They prefer to roll in mud, but we tend to keep them in shit-strewn pens, so they have little choice. In any case, *you'd* roll around in the first effluent you came across if I ripped out your sweat glands and you had no other means of cooling down. Needs must, even for a pig.

Are we, perhaps, offloading some of our less desirable traits onto the poor animal, inventing for him a personality that merely combines the worst of our own traits? Hence, selfish drivers become road hogs (pigs, we must therefore assume, are selfish), and those perspiring heavily are said to be sweating like pigs, although pigs cannot sweat (or drive). We even call police officers pigs, a curious irony in that their job is essentially to prevent us from behaving 'like pigs'.

Despite all the bad press, then, it comes as a surprise to learn that pork is by far the most popular meat on the planet. About one hundred million tons are produced annually, in comparison to around sixty million tons of beef (including veal and buffalo). This is partly a result of the ease with which the odd pig can be kept in a normal domestic setting, especially in the countryside. China accounts for roughly half the world's annual pork output, indicative of a massive preference for pig production, although this might be on the point of changing, now that the People's Republic has embarked on a quest to provide all 1.3 billion of its citizens with one *jin* (about a pint) of cow's milk per day.

Over in the USA, beef is slightly in the lead, but Japan produces twice as much pork as beef, with Chile and Cuba returning comparable figures. The Germans do even better, putting out three and a half times as much pork. With their neighbours the Belgians it's four times, same as in Thailand. Poland hits a sweet six, Vietnam ten, Denmark nearly thirteen, and Papua New Guinea a frankly excessive twenty-one times as much pork. In Papua New Guinea, tribeswomen sometimes suckle piglets together with their babies, which seems as if it might explain the data here, although I have no idea how.

Rightly speaking, then, the pig is man's best food friend. And it's easy to see why. Cows gestate for nine months and give birth to one calf. This is great if you are making a substantial emotional investment in your animal; it gives you time to redecorate the spare barn and to start thinking about a college fund. If, on the other hand, you are already sharpening the carving knife when the animal is conceived, a nine-month time frame for a single beast is ridiculous. The pig gestates for four months and produces litters of about ten. A sliceable, diceable godsend.

Unlike most of the mammals we eat, the pig is not a ruminant. He has a digestive tract very much like a human's, suited to the same low-cellulose vegetable diet. The valves from pig hearts have been used to replace worn-out human ones for years, and if the transplant of full animal organs to humans ever gains medical and ethical acceptance, pigs are the likeliest donors. Our flesh is even said to taste somewhat porklike. In Polynesian and Maori culture human flesh is sometimes known as 'long pig', although when the

31

writer Paul Raffaele travelled into the heart of Indonesian New Guinea to meet members of the Korowai tribe, thought to be among the few peoples still practising cannibalism, they told him that it tastes more like the meat of a young cassowary, a bird similar to an ostrich. Pig or ostrich, I guess it's pretty much academic to us, either way. Unless our plane comes down somewhere awkward.

The pig traditionally snaffles up everything we don't want: cheese rinds, kitchen slops, stacks of returned love letters. A semi-domestic vacuum. And he enjoys a good forage, so you don't even need to put your scraps in a dish; just toss them out the window. Pigs are also great converters, turning about one-third of all the energy they ingest into more pig. That's a stellar conversion rate: sheep manage around 13 per cent and cows a miserable 7, presumably because they are too busy converting their cud into ozone-layer-destroying methane. (Take note, Al Gore: turn down your lights *and* eat less beef rump.) Then, after all that, you can slit your waste disposal unit's throat and eat him, every last bit of him, snooter to tooter. You can eat him at a fortnight old, or as a hoary teenager; he's easy. However you slice it, a pig is a tremendously efficient beast to have around.

The animal's main (perceived) defect, vis-à-vis the cow, is the absence of milk, a substance that humans do not need in the slightest. It's crazy.

Human beings don't produce enough enzymes to break down and metabolise the lactose in milk, and only in the West have we trained ourselves to tolerate cow's milk in large quantities. Elsewhere in the world, it has never been very popular, since all that undigested lactose ends up in the gut, feeding the bacteria there and leading to excess gas and bloating. (That'll be 1.3 billion new gassy Chinese citizens, then, not to mention several hundred million extra methane-pumping cows. Al, China needs you!) We do need mother's milk when we are very young, but that's *our* mother, not a two-ton Holstein-Friesian hooked up to a great big teat-sucking machine that keeps her lactating unnaturally her entire life.

Yet if the pig beats the flatulent, slow-growing, cream-dripping cow on so many counts, why do we diss the porker? Pork is the world's most proscribed meat, banned in both the Torah and the Quran. One theory that seeks to explain these prohibitions is deforestation. Pigs were kept for thousands of years in the Middle East, but as the region became drier and drier, this gradual loss of the pig's natural habitat made it increasingly impractical to keep the animal. Unlike ruminants, the pig does not thrive in semi-arid conditions, and the ban on pork in Leviticus may have been no more than sound practical advice; the pig eats what its master eats, not the kind of company you want to keep if food is likely to be scarce, on a forty-year trek in the wilderness, for example.

Later on, when Islam began its expansion through the Middle East, eventually reaching as far as the Bay of Bengal, Mohammed's ban on pork meat – the only food prohibition in the Quran – would have presented the peoples of these by now semi-arid regions with few problems; the sheep and, more to the point, the gloriously hardy and omnivorous goat, already reigned supreme.

No, the pig is made for cool, damp conditions, where tubers, root vegetables, and leafy greens abound. A place where there is lots of moist, cool shade. A damp, verdant place. Where it rains a lot.

Don Porco, welcome to Galicia.

EXALTATION OF THE SAUSAGE

We arrive early. Two braziers throw out massive plumes of smoke, and a crew of burly workmen in blue overalls plies the fires carefully with wood. Whenever the wind picks up, white clouds race about at ground level, chasing through our legs, filling our throats with tickly memories of childhood barbecues. More blue men appear. They carry large cardboard boxes, which are set down close to the braziers. Then they hang about, solemn and straight-faced, standing guard.

The braziers form one side of a rectangle, perhaps twenty feet by fifty, the other three sides made up of trestle tables covered in white paper. Farther back, along the edges of the town square, are sales kiosks. And now, as the chill of the morning is crisped up by strong but not very warming sunlight, women in overcoats are stocking their stalls with trays of freshly made *cañas* (cream horns), *orellas* (discs of deep-fried batter, shaped like big, floppy ears), *flores* (ditto, but flower-shaped), *rosquillas* (aniseed-flavoured biscuit-like rings), all the traditional sweet fancies of Galician feast days. Then there's dark home-produced honey in jars that still bear old labels for sweet-corn and asparagus; there is creamy white local cheese, almost oozy, the kind that has a whisper of acidity chasing its silky smoothness, and right next to it the trinkets of an itinerant faux-hippie artisan; farther off cheap slippers are piled up chaotically on a long table in a sort of rubber and nylon wasteland – find a matching pair, it's a game as well as a purchase opportunity.

Vila de Cruces, literally 'the town at the cross-roads', lies in the beautiful, sweeping Deza valley, in central Galicia. Carnival is not far away, and in Vila they've decided that a little limbering up is in order. They're having a sausage party, and this is where my mission to eat the whole pig starts in earnest.

Public festivals in Galicia have several distinct origins. First, there is the ancient tradition of *feiras*, local markets where local produce is sold and live-stock traded; these continue to this day in towns and villages, normally twice a month. Second, festivals have always been held on local saint days, and usually involve dancing and eating in addi-tion to the saintly stuff. Then there's Carnival itself, *Entroido* in Galician, literally 'entrance' or 'entering'.

More recently, local councils have started thinking up even more excuses for celebrations. And, this being Galicia, the best excuse is eating. Many places now have their own food-themed festivals (*festas gastronómicas*). Some are glorified versions of the original markets, centring on the sale of a locally produced product. Others are just eating extravaganzas. The town of Vilalba, for example, celebrates its home-produced capons, and Baiona has a honey and walnut gala; there's toasted chestnuts in Pontevedra, tripe stew in Vilanova, cockles in Foz. Two *grelos* festivals take place on the very same day later this month, one of which goes by the rather grand title Expo-Grelo, and I have counted six pancake parties in one place or another over the course of the year; there may be more. On it goes, *festas* for pig's ears, firewater, oysters, *caldo*, lamprey eels, cheese, wild mushrooms, octopus, giant potato omelettes, crayfish, cider, goose barnacles, sweet squid . . . We once attended a stewed pork knuckle festival in a place called Mos. Just how festive can you get about pork knuckle?

Today's sausageathon, the Exaltación do Chourizo – Exaltation of the Chorizo – has a nobler history than mere greed. For centuries an annual pig market was held in Vila de Cruces. Local farmers would come to sell their fattened hogs, gathering in front of the church before the fair to pray for good prices. The *feira* eventually dwindled and died, as the trade in pigs became more industrialised, forcing out small breeders. However, it has now been firmly restored to the calendar as a local tourist attraction, although these days the pigs arrive in a more convenient form: diced, spiced, and wrapped in their own intestines.

The chorizo feast here falls just before the pre-Lenten gluttony-fest of Carnival. It's a sort of head start for those who just can't wait, a pre-pre-Lenten knees-up. It's also the perfect way to exalt the lightly spiced, smoke-cured pork sausage that hangs in just about every kitchen in Galicia, and into which a large and varied amount of Don Porco is traditionally squeezed. Particularly the less desirable bits, you might think. But that's not really the case, because there are no less desirable bits on a Galician pig, as we shall see. What definitely is the case: after devouring a few good quality Galician chorizos I will be able to strike several parts of the pig from my to-eat list.

The braziers are now surrounded by blue-hued activity. The smoke drift intensifies, carrying splendidly greasy smells to all parts of the square as the dark little sausages drip their paprika-steeped fat onto the sizzling embers below. More and more of them are being taken from the cardboard boxes and laid out on big iron racks to roast.

We stand close by and watch the spectacle. I am drooling, whereas Susana's expression is blank and uninterested. To a vegetarian, the spitty hiss of the fat, the smoky aromas, the meat-suffused air that hangs about us like a pungent bacon cologne wafting on the breeze, none of this triggers anything inside her head. The prehistoric meat lust of her hunter-gatherer forebears has been completely expunged from her psyche. On the other hand, she would cleave you through the heart with a carving knife to get at a well-roasted eggplant.

I try to keep Nico close to the sausages for as long as I can, to make sure all those primordial triggers start triggering for the future. Quite simply, I do not want my firstborn ever to have to utter the words *I'll have the veggie option, please.*

We then wander over to the town hall steps and I ask for José Ramón, the mayor's secretary. I rang the council last week after hearing about the upcoming *exaltation,* and he's the guy I am supposed to meet to get some background on today's festivities. He's not there. With typical Galician imprecision, nobody involved in today's proceedings can even confirm that he's going to turn up.

Just off the main square is a stall doing a brisk trade in farming tools. There's a mix of people here today, mainly locals, including farmers from the surrounding district, people who might well have need of the scythes, axe heads, and cowbells on display. On the stall there's also an impressive selection of brutally uncomplicated knives with unvarnished wooden handles. What kind of murderer would use a knife with a bare wood handle? I ask myself. One who wants a good grip? One who doesn't care about blood stains or splinters? One with a penchant for doing things the old-fashioned way?

A little way up the street someone has parked a brand-new tractor, and a brand-new mini-tractor right next to it; they look like father and son out in their Sunday best. The machines appear to be for sale, although no vendor is about. He's probably breakfasting with José Ramón.

Farther on still and a man is hawking slippers in another chaotic pile, only his slippers are precisely one half the price of those down in the square, which just goes to show. Then there's a music stall blasting out *paso dobles* far too loud, and a man selling stout earthenware bottles in which to keep your *orujo*, the local grappa-style firewater. They are arranged on the bonnet and roof of his car, which from a distance looks as if it's covered in the pustules of a pretty nasty tropical disease. Like grappa, *orujo* is distilled from the residue of wine making, the seeds and skins, and it is illegal to make it without a license. This law, though, is actually a sort of inverse purity law. Everyone in Galicia buys illegal, homemade firewater direct from country folk. Legally produced stuff exists only in airport gift shops.

Several *churro* stands are already at work, making what seems like far too many of these deep-fried dough fingers. At one stall the *churros* are then dipped in an incredibly dark-looking chocolate: 'artery plugs', I think they're called. Meanwhile, a number of *pulpeiros* (octopus sellers) are bringing their big copper drums to the boil, the purple monsters inside bobbing and diving to the lively swell of the steaming water. One lady, who has her drum set up by the back doors of a white van, is tucking into a plateful of cephalopod as we pass. If this weren't sausage day I would be stopping off for an eight-legged breakfast myself.

If you like octopus, then you really need to come to Galicia. As close to a Galician's heart as pork, octopus (*pulpo* in Spanish, *polbo* in Galician) is *always* available here. You just can't have a festival of any kind without these big copper drums full of dancing *pulpo*. It matters not that we are currently at a chorizo festival; there simply must be octopus. Galicia is probably the only place in the world where you'll find octopus bars (*pulperías*) serving 'fair-style octopus' (in Spanish *pulpo a la feria*, in Galician *polbo áfeira*), one of Galicia's best-known gastronomic exports. The whole octopus is boiled for about an hour, then its tentacles are cut into small discs, arranged on a thick, wooden plate, drizzled with olive oil, and sprinkled with sea salt and paprika.

Octopus is fished off the coast here, but the reason for its popularity at festivals is that in the past they were dried, making them ideal for the long, slow transportation inland to Galicia's rural hinterland, where fresh fish and seafood almost never reached. These days it is frozen, and is one of the few foods that actually benefits from spending time in the deep freeze, becoming more tender. It's a challenging mouthful, at least the first time. Beneath the purple skin, covered in little round sucker pads,

41

is a layer of squishy, slippery fat that has a creamy presence in the mouth. Under that is the meat itself, white and robust, quite chewy, with a taste like fishy chicken, or chickeny fish (I can never decide). Some people, when they are bemoaning the cost of living, talk about the price of eggs; with Galicians it's the price of a plate of octopus that serves as a yardstick.

We return to the main square, still looking for the frustratingly elusive José Ramón.

'Do you really need to talk to him?' Susana asks, as she looks out across the square, now filling up with people, most of them standing close to the trestle tables, which are empty. 'Isn't it just going to be a lot of people eating chorizos?'

She's right. That's all it's going to be. But you can say that about anything. Joe Frazier versus Ali in 1971? Just two blokes hitting each other. The *Mona Lisa*? A painting of a girl with the toothache. Besides, today's festival perfectly illustrates the best way to draw a crowd in Galicia. You will need an awning, or trestle tables, or indeed any kind of place at which free food can be served. If you build it, they will come.

A gaggle of raucous teenage girls call us over to their stall. They have the wine bowl concession, a nice touch from the council, who will be providing free *vino* during the celebrations but will not be handing out drinking vessels of any kind. Hence, the local school kids get to sell small glazed pots for two euros, and that includes getting your name on the cup in permanent black marker pen. Funds go toward the school's summer trip, and judging by the size of the bowl-bearing crowds that are now congregating, this year it'll be fishing barracuda off the Madagascan coast. The girls, aware that the splendour of summer depends on their efforts, are haranguing passers-by shamelessly, bawling right across the square whenever they spy a bowl-less individual. We get a bowl and have it inscribed with Nico's name. Susana examines it, and – slipping effortlessly into language teacher mode – hands it right back to the girls, chiding them for spelling Nicolás without the accent.

With the fire in the braziers now settling down to a glow, and the square rapidly filling up, I make a last-ditch attempt to locate José Ramón for an interview, but instead find myself talking to Florentino Varela, today's master of ceremonies and de facto supremo of the festival. He's just finishing up a *carajillo*, black coffee spiked with *orujo*, and looks remarkably calm for someone in charge of a sausage party for a couple of thousand hungry souls. Despite the approaching chorizo hour, he lights up a cigarette and offers to give us an impromptu tour of the parts of the fair that we've missed. Strolling up past stalls selling clothes and leather goods, we turn onto a narrow, cobbled side street given over entirely to the pig. It is a magnificent sight: a line of some half-dozen covered kiosks are all selling pork, every bit imaginable, from salami-like sausages a foot and a half long and as thick as your arm, to hams and hocks, dry-cured loin, shoulders and ribs, sides of bacon, trotters, as well as *cachuchas* – the entire head, deboned and debrained, then dried until it looks like a great knobbly Frisbee with ears and a snout. The grinning *cachuchas* hang from the eves of the kiosks. Boiled pig head is highly desirable in Galicia, often eaten in tapa-sized chunks, or thrown into the *cocido* pot. As we watch, an aged *paisana* dressed all in black and no more than five feet tall is moving along the line, prodding the pork Frisbees overhead with her walking stick, as if she's playing some exotic mammalian marimba. Around Carnival time, the window displays of almost every butcher and delicatessen in Galicia will feature dried pig heads, many bearing comedy moustaches and glasses, or sporting knitted bobble hats and scarves in the colours of the local soccer team. Galicians are not cruel to animals, but neither are they sentimental.

The panoply of pork before us also includes a great many chorizos. Unlike most kinds of sausage, the chorizo is not simply a receptacle for all the bits of the animal too vile to use elsewhere. It will not contain any MRM, 'mechanically recovered meat', a sloppy paste that includes the matter that only a high-pressure suction machine can separate from an animal's bones. Even if it is mass produced, there will be no pulverised gristle and skin. The filling of a chorizo is very coarse grained.

44

If you use one in a stew, you might subsequently cut it open on your plate, and at that point you'll expect small pieces of meat to fall out, not congealed gristle sludge. Chorizos will not contain head meat or ears either, because these play their own part in Galician cooking, to which the pork-filled alley here in Vila de Cruces bears testimony.

What the chorizo does offer is diced off-cuts of meat. In his classic cookbook *Cocina Gallega* ('Galician Cooking'), the gourmet and intellectual Álvaro Cunqueiro (1911–81) suggests you use loin meat, one of the *noble* cuts from the animal, and considered the best. But less prized parts can be used, such as the 'spare rib roast' (aka the 'blade shoulder roast'), the fatty but fabulously succulent meat from the neck and shoulder area. Belly meat is also common, although in practice absolutely any off-cuts are allowed. Add plenty of finely chopped belly fat to the mix, then marinate in lots of *pimentón* (paprika), and perhaps crushed garlic and cloves. *Pimentón* comes in two varieties, made from either sweet red capsicums or from spicier peppers, in each case slow-roasted then dried and ground to a powder. Many chorizos contain both sweet *pimentón* plus a touch of hot, although producers generally do an in-your-face, all-hot sausage as well.

The *pimentón* gives the chorizo its powerful red hue and a deep, roasty backtaste. The light smoking that it normally undergoes adds yet more depth, making the chorizo your most versatile friend in the kitchen. Soft, fresh ones with a minimum of smoking and curing are used for cooking, and the darker, harder ones that have been left to cure until they look like hardy-sized bars of gnarled mahogany are for slicing and eating cold. Between the soft and the hard, the young and the old, these unassuming sausages crop up everywhere. On my first visit to Galicia, all those years ago, I sat in a cellar bar late one night drinking Rioja and eating slices of a moist, spicy chorizo and lumps of creamy, acidic cheese. I thought I'd died and gone to heaven. A chorizo can be sliced in a sandwich, used in meat or bean stews, as a flavour booster in any number of broths and soups, pan-fried with fried eggs and potatoes . . . I particularly like the way that boring old green lentils, cooked with onions and garlic, spring to life when you throw in a few chunks of chorizo. You can even add a bit to Galician red sauce (olive oil, paprika, garlic, onion, bay leaves, a dash of lemon), which is dribbled over poached fish – monkfish, hake, turbot – for extra depth and richness.

Making chorizos was traditionally done by the women of the village on slaughter day or soon after. The chopped, spiced meat mix – known as *zorza* – would be stuffed into the intestine skins of the same animal. And if there was any filling left over, it was fried and eaten just as it was. These days, a version of *zorza* figures on almost all tapas menus here.

The cry goes up. We scurry back to the square. The blue overalled men, now stationed inside the rectangle of tables, have started piling grilled chorizos onto plastic plates, which are then deposited at intervals along the tables, together with chunks of dense, chewy rye bread hacked from enormous country loaves by yet more blue men. Another man comes around handing out *filloas* (thin savoury pancakes made with pork stock instead of milk) as big as handkerchiefs. Then there are jugs of local red wine straight from the barrel. If you haven't bought a bowl from the girls, you've made a big mistake.

Eating begins. In theory, you take a chorizo with your fingers, still piping hot and dripping its deep red, smoke-suffused juice, pop it on a piece of bread, or wrap it in a pancake. And, voilà! With your bowl of wine in the other hand, off you go.

Galicians, though, are seasoned festival fighters. And the older they are, the harder they fight. Even before the chorizos start coming, every inch of the table is taken by granite-faced retirees. Behind them, five or six deep, the rest of us huddle and wait. When the plates arrive, those up front tuck in, remaining right where they are, one hand on their much sought after spot at the table, the other grabbing sausages. The rest of us try with little success to make progress toward the plates, just a few feet away from us yet miles off in the space-time-chorizo dimension. Within a matter of seconds the plates contain nothing but smears of dark

47

grease. The best I can do is make a lunge for some bread, but even that vanishes before I get my hand on it.

More plates arrive. The table hogs are noshing with stern, unhurried pleasure while those behind can (and must) wait. There is no passing back, no camaraderie, no sharing or ceding of one's front-line sausage rights: it's pig eat pig and damn the rest. As the serving men continue to make their deliveries, second and third lines push in closer, every single person (with the exception of me) taking the urgent intimacy of the crush with equanimity. Actually, it's not equanimity, there's a becalmed air of single-mindedness to the proceedings; when hot chorizo fumes are in the air, it seems, people simply do not notice that they are rubbing shoulders, chest, and rump with countless strangers.

Somewhere out in the deep, Susana and Nico wait. This morning I am providing for the whole family, and thus far I am failing completely; this is exactly what happened to the Neanderthals. 'Just a piece of bread,' she said to me as I prepared to dive into the throng. It was rather touching. I mean, she could have stayed at home and read the Sunday papers. Would you have come a hundred miles on a cold winter morning to stand about outside eating a hunk of rye bread amid hordes of discourteous golden agers?

The old people at the front begin shouting for more. *Here!* they cry. *You've forgotten us, here, here!*

48

They wave and gesticulate at the man who teeters toward them, a dozen plastic plates of chorizos balanced in his hands, one on top of the other. He sets a plate down near us. Arms dart out like crafty salamanders. The hot food disappears immediately. I am no nearer to a chorizo than this time yesterday.

By now the wine man has done a number of circuits, and finally, by tipping my upper body clean over a squat lady in a red coat to my immediate right and holding my arm out so far that my armpit caps the crown of her head, my wine bowl is filled.

Then a gap opens up. I sidle in, not getting quite as far as the table edge, but almost: I get a hand on it. There are no chorizos just now, so I tighten my grip on the table and wait. With my free hand I sample the wine, a robust local red, good tannin-laced stuff, about as cold as the morning, but it quickly warms my stomach through.

As I sip, a tall woman in an overcoat as thick as a carpet nudge-shoves me with her powerful body. I struggle to hold on to my wine, not quite believing what's happening. But I have to do my double takes from the second row, because that's where she's pushed me. Meanwhile, she herself has wriggled right up to the table edge, where she and the lady in red now munch away on hot chorizos. I've been utterly outflanked. The two of them have an entire plateful of sausages, which they have drawn right to the edge of the table.

They stand close over it, clucky and sharp eyed, like mother hens watching their brood. The plate has a pancake draped over it, and the ladies slip their hands (painted fingernails, flashy rings) under the pancake to extract juicy, gleaming sausages. People nearby cast jealous glances, but the ladies are not making eye contact with anyone at this point, and to be honest, we are all just a little bit impressed by their ruthless efficiency.

At last, I lose all inhibitions, windmilling through to the front and grabbing my first chorizo. It is gloriously pungent, smoked twice – in the smokehouse and then again over today's grill – and soft on the inside, a real youngie with a good, coarse grain. The hot grease, soaked up in bread, would be a meal on its own. At this point I understand the crush, because the struggle, in some ways, is part of the challenge: you *earn* your chorizo, and the achievement adds something to the flavour. The lion, I think, must experience something similar as he savours the still-warm flesh of the caribou. Emboldened almost to wildness, I seize a second sausage, leaning over whomever gets in my way and snatching the goodies from right under his or her nose. At some point I pass bread back to Susana, who can do nothing but nibble it and dream of eggplant *festas*. Nico, meanwhile, is going two-handed with a banana. At least it's shaped like a sausage.

At chorizo number six I relax. It's as hard getting out as it was getting in. I fight my way back through the crowd, and the three of us wander to a bench a little way from the fray, my last chorizo wrapped tight in a pancake, like a red-faced baby Jesus in savoury swaddling. Susana still has some bread, and Nico has the banana. It's his first *festa*, but our paediatrician has been stern about the chorizo. I can only agree; that table was no place for a youngster.

A woman of a certain age, in skintight jeans, an enormous shocking pink shawl, wraparound Ray Bans, and pink stilettos, totters past us. Balanced on her palm is a plastic plate full of chorizos straight from the table, plus a large quantity of bread, piled precariously high right on top of the sausages. *Hola*, she says, quite unabashed, as she pulls a plastic bag from her expensive-looking leather purse and tips the whole lot into the bag. Bright red oil trickles from the plate at the drip rate of a medium-severe nosebleed. She ties it up, and it goes right inside the designer purse. Off she goes.

A gypsy now makes his appearance, pushing what looks like a hot dog cart. On it, making a *putt-putt* sound, is a little gasoline-powered generator, and hooked up to the generator is a loudspeaker and a keyboard, one of those that plays its own rhythms, the kind that your neighbour gets for Christmas, turning your life into bossa nova hell. In this case, though, the music is upbeat and only slightly tinkly, an anaemic Shakira. His left hand sits crablike on the lower end of the keyboard, moving occasionally, as the ingenious keyboard does the rest. Then he pulls a trumpet out of nowhere, conjurer-style, adopts a boxer's stance, and places the instrument to his lips. The mariachi-cum-Herb Alpert effect is evocative, but also deafening, since the trumpet is hooked up to the speaker too.

This musical setup is common in Spain, especially at Christmas, when Gypsies play loud, loud keyboard music in the street with a goat at their side (no one seems to know why the goat comes along; it doesn't dance). Today there is no goat, but instead a young woman in extravagantly curly-toed snakeskin boots and a buttock-clenching skirt split up the thigh on one side. She sings along to the gas-powered organ. The temperature cannot be much above forty degrees, but she doesn't appear to be feeling the cold.

The gypsies move off, and for the rest of the morning they work the nearby streets. But what with the agitated lowing of the tumultuous, chorizo-gobbling masses up on the square, all that can be heard of the ambulant Gypsy performers is the plaintive strains of a lone trumpet. It all starts to feel as if we're in a Sergio Leone sausage western.

I finish off my last chorizo. They were excellent, really good quality, and smoked to perfection.

'*Lomo* and *aguja*,' I tell Susana, as we prepare to leave. Loin, plus shoulder and neck meat. I can cross them both off the list. I'm making good progress toward everything but the squeal.

Off we drive. And all I can think to say to my endlessly understanding vegetarian wife is, Thank you for being in my chorizo movie. Yours was never going to be more than a walk-on part. Tonight we'll have eggplant.

THE CASTLE AND THE
ENCHANTRESS

Have you ever been to Stratford-upon-Avon? This modest English town, birthplace of William Shakespeare, is a walk-around shrine to the Bard, heaving with day visitors all conscientiously *doing* England. They file reverently past the playwright's remains in Holy Trinity, said to be England's most visited parish church, before getting their tickets for *Hamlet* at the Royal Shakespeare Company, housed in a large riverside bunker that looks as if a five-year-old designed it out of cornflakes boxes but didn't quite know whether he had a theatre or a landlocked oil tanker in mind.

Shakespeare's birthplace, a nearby Tudor town house, serves as HQ for Operation William. After you purchase your postcards there, you can stroll along to Hall's Croft, where his daughter Susannah lived; thence to Nash's House, once owned by his granddaughter's first husband, and on to New Place next door, of which only a few bits of foundation stone remain, but they were all Bill's.

About a mile from Stratford is Anne Hathaway's

Cottage. Anne Hathaway married William after becoming pregnant (she was twenty-six, he eighteen). She moved to Stratford to live with Bill, where the arrival of their first child was closely followed by twins. At this point Bill dashed off to ply his trade on the London stage (in one brilliant career move avoiding triple-nappy duties). If you want to see the house that Shakespeare never lived in, it costs six quid. Stratford also has a butterfly farm, if you tire of Shakespearean stuff.

This kind of thing is not confined to Shakespeare. In the small Yorkshire village of Haworth, where the Brontë sisters lived quietly with their clergyman father while penning some of the greatest novels in the English language, there are road signs in Japanese. Walk down the stone-cobbled main street, which looks much as it did two centuries ago (minus the bloodstained phlegm of consumptives), and you can buy Brontë biscuits and gingerbread, Brontë fleeces, and Brontë flagstones (for your literary-themed driveway). You might then want to take refreshment at the Villette Coffee House (*Villette*, the novel by Charlotte they don't even force you to read at school), before stocking up on Brontë dish towels – just impossible to get in Osaka. The Brontë Hairdressing Salon salvages some local pride by refusing to call itself Jane Hair (at least two salons in neighbouring towns, though, are guilty), and the Brontë Balti House is there for all your literary-themed curry needs.

Dead writers are big business. So let's take our air-conditioned tour bus across to Spain, where Shakespeare's contemporary, Miguel de Cervantes, rules supreme. Cervantes is the father of the European novel, with *Don Quixote* again and again topping those 'best books ever written' polls, as well as being one of the few books on the list that people actually read for fun. He is box office. A towering literary figure. So when I journeyed to the rural municipality of Cervantes, in east Galicia's mountainous borderlands, it was with a certain sense of anticipation.

The great writer's family, it is said, originated in Cervantes. The author of *Don Quixote* a Galician? Who knew! The evidence is not conclusive: his surname is de Cervantes – 'from Cervantes' – and the Cervantes in Galicia is the only one on the Iberian Peninsula. Little, though, is known for certain about the man's ancestors. Then again, Anne Hathaway left her parents' cottage after Bill's Tudor rhythm method missed a beat, never to return; plenty of willing souls traipse a mile out of Stratford and cough up six quid to see the place anyway. At least Cervantes is *called* Cervantes.

Don Quixote is a book very much influenced by the events of 1492 and what followed. Apart from the discovery of the New World, it was the year in which the 'reconquest' of Spain was finally won, an eight-century battle to kick the Moors out of their strongholds in the south of the country.

In the same headline-grabbing year, the country's 'Catholic monarchs', Ferdinand and Isabella, expelled the Jews. From then on, Muslims and Jews could only remain if they converted to Catholicism.

By the time Cervantes was writing *Don Quixote*, a century later, Catholic Spain was gripped by the Inquisition, a religious court originally set up by Ferdinand and Isabella. It hunted down secret Jews and Muslims and forced them on pain of death to convert. (In fairness to the Inquisition, they burned Protestants as well.) The persecution of Jews and Muslims is where pork comes in, because what better way to escape the suspicion of the Inquisition than to eat the flesh of the pig? One theory goes so far as to claim that cured ham, loin, chorizos, and the myriad other pork products eaten in Spain became so popular precisely because the threat of the Inquisition made it prudent to openly demonstrate one's consumption of a meat proscribed in both the Jewish and Muslim faiths.

The character of Don Quixote himself may be a converted Jew (a *converso*). He steadfastly refuses to eat pork, while his squire Sancho Panza (the 'old Christian') stuffs his face with bacon and eggs. Indeed, Cervantes makes repeated reference to food as a cipher of secret religion; even the fictitious Moorish-Muslim author of the book (a literary game played by Cervantes) is called Benengeli, a pun on the Spanish *berenjena*, eggplant, at the time associated with both Jewish and Muslim cuisine.

The novel itself is cram packed with food: good food, bad food, feasting, fasting. And there's something gluttonous and tastelessly surreal about the way Cervantes writes about eating. Ever since I read his description of Camacho's wedding I've wondered whether a modern-day reconstruction might be possible:

> The first thing that offered itself up to Sancho's gaze was an entire heifer, spitted and roasting on an elm tree . . . there were six pots, each of which could have held a slaughter-house of meat; whole rams were swallowed up by the pots, disappearing without trace as if mere pigeons . . .

It could almost be one of the 'gigantic' cooking events that are still popular in Galician towns and villages, where they do *cocido* for five thousand in Dumpster-sized stew pots, or gigantic potato omelettes in specially engineered frying pans. The highly respected Galician chef José Rivera got his hometown of Padrón in the *Guinness Book of World Records* in 1990 for an omelette made with four and a half tons of potatoes and twenty thousand eggs; two small cranes were needed to flip it.

The wedding scene from *Don Quixote* could easily stand as an account of the Galician approach to eating. Because Galicians do tend to be, well, *larpeiros* (greedies). When someone here tells you about a fantastic place to eat, odds on they mean the portions are fantastically large.

> In the distended belly of the heifer a dozen small, soft suckling pigs had been sewn to add savour and tenderness. The various spices seemed to have been bought not by the pound but by the stone, and all lay in a large open chest. Thus, preparations for the wedding were rustic, but enough to feed an army.
>
> (*Don Quixote*, Part Two, Chapter XX; my translations)

Could Cervantes, then, be giving expression to his distant Galician inheritance, seasoning it with the kind of gross exaggeration that only he can achieve? Perhaps I'll find out in Cervantes.

One reason that explains why Galicia is so different from the rest of Spain is that for centuries it was geographically cut off from the plains of Castile by mountains. Os Ancares, part of this mountain frontier, in which the municipality of Cervantes can be found, is roughly sixty miles of breathtaking, high-altitude terrain abutting Galicia's eastern border, where heather purple peaks and hillside pasture give way to thick oak, birch, and hazel forests below. Little has been built here since before the invention of industrial concrete mixers, lending it the aspect of a rugged but fabulously majestic alpine paradise.

Winters in Os Ancares are long and cruel, and before the advent of asphalt, a fairly recent innovation in these parts, the terrain was all but impassable. People hardly ever left, surviving in tiny, isolated communities through a combination of small-scale agriculture and hunting. Not surprisingly, it was sparsely populated. Those who did manage to leave seldom went back.

My trip here today has two purposes. First, to see the village of Cervantes, and second, to meet a lady called Doña Marisol, of whom I have great expectations.

But to begin at the beginning. I lay one morning in the treatment chair of my mother-in-law's chiropidist as he chipped callused skin from my feet with a scalpel and told me to wear better shoes. Some of the chippings fell into the cuffs of his trousers. (The dry cleaners, I thought. What do they *make* of it?) As he chiselled at my heels we chatted. I mentioned the book I was planning.

'Eating pork!' he exclaimed, the scalpel suddenly immobile in midair. 'Pork! You've got to go talk to Doña Marisol!'

I was not in a position to argue.

He called for his secretary and got her to bring him a slip of paper. *Doña Marisol, Doiras,* he wrote. No surname, no telephone number.

'Just go to Doiras and look for the white building,' he said, still brandishing the scalpel with irresistible conviction. 'Doña Marisol's place. She knows all about Os Ancares. It's real eating country. Real pig country. Doña Marisol will put you right.'

Thus it is that today, on a bracing February morning, I shout the foot doctor's praise as I pull off the motorway and enter the foothills of the glorious Os Ancares mountain range, where unbeknownst to me I am about to have what must rank as one of the worst meals of my life.

The sun is dazzlingly bright, and I wind my way along a valley bottom, following the course of a gently moving river as it makes its way between some pretty impressive purple mountains, tipped with pure white. Light dances off the crystal clear water; trees seem to be hunched up, brown and denuded, but ready to leap up and dance when spring arrives. I feel incredibly fresh and alive, and roll down the window to take in a big lungful of life. It's cold.

The road climbs a little. On a corner I pass an old man in a black Galician beret (just like a French one). He stands in the front yard of his house, a couple of scrawny Alsatian-like mongrels lurking at his heels, and watches me go. His abode is sprawling and ramshackle, piles of firewood everywhere, the whole place like an abandoned junkyard. I almost stop to take a photo. But there's something in his stare, something that leads me to think that I would not be the first. He also has that shotgun-owner look.

On I go, and before long I see a tractor up ahead, parked on the road. It is just about old enough to be in a farming museum, and stands adjacent to a large building with stable doors that give onto the road. The doors are wide open, and a stout woman in a blue apron is there alone, bent over a plastic bucket, stirring with a stick. I slow down to pass. The bucket is full of a dark liquid. Steam rises as she stirs. She doesn't look up.

Half a mile on and I see a wolf emerge from the side of the road. It might be another mongrel, but the white on its forelegs and the curious nobility of its demeanour say *lupus*. A thought occurs to me: real country has real wild animals in it. If I bring Nico here walking in a few years' time, and if a wolf shows up, what the hell am I supposed to do? Snarl? Wave a stick? As for bears, the last native Galician bear is said to have been shot and killed in 1946 (I ask myself how and why this date was recorded), but recently they have begun to stray back here from the forests of Asturias, the neighbouring region to the northeast, green and rural, just like Galicia. In one recent case a bear greedily trashed honey hives in the village of Quiroga and became something of a local celebrity. Quiroga is only forty miles away. Wolves, bears . . . It's all a big scary safari park to me. I'm going to have to read up about all this on the Internet before my son develops a taste for the outdoors.

I drive on. Road signs are not much in evidence. Then I spot the square-tooth battlements of a medieval castle breaking through the blue grey mist that fills the valley before me. The castle seems to hover in the air, evocatively unreal and not quite congruent, dwarfing the trees at its feet. Doiras Castle is set high on a hill just big enough for the purpose, and as medieval castles go it is well proportioned and rather attractive, with an eerie look of quiet impenetrability. The author of *Don Quixote*, it is said, had his origins in the noble family who built the place.

The possibilities for literary tourism here are plainly immense. The castle not only dates back to the Cervantes family, but Doiras village itself is in the municipality of Cervantes. It could hardly be better. Just imagine it: the Don Quixote Experience, with computer-simulated tilting at windmills for the teens and rides on Sancho Panza's donkey for the kiddies, a hotel and cultural centre next door, with ten acres of forest cleared for parking. In the real Doiras, however, there is just the castle. No sign announces its significance, although apparently you can scramble up the hill and take a look if you like.

The village itself is no more than a fork in the road. There is a bar, and on the other side of the road, a little way up, a white *hostal*. That must be Doña Marisol's place. However, I nip over to the bar for a quick coffee first. Inside, a group of ladies of varying ages are talking in loud

Galician, which is still the mother tongue of a sizable percentage of Galicians, especially those living in the countryside.

The Galician language is emphatically not Spanish. It shares its roots with Portuguese, and in the Middle Ages was also the language of love poetry and of troubadours right across the Peninsula. As Portugal and the old kingdom of Galicia separated politically, Galician and Portuguese began to develop into two distinct though closely related languages; speakers of Portuguese and Galician today can usually understand each other.

In the fifteenth century, Galicia was annexed by Ferdinand and Isabella's kingdom of Castile and León (what would become Spain). Thus began the dark ages for the Galician language, with the arrival of a Spanish-speaking nobility in the region. For almost four hundred years Galician was hardly ever written down; it was relegated to the countryside, the language of illiterate peasants. You would hear Spanish in church, if you happened to go to school you would learn Spanish, and whatever legal documents you might possess – the title deed to your farm, for example – would be in Spanish as well.

The second half of the nineteenth century saw the beginning of a cultural and political Galician renaissance. From then onward, the language has undergone a slow process of recovery, put on halt during the years of General Franco's regime

(1939–75), during which the Galician language was ignored. In 1981 Galician become recognised, alongside Spanish, as the official language of Galicia.

To my ears, modern-day Galician doesn't sound much like the dulcet tenor of a troubadour, more the sweetly lyrical yelping of a friendly dog, full of helter-skelter swoops of intonation and big, hudumphing word stress. Whereas Spanish can often sound like the monotonous rattle of a machine gun, Galician gives you the impression that you're being wrapped in a thick blanket of rhetoric and playfulness, the result of all those long, lingering syllables and steeply falling-rising pitches.

Conversation in the bar is about the merits of a skirt that one of the ladies has just bought. She calls one of the others 'cousin', which I like, jotting it down in my leather-bound Moleskine notebook.

There is a faint smell of burning wood in the bar, the default smell of Galician villages. I try to ring Susana to tell her about the wolf, but there's no signal.

I stare at the word 'cousin' on an otherwise empty page, and wonder what I am doing here: a thirty-nine-year-old college graduate with no career to speak of and a young family to support, loafing about in one of the least known corners of Western Europe on a Tuesday morning, about to confront an old lady who has no idea who he is, and who will not understand why he has made the three-hour drive from Coruña on the advice of his foot doctor to ask her what to have for lunch. I feel like a fool who, for reasons unknown, is humouring himself. Only, it's not funny. I feel seriously and disconcertingly *unsensible*.

I drink up and make my way across to the white *hostal*. Outside it's freezing cold. The white *hostal* has a large and comfortable bar area, and there is a sweet aroma in the air, baking perhaps. A lady is sitting by the window, sewing something with needle and thread. She is in her middle years, well dressed, her hair perfectly in place. She puts down her sewing, looks up at me, and waits, quite calmly. Her demeanour is serene, beatific almost. I ask for Doña Marisol.

'I'm Marisol,' she says.

This throws me, although it doesn't take much to throw me right now.

I had been expecting an eighty-year-old peasant with a hooked nose, a hairy chin, and a wealth of anecdotes about how they used to eat fried bat wings in the old days. What I find is a woman who glows with a quiet inner warmth, a tranquillity, you might say, and a hint of irony in her dark eyes. That's why the chiropidist has been calling her Doña (a title these days reserved for formal contexts): she's enchanting.

I launch into a long explanation of why I am here. My voice is stuttery, and I'm already doing that breathless-swallow thing that children do when they're trying to lie their way out of trouble.

66

My arms flap a bit in front of me as I speak (men in my family have a history of not knowing what to do with their arms). I cannot remember the name of the chiropidist, only that he stays here sometimes, and that he told me about her, and that I am trying to eat all the different parts of a Galician pig.

Finally she moves across to the bar.

'Yes, yes, I understand,' she says at last, looking (not staring) at me with something between mild surprise and pity, as if she just wants to help me stop making a fool of myself. I order another coffee, fumbling with my Moleskine as she turns to the espresso machine.

As I sip my second powerful dose of caffeine, she begins. Not in Galician, but Spanish, the language that in Galicia is still sometimes associated with education and metropolitan sophistication, a vestige of centuries of dominance by Spain. Her delivery is slick, almost professorial, as if she's giving me a lecture. I try to take notes, but she really is distractingly enchanting, with an everything-will-be-all-right smile, and I miss the greater part of it. Then I hit lucky.

'Piornedo,' she says, 'they eat the feet there.'

As for recipes of the most ancient and curious kind, she says, you'd have to speak to someone from the older generation. I know, I almost tell her, you're too young, Doña Marisol, you're too young. Which, come to think of it, would make a great song title.

Now, the foot doctor comes to Doña Marisol's place to eat, so by far my best option today is to have lunch here. But cooked pig feet are, strangely, not that common in Galicia, and the lure of a plate of trotters is too strong. I thank my enchantress and head off in the direction of Piornedo.

Of the next three hours, I will be brief. I continued for a while, the road taking me gradually higher and higher, and soon I realised that there were no other vehicles in sight. Then the asphalt stopped. This was a sign to turn around and go back to Doiras; resurfacing was in progress. However, I took the russet-coloured bare earth ahead of me to be a good sign, a sign that improvements lay ahead. This was the wrong sign.

The road got so narrow that the idea of meeting someone coming the other way was chilling. Up it wound, getting more tracklike as it went, the kind of road that goats would just love. Then, as I rounded a curve, there was a mountainside, and I was most of the way up it. To my right, about two feet from the road's snow-flecked edge, the drop was what I suppose amateur cartographers would describe as a bastard of a long way down. I was almost at the summit and could not turn the car around. So on I drove. Melted snow had spread across the road then frozen, forming solid sheets of ice that threw off blinding white sunlight. The sound, well, there was no sound, and if you live at the centre of a busy city, silence of the absolute kind is tremendously unnerving, especially if you are driving at five miles per hour, white-knuckled, stiff-backed, and murmuring, *Concentrate, it's just a road ... look straight ahead, straight ahead ... Oh, Jesus Christ, one pothole and I'm dead ...* And although I didn't know it at the time, bovine flatulence had saved me from a fatal plunge. The unusually mild winter – blamed on global warming – had meant that there was a good deal less snow and ice about than normal.

The terrain eventually softened, and although I was still lost, a stratagem of taking all the turns leading downward began to pay off. About the time I descended below the tree line I spotted what was either a huge, fat-faced domestic cat miles from home, or a genuine wildcat. It paused as I drove past and gave me a look of bored conde-scension, which was unnerving and also obscurely humiliating. Not long after that I had to stop the car as a herd of long-horned cows was ushered up the road past me by an octogenarian *paisano*. They were Galician Blondes (*Rubia galega*), the principle meat-producing breed here. They lumbered toward me, their immense, muscular shoulders rolling, their heads dipped, like a pack of lugubrious Mike Tysons circa 1988. Neither man nor beasts were in any sort of rush, and the cowherd nodded as he walked slowly on, looking amused to see me, rather like the wildcat. Beneath the Tyson-Blondes hung stomachs and udders of such staggering proportions that a loose swing of one of those undercarriages could have sent me over the edge, car and all. As it was, I survived, although the animals showed scant respect for the bodywork of my vehicle.

At three in the afternoon – Spanish lunchtime – I stopped. I was back on proper roads in the lowlands, still two whole mountains away from the pig feet of Piornedo, and I was hungry. There was only one establishment to get fed at, a small eating room adjoining an otherwise unremarkable bar. It was empty. But so was I.

A scowling lady slouched across to my table; it appeared that I was about as welcome as a tax collector with an infectious disease. She reeled off the menu disdainfully. *Botelo*, she said, almost as an afterthought. I asked her what it was. Tired and hungry, I only caught the words 'ribs' and 'traditional' from her mumbled Galician. *Botelo* it was.

What came was the most peculiar rib dish I have ever tasted. On the plate sat a dark brown bag, what looked like, and in fact was, part of a pig's lower intestine – the stomach sack will also do, I have since learned. It was filled with broken bones, off-cuts of meat, and paprika. Now I am no expert on bones, but when she said 'ribs', she probably meant to say 'smashed-up vertebrae and other stuff,' because that's what was inside my boiled *botelo*. A variety of bones, cracked so that the marrow could escape, plus little odd-shaped meaty twists, jowl scrapings, perhaps. Perhaps worse.

70

I cut into the bag and sampled a bit of meat. It was powerful and salty to the taste, almost fishy, a concoction of bone marrow and face meat that had in effect been steamed inside a hermetically sealed sack. I very nearly put down my knife and fork, for there are some places that a person should not be asked to go, and for me the insides of a pig's bone-stuffed bowels is one of them. But in I went, searching for those fragments that most closely resembled flesh.

The smashed bones? I had no idea how to eat them. Suck? No way. I devised a plan. Each scrap of paprika-soaked, unidentified pig was accompanied by a little of the boiled potatoes, then some bread, and finally a slug of a rather nasty red wine from a labelless bottle. A combination of seeping marrow, congealed meat juices, and paprika had produced a sort of pâté run through with sinews and knots of crunchy gristle. I picked at the contents judiciously, like a hyena with delicate digestion, chasing each morsel down with potato, bread, and wine. As soon as I ran out of potatoes, I stopped. The lady cleared away my plate. She did not ask whether I had enjoyed my *botelo*.

As I drove away from the site of the *botelo* incident, the bone meat, its weirdly fishy taste, and the urgent resurfacing of paprika fumes all convinced me that Piornedo and the pig feet would have to wait for another day. In any case, my trip hadn't been completely wasted; I could tick off bone marrow, intestines, rib meat, and vertebrae, and that was some consolation.

On the way home, and by now firmly back on the map, I made my long-anticipated stop at the village of Roman de Cervantes, administrative centre of the municipality known by the same name. The council building was newly painted in white and cream, cervantes in bold letters above the door. So here I was, where the great man had his (distant) Galician origins. Quite possibly he never once set foot here, yet in a kind of round-about way this small village is the birthplace of the European novel. The kind of roundabout way that a local tourist department can turn effort-lessly into certainties and hard cash. Would there be a Don Quixote museum? Or a statue at least? In Stratford-upon-Avon there are statues of Shakespeare's *characters*, never mind the Bard himself. So how about a statue here? Don Quixote? Sancho? His donkey?

Nothing. Not a plaque. Not a park bench with his name on it. And all I wanted was a couple of souvenir dish towels.

WHY GENERALISE?

Some time ago . . .

I'm in Coruña's maternity hospital, a tatty, ugly-as-hell building dating from the years of General Franco's reign. (Name me a dictator with a flair for architecture. Just one.) It's midnight, and I'm sitting alone on a bench down a deserted side corridor. All I can hear is the hum of a vending machine on the main corridor off to my right, also deserted. Green-tinged strip lighting high up in the ceiling lends the scuffed grey walls an anaemic pallor. To my left are some brown frosted glass doors that I am not allowed to go through.

Nico, clearly a foetus with taste, has decided that faded Fascist Brutalism really isn't a fitting backdrop for his world debut, and is not coming out. So, after a long day's negotiations, they're going in to get him. Papá is not invited.

Opposite me is a small aluminium window. I stare at the indigo night sky beyond, trying in vain to make out a star, or a cloud, or anything. Next to the window are two lifts, one of which stands open. Glancing in it I see a small sign. It is written in Galician, a language that I understand tolerably,

73

but not a language I use very often, despite so many years in Galicia. Some of the letters are missing, rubbed out, or graffitied, lending the text a Cyrillic aspect. For a second or two I don't understand a word.

The moment unnerves me. The incomprehensible sign, the featureless sky, the bleakness of everything . . . I feel an enormous sense of displacement, as if I have no idea where I am, on a dark night in a foreign country, sitting in a place that looks like a Romanian mental institution circa 1960. How in God's name did I get here?

There are times, no matter how long you've lived abroad, no matter how far you've gone toward integrating yourself, times when you feel utterly lost. And alone.

Travel writing is about trying to extract something general from your personal experiences, about summing a place up, capturing the essence of how life is lived there. And for the purposes of making generalisations about a whole region and its people, you can do a lot worse than go to a hospital, a sort of microcosm of society in green pyjamas.

The arrival of your first child is probably not something you're going to want to treat as an opportunity for general comments. On the other hand, my firstborn was going to be a Galician. And that set me thinking . . .

So let's start with a generalisation. When it comes to health, Galicians are a little nuts. They're not as nuts as the French (to extend our generalising still further), but being less hypochondriacal than the French is hardly a boast. The French go to the doctor when they have *crise de foie* ('liver crisis') and are taken seriously. *Crise de foie*, dear reader, is a hangover, it is 'feeling a bit shitty because I consumed the engorged livers of six geese and a bottle of Armagnac for dinner'. It is said that the French seek medical attention every now and then just to check that they are still French.

Galicians are not hypochondriacs. But they do tend to take a strong stand on medical issues. For a start, they all seem to have at least some basic knowledge of physiology and pharmacology, as if the entire population has done the first year at medical school. They'll question the decisions of qualified doctors, debating among themselves whether a diagnosis was a good one, advising second opinions (a whole army of private doctors live off the second opinion trade). They like to chip in with their own advice about the medication prescribed, scrutinising the counterindications information inside your box of pills and quizzing you unashamedly about your symptoms.

The weather is also a source of great concern here. Galicians fear draughts like you or I fear the Andromeda Strain. Not just cold draughts, either; anything invisible that moves is considered mortally dangerous. The merest summer breeze could easily give you flu. And it would be flu, because Galicians never get common colds, they always get *una gripe tremenda*. The common cold is far too mundane, almost an embarrassment, like winning fifty pence on the lottery. *Tremendous flu*, on the other hand, is widespread, and to avoid its devastating effects (which are curiously similar to those of the common cold) windows are constantly being slammed shut and lapels pulled tight around necks. At my in-laws' place, if you want to open a window even an inch (which is more or less the maximum permitted, and only in August) you must first close all the doors in the apartment, just to be sure that a draught is not allowed to dart through the window and slice right across the room, killing everyone.

There's an old Galician refrain: *Se queres criarte gordo e san, a roupa do inverno pouna no verín.* 'If you want to grow fat and healthy, wear your winter clothes in summer.' Need I say more?

About a year before the arrival of Nico, a friend of ours fell ill and spent six days in Coruña's general hospital. I visited twice a day for those six days. The hospital's main vestibule served as a waiting area as well as an entrance, and everywhere you looked were signs saying SILENCIO. Signs requesting *silence*? In a Galician building? In a Spanish building? Really, you might as well cover the walls with THE USE OF INVOLUNTARY MUSCLES IS STRICTLY PROHIBITED. Was it a joke?

76

On that occasion I was given a credit-card-sized authorisation pass, which you swiped through a security barrier that controls access to the wards. Only you didn't. The barrier didn't work. Instead, you walked freely through a permanently opened gate, above which a sign read SO PERSOA ('personnel only'). By this point I was beginning to think that the hospital signs had been designed by René Magritte.

I was now spending a lot of time looking at a door. It led into the observation room of the A and E department, where our friend remained for nearly half his stay; occasionally a doctor would come out and tell you the latest news, so friends and family tended to gather there. On the door was written: ENTRY RESTRICTED – RING THE BELL. There was a bell. Now and then someone rang it, to no avail. But most visitors ignored the bell. Instead, they loitered with criminal intent, inching the door open to peep inside. If the coast was clear the whole family crept into the ward to look for their ailing loved one, only to be manhandled back outside by no-nonsense staff nurses, the whole unapologetic lot shooed away like a gaggle of straying hens. Everyone took this process with equanimity. Those who had been chicken-walked out simply regrouped in the corridor, waiting for their chance to creep back in.

Now personally, when I see a door that tells me that I shouldn't go through it, and I know that on the other side is a hospital ward full of ashen-faced, drip-fed human wrecks groaning as their kidneys twitch to a halt, I am disposed not to walk through it. Galicians, by contrast, see the six-inch letters barring their entry as a trifling obstacle. 'Do not enter' simply means 'We're not actually inviting you in, but by all means give it a go'. The nurses know this. Everyone knows. It's a confrontation that no one can win. Or lose. It is a system.

But what kind of system? As I watched families planning their sorties into Observation, I noticed that the door also had the word PULL on it. On the other side was the word PULL. Had Magritte been here too? No, the pull-pull system is smart, because the door always opens *into* the person doing the opening, and never crashing into those on the other side. Yet by my reckoning 75 per cent of those going through the door over the time I was there pushed. That's more than random distribution; that's wilful. The injunction to pull, then, was it also a joke? A suggestion so unlikely to be followed as to be amusing? Staff were just as likely to push as visitors, and on several occasions the door was pushed and slammed right into a sick person in a wheelchair or gurney on the other side, occasioning cries of 'I'm sorry, didn't see you there!' No one got angry. That was the system.

The nonbarriers, the silence signs, the push-me-pull-you doors . . . Are Galicians anarchists? Beneath their generally tranquil and modest character, does there lurk a deep contrarian instinct, a transgressive gene coiled up somewhere within the DNA? Or are straightforward rules simply too clear-cut to hold their attention, routinely ignored because they leave no scope for doubt?

Álvaro Cunqueiro, who we have already met in the guise of cookbook writer, was also a prominent literary figure here, and he explained the aversion to straightforwardness in the Galician character as the result of over two thousand years of being invaded. If you take a look at the history of Galicia, it's more or less a roll call of European pillage and land grab. And until 1492 Galicia, with its dangerous, rocky coastline (known as a Costa da Morte – the Coast of Death) was thought to be the western limit of the Old World, the farthest point you could go. *Finnisterrae*, the Romans called it, 'the end of the world'. They also thought that the river Limia, near Ourense in the southwest of Galicia, was the Lethe, the mythological river of oblivion in Hades; several Roman legions refused to cross it.

Galicia really was the last stop west, and many invaders, having worked out that there was nowhere else to go, stuck around, being bossy and acquisitive, as is the way with invaders. Those already here had little choice but to negotiate, to accommodate, to trick and manipulate the latest unwelcome guests as best they could.

The Galician character, Cunqueiro argued, is

hence one of defensiveness, of noncommitment. The aversion to saying yes or no derives from a suspicion of the invader, of the external power, the outsider, and a determination not to be tricked. *Retranca* – literally the brake strap on a carriage wheel – is the term used to describe this manner that Galicians have of putting the brakes on things when they talk. Their conversations take a circuitous, rambling course, full of shrugs, indecision, and irony, with a sense of uncertainty always close by.

So, I think the mystery of the hospital signs does have an explanation, of sorts. If you don't like saying yes in a rush, if the whole tenor of your approach to life is historically one of prevarication and delay, perhaps you don't much like agreeing to abide by a sign on the wall, or the door. Or anywhere. Perhaps after two thousand years of evasive action you just don't see the sign at all. How's that for a medical condition?

The following morning I marched proudly toward the neonatal room to pick up my Galician boy.

As I got to the door a nurse came out.

'Room two forty-eight?' she asked, a newborn bundle in her arms.

Sleep deprived, and consumed by anticipation, I nodded. She handed me my prize, and we walked slowly back down the maternity ward. The previous night's feelings of displacement were suddenly wiped away. I kissed the tiny bag of beauty on the forehead, holding him close to my chest.

'Where are you going?' said the nurse, as we arrived at Susana's room, the number on the door 242.

I don't know who the kid was, but I hope he's on solids by now and sleeping properly.

DIRTY DAY IN LAZA

The low-arched bridge that straddles the river Tâmega is solid with traffic, and we're stuck in the middle of it. Susana gets out to have a look. She thinks the road up ahead is cut. More cars arrive behind and join the queue, but it is now evident that the bridge is indeed closed. We decide to turn around. So does everyone else. A dozen or more vehicles nudge backward and forward, shuffling tentatively this way and that. It's like a foxtrot class for novice automobiles.

Next, we try our luck down a side street, only to discover that it leads us a half mile along the banks of the river, parked cars taking up every available inch. Getting out again takes some time; a medium-large Winnebago has followed us in and is now trying to turn around in a space slightly narrower than a medium-large Winnebago.

As we escape the riverside we see that the bridge is again filling up with cars, whose expectant drivers will soon realise that there is no way through, and will begin edging backward and forward in little prancing movements. To make matters worse, a *paisano* is double parked in his rusty old Citroën van right where everyone needs a bit of width to swing around and leave. He sits at the wheel, dozing to the radio.

This is typical of Galicia. If you attend an event in a place which is plainly inadequate for the weight of traffic that it will attract, no traffic cones will have been put out and no designated parking area will have been designated. Just leave your vehicle sprawled diagonally across the pavement (pedestrians have no rights, which makes this easier); ram the rearing, bucking thing up onto a grass verge so high that when you try to get out your legs dangle in thin air; scrape your gear box, gouge your undercarriage, graze your paintwork . . .

We continue not parking, which is the accepted technique: just carry on failing to park, doing it a little faster and a little more desperately as the sun climbs higher in the sky. We drive right out of town again and investigate a steep lane that runs off from the main road. It is bursting with parked cars all the way up. But finally we come to a large, concreted car park that is almost empty. It is the Guardia Civil's HQ. Theoretically, the Civil Guard oversees traffic issues in rural Spain.

Today's parking games are in Verín, Galicia's southernmost town, just a few miles above Portugal. I don't want to be unduly mean about the chaotic roads here. On this, the big festive Sunday of Entroido (Carnival), the whole of Galicia will be awash with parades, music, and street festivities of one sort or another. It will also be awash with cars that cannot find a place to park. Finally my patience is spent, and we drive to a castle for lunch instead.

Monterrei Castle, an immense, sprawling medieval fortress set atop a mountain peak just outside Verín, and dominating the plains for miles around, is where we'll be staying for the next couple of nights, as Galician Carnival reaches its hedonistic climax. Actually, we're staying next door in a manor house. It's a *parador*, one of the high-end hotels run by the Spanish state that are usually ancient buildings converted for the modern traveller. Ours is simple yet grand, heavy stone walls hung with fusty old oil paintings, and with cannonballs and other museum pieces lying about everywhere. You soon get a taste for *paradores*, and it comes as something of a disappointment to walk into the lobby of a lesser hotel to find that there is no coat of armour standing to attention by the door.

We are here not only to see the celebrations in Verín, but those of Laza, a village about a dozen miles up the valley. Entroido in Laza is said to be among the oldest folk festivals in the world, and on offer there will be a part of the pig that I have never tasted before, but which I definitely need to include on my itinerary: the head.

During the years of General Franco's rule (1939–75) Carnival was banned throughout Spain, considered altogether too naughty for a good Catholic dictatorship. However, a handful of towns and villages managed to continue with their traditions right through that period. No one knows how or why, although they were generally small, out-of-the-way places, and perhaps they simply fell beneath the Generalissimo's radar. Here in the very south of Galicia, three such places – Verín, Limia, and Laza – kept going with their ancestral festivities. Entroido in these parts therefore represents a continuous line back to the ancient folk festivals that have been going perhaps a thousand years. Of the three, Laza is the most . . . unusual.

'Laza!' exclaims the lady working behind the hotel bar. 'But tomorrow's Dirty Day. The worst day!'

She goes on to tell us about a young woman from a Barcelona-based TV station who came to report on Laza's Dirty Day a year or two back, and was so appalled at the way she was treated that she vowed never to return. Susana listens to all this, holding Nico in an increasingly tight bear hug of maternal protection. The lady behind the bar also becomes the first hotel employee ever to insist to me that as soon as I return to the premises I take a shower.

The manor house, Susana finally decides, will be a great place to spend tomorrow. So I'll be going to Laza alone.

The next morning I climb into the car good and early. Outside, the temperature is thirty-five

85

degrees, and the rain is coming down fast and hard. It sounds like there's a troupe of monkeys on the roof of the car drumming with their fingers. *D-O-N-T – G-O!* they tap out in rapid-fire monkey-Morse. And they're right. I don't really want to go to Laza on Dirty Day. Yet I must go, because if Entroido is about letting your hair down, then in the remote village of Laza they've been letting it down longer and farther than anywhere else in Europe.

Preparations have been afoot for weeks. At midnight on the first of January cleansing rites were performed to rid the village of malign spirits, with ash thrown at houses and sheaves of burning straw carried through the streets. These noisy midnight processions – *foliones* – have continued throughout January. But the main event falls on five intense days of Carnival leading up to Ash Wednesday. There has already been goat roasting, all-night partying, and a lot of getting whipped (see below). But today, on Monday, is when it starts to get a little bizarre. In theory, I am here to get my first taste of *cachucha* – boiled hog head, ancient festival food par excellence – but there's a lot going on before we get to that.

There's also a lot going on in my mind as I drive along the deserted road to Laza. The woods in this area are where the real-life 'wolf-man' Manuel Romasanta prowled in the early nineteenth century. A wandering soap seller, he murdered thirteen locals, devouring the flesh of each one.

The deaths were at first thought to be the work of wolves, such were the ragged teeth marks on the remains of the bodies. But eventually Romasanta was captured and confessed, claiming to have been possessed by wolves. The wolf-man is prominent in Galician folk myth, as it is across Europe, and the soap seller from these parts helped keep the nightmare alive.

When I arrive in Laza, hardly anyone is stirring. It is still thirty-five degrees. The village has seven shops and seven bars, and a hint of the Wild West. There's a mishmash of very old houses, some of them in ruins or close to it, and others renovated but generally retaining the same style: a medieval cottage feel with gallery-like balconies on the upper level, where by tradition you live, the beasts providing a sort of rustic under-floor heating system from the stables below.

I make straight for the Squirrel Tavern, which is adjacent to the village square, Praza Picota (Pillory Square). A *picota* is a pillory stake or whipping post, where petty criminals were tied up so the good citizens could throw rotten tomatoes or take free kicks at the offending ass. I get a coffee, then stand on a small covered terrace at the front of the tavern that looks out onto the square, thankfully bereft of all pillory equipment. A young, blonde reporter from Galician TV is here with a cameraman. She rebuffs my attempts to bond with the press corps, and I begin to wonder if a similar fate awaits her as that of last year's reporter from Barcelona.

Packs of adolescent males begin to emerge onto the streets, a slow, ominous bounce in their step. Many of them wear overalls, and regulation cigarettes hang from their lips as they stalk about. One boy has on a hooded leopard-skin jacket and Day-Glo yellow overalls. Another sports a Mexican sombrero. There's a touch of edgy anticipation in the air, of young men gearing up for action, and no one's laughing.

Groups of the lads call in the Squirrel for coffee, or beer, or coffee liquor. Others are carrying plastic supermarket bags with litre bottles of Coke and bottles of rum – the party starts nice and early in Laza. One boy in pristine blue overalls passes by the tavern several times, looking right at me and glowering. He seems to be wearing a mask, but it's just that he has very pale skin and very black hair. He might be fifteen. I don't know what he's got against me in particular, but I start to avoid his stare as the morning wears on.

The Squirrel fills up with villagers of all ages, plus tourists, several of whom I recognise from the hotel (where yesterday I had eaten the daintiest *cocido* of my life – all of it fitting comfortably onto a single dinner plate). A group of about a dozen well-heeled tourists in nice shoes arrive. They are all wearing plastic capes of varying colours.

Someone puts 'Y.M.C.A.' on the jukebox. An inebriated new-age grungester dances alone. He has with him a shopping basket on wheels, the kind that pensioners have, and he is drink-spilling coffee liquor as he dances. These rural festivities are popular with hippies and the hardier brand of new-age traveller, because there's often free food in the evenings, and people usually let them sleep downstairs in the stables.

Brushing past the blonde TV girl, who has her head down and is talking to absolutely no one – a novel way of reporting – I wander a little way back down the main street. One house has its ground-floor doors open, and several tourists are snapping yokel shots of the clumps of golden corn that hang inside, probably pig fodder. (Susana's grandmother always refused to eat sweetcorn, saying it was fit only for pigs.) On the first-floor balcony, four of the house's inhabitants stand holding mugs of coffee and watch the photo-taking right below them. This all takes place in silence.

Suddenly, a noise. It sounds like an army of biscuit tins looking for trouble. And it gets louder very quickly, echoing off the walls of the empty lane that I am staring down. It's a frightening noise, auguring danger, mischief, threat.

Then they run around a corner: *peliqueiros*. Grown men in black shoes, white tights, coloured garters, knickerbockers with four layers of fluffy woollen bobbles all the way around, a bright blue or red silk cummerbund swathing their midriff; a short-cropped, gold-tasselled jacket, white shirt with tie, and a finely decorated silken shawl over the shoulders and down the back (by tradition the shawl should belong to their sweetheart). They wear brightly painted masks, fashioned from birchwood, with two malevolent eye slits and painted with bright red circles for rosy cheeks, a black moustache, and a sardonic grin with something startlingly pagan in its awful simplicity. Above the face mask extends a mitre, about a foot and a half high, painted with the image of a wild animal (fox, wolf, leopard). At the back the mitre is covered in an animal pelt, often that of a cat, its tail hanging down the wearer's back (the word *peliqueiro* derives from *pelica*, pelt). Meanwhile, attached to the *peliqueiro*'s waistband at the back are six *chocos*, large bronze cowbells that make a clunky ringing sound that is both very loud and very unnerving; if there are five or six *peliqueiros* together, that's a lot of loud clunky bells. The *peliqueiro* also carries a *zamarra*, a two-foot wooden stick with a heavy, double-sewn calf-hide strap of equal length dangling from it. He beats people with this.

These clown-monster-avenger figures are unique to Laza, although nearby Verín has similar figures known as *cigarróns*. The tradition is taken very seriously, with costumes handed down from father to son. Baby boys are given a set of mini-belt bells, and spend their childhood looking forward to the time when, as young men, they can start a-whipping their neighbours. *Peliqueiros* – 'the pelt-wearing ones' – cannot talk, and they cannot stop moving once they're in public view. Rather, they must trot in formation everywhere they go, one right behind the other, using short strides, which maximises the horrid cacophony of their bells. They are permitted to clout anyone they want with their whips. You, on the other hand, can shout and jeer, but you cannot retaliate: no one is allowed to touch a *peliqueiro*. They traverse the village streets in a representation of cruel, arbitrary power, instilling fear wherever they trot, and whipping people at will. The symbolism is pitifully reflective of real life; even if you escape, they just get you the next time. Essentially there is no avoiding the shit. That is the *peliqueiro*.

The colourful uniforms and grinning masks somehow succeed in communicating the accumulated malice of a millennium, of sneering, wanton injustice and cruelty. Yet there is also a note of carnivalesque fun to it all, not least because these men, although in theory anonymous, are actually your neighbours. Frightening but thrilling. It's like being a child again, knowing that the man in the bogeyman costume is your dad, but that petrified-electrified adrenaline rush still sending you deliriously giddy as you sprint off.

Anthropologists don't even pretend to understand the concoction of symbolism and deep folk meaning that lies beneath the *peliqueiro* tradition. Some say the figures originated as parodies of local tax collectors in feudal times, but others talk of pre-Roman origins. Whatever, they appear from nowhere with great, frightening effect, using certain houses throughout the village as stopping-off points. There's a lot of laughing and smiling when they're about, but a lot less bravado, and absolutely no standing your ground; everyone runs. As the *peliqueiros* jog deafeningly past me for the first time, I flatten myself so hard against a door that one of my buttocks pushes partway into the letterbox. But I avoid a whacking.

At midday a chorus of cow horns announces the arrival of a donkey cart just next to Pillory Square. Masses of soggy rags are forked from the cart into an awaiting bathtub, along with large amounts of mud and water. At this point I detect a subtle but definite backward creep in those watching, and I instinctively creep back with the rest. The village's youths, meanwhile, are now congregating in earnest, looking serious, eager, dripping with testosterone.

The *farrapada* begins. It is, quite simply, a cloth-throwing fight. The rags, some as big as bath towels, heavy with watery mud, whiz-spin high into the air before slapping down just a few yards away. The battlefield itself is right next to the square, where the four principal lanes of the village converge, and is perhaps thirty yards at its widest. There are two notional sides in this soggy towel war, and they make spontaneous charges forward as they launch their brown cloths, newly soaked in sludge. This, then, is Dirty Day in Laza. Or so I think.

The fighting intensifies, spreading gradually

outward. '*¿Para que?*' (What for?) says a man standing next to me. He looks on incredulously from the safety of the Squirrel as two lads, standing six feet apart, fling the same sodden cloth back and forth at one another, pausing each time to soak it in a puddle between them.

It is raining, but this doesn't matter. The battle is serious but not vicious. There is a degree of precision in the hurling of the muddy rags, and the tribal roars that accompany each sally toward the opposition have an exultant quality. The faces of the fighters are striped with mud and rivulets of rainwater that run down from their soaking-wet hair, and the colourful outfits of just a few minutes ago are turning quickly to a uniform brown. Just off to the right in Pillory Square onlookers congregate. On the terrace of the Squirrel too. But those of us observing the spectacle are not targeted at all. The local lads don't give a toss who watches.

The great dream of 'tourism', then, comes close to fruition today in Laza. As tourists we want to taste the authentic, the local, the genuine. Effectively, we want to go where there are no tourists. Well, the *farrapada* fighters are pretty much oblivious to their audience. From my vantage point up on the Squirrel's terrace it's like being in a caged Jeep watching a clash of feuding orang-utans in Borneo.

After twenty minutes of observing the warring primates I need a drink. I retire to a small, low-ceilinged bar down the main street. It's full of villagers talking about the *farrapada*, comparing it to last year's, and looking forward to this evening's event. Suddenly a *charanga* band pushes in through the doors, its six players managing to elbow themselves and their instruments enough free space to break into 'Brazil'. It is deafening, and since conversation is now impossible, those of us in the bar sway a little in time to the music and grin.

As the band plays on, I notice two young men slumped in plastic chairs over by the door. One of them wears an enormous circular loaf of bread on his head, about the diameter of a Stetson. He's on that particular plateau of semiconsciousness that follows a wicked all-nighter (I heard that yesterday's revels went on until this morning). The bread hat has been hollowed out to fit the dome of his head. From time to time he takes it off and picks at the hollow, nibbling the crumbs. Neither he nor his companion shows the slightest sign of having noticed the lively samba that fills the room.

Eventually the *charanga* leaves, after garnering some pretty enthusiastic applause. I get another wine and take it outside. I can see in the distance that the cloth throwers are still at it, now head-to-toe brown. The white walls of the buildings that form the perimeter of the war zone are covered with abstract brown stains, like a walk-through Rorschach inkblot test ('I see a butterfly . . . a vagina, no! I mean . . . a towel!'). Sloppy rags have found their way far and wide.

An enthusiastic tourist picks up a stray scrap of muddy cloth between finger and thumb and, with a delicate flick of the wrist, slaps his friend limply on the chest with it. No doubt the guys back at the office are going to hear all about how Juan and Pedro were in the very thick of things down at the *farrapada*.

After about an hour the cloth-slinging peters out. I take a walk down one of the lanes leading off from the main area. A group of youngsters, all of them entirely brown, and surrounded by a sea of beer cans, are tossing muddy rags at a large house. A stout woman in an apron hangs from one of the balconies and warns them off. They (literally) fall about laughing as her angry, warbling alto ratchets swiftly up to a shrieking and uncontrolled soprano screech.

Down a quiet street I find some of the oldest houses in the village, many of them abandoned. The population of Laza, including its outlying parishes, has halved to under two thousand over the course of the last generation, and it is unlikely that the oldest of these buildings will ever be restored. As I take pictures of sagging wooden balconies and timeless stone cellars, four donkeys approach me from behind. One is sporting an enormous Mexican hat, a cravat around its neck, and has four green balloons tied to its tail. Astride the beast is a gent in a blue suit who is carrying a large bunch of flowers. He looks a little like Harpo Marx. Another of the donkeys is ridden by a man dressed as an American Indian. A third rider is simply in an anorak, although his donkey has a blue and yellow '46' stuck to its rump, the number of Italian motorbike champion Valentino Rossi.

I stand against the wall and let them all pass, wary of their lively back ends. As the donkey parade makes its way down the rain-soaked lane, a *moo* reverberates around us. Four brown cows emerge slowly from a house, followed by an old man, who presumably lives upstairs. The cows amble right past the donkeys, ignoring their fancy dress, before sauntering out of town to pasture.

Running along the outer limit of the old village is a main road. The drizzle has almost let up, and lots of people, mainly young, are now having tailgate picnics there: *tortilla* (potato omelette), *empanadas* (pasties), plus an array of unidentifiable things stuffed in long sections of breadsticks. One Citroën AX has a trunk full of Mahou 5-Star lager. The AX is not a very big car, but that's still a lot of beer, especially Mahou, which is nothing special.

Wine bottles stand open on the sidewalk, and the hoods of cars are dotted with white plastic cups. Many of these picnickers are in fancy dress, the most impressive of them a tall young man in a red military jacket who wears a top hat fashioned out of a grain sack. It stands two feet high on his head, and the brim is almost as wide.

In a nearby café the barman is in a red silk jacket

and yellow-red tights (one leg in each colour). Sackman appears with a friend in a Tibetan skullcap. They drink Martini Rosso with gin. Everyone is in fancy dress, and everyone is smoking. There's a sweet, Jamaican smell wafting around. Although I don't know it, this is the calm before the storm. These people are girding their loins. The muddy towels? Nothing but morning games. Dirty Day has hardly begun.

I drive back to Verín, where we have lunch with our friends María and Paco. They have made the three-hour drive down from the city of Coruña (where we all live) this morning and are staying at the *parador* tonight. Paco and I share a plateful of frog's legs. Like Mahou beer, frog's legs are nothing special, a cross between cod cheeks and chicken wings. But you find them so rarely on menus that it seems like a missed opportunity not to order them. María, meanwhile, is talking to Susana, and soon decides to forgo the dirty delights of Laza in favour of a quiet night with Susana and Nico at the hotel (she's clearly never tried putting our son to sleep).

So, it's just the boys. After lunch we bid them all a brave farewell, pay a quick visit to a general store that has set up a fancy dress section for the duration of Carnival, and head back up the valley.

When we arrive, the rowdies are already gathering on the site of the mud battle. Orquesta Europa, a seven-piece band, strikes up on a large stage at the back of Pillory Square, right above the dirty zone. The lead singer looks as if he's barely entered adolescence, but he has a great – and broken – voice, perfect for the band's repertoire of old melodramatic Spanish songs. Incidentally, one of the show bands playing in Verín this weekend is called Los Cunters. I would have liked to have spoken to the band members about the name of their combo, but traffic issues intervened and made this impossible.

The postpubertal singer finishes his opening number with a long coloratura flourish. Despite the growing throng in front of the stage, few people clap. The stage is right at the back of the square, and the real action is now down in the adjacent area, where the revellers are closely packed and drinking enthusiastically from beer cans and wine bottles. They are also tossing muddy cloths up at the telephone lines overhead. When a cloth gets caught on the wires, a great cheer goes up.

In our mad dash to the fancy dress shop I had grabbed an old-fashioned round-rimmed hat and a black beard; together with my thigh-length black waterproof I make a pretty convincing rabbi. Paco has on a red monster skullcap and a bright green windbreaker, plus a black beard. Dirty Night doubles as fancy dress night in Laza.

We requisition some beer, then take in the scene. An incomplete inventory: a big-boned caveman;

a mouse; a young man in a latex purple miniskirt and a knitted Rasta hat (he keeps tugging at his balls for effect); a surprising number of men in Colonel Gaddafi desert garb, although tonight a multicoloured wig is also de rigueur; two devils, one in fluffy boots; several medieval noblemen (one wearing black leather biking trousers, which is *very* effective); a man in a yellow crash helmet, a black skirt, and a blue apron (no obvious theme here); a girl carrying a mock TV camera made from cardboard and a friend with a mic, the two of them doing spontaneous interviews wherever they go (TV Galicia could learn a thing or two); a man with *five* six-packs of Mahou beer tied together and dangling from a rope over his shoulder like the spoils of a very successful hunting trip to the local off-licence; a butcher with a cowbell around his neck; a skeleton; numerous witches, maids, clowns, nurses . . .

No Superman! It has taken me a while to realise that no one is dressed as a superhero or cartoon character. A few children do have full outfits from the fancy dress shop, mainly princesses, but in general the costumes here are individualised, from the slick satin of the blue nun's robes and her black priest husband, to the utterly improvised and seemingly random, like the young man in a battered old fur coat, a long grey skirt, and green socks, swigging from a bottle of crème de menthe as he goes. There are a good few poncho wearers, many sporting cowboy hats, which at least hints

99

at a broad kind of thematic cohesion. One man has brought two fancy-dressed daughters but is himself in regular clothes. At the last minute he must have borrowed some lipstick and reddened his cheeks and forehead, just to enter into the spirit of things. Yet he has done it so convincingly that he appears to be heading for a serious cardio-vascular event; by his side the two little girls look like Orphan Annies in waiting.

There are also a lot of people in waterproof capes and overalls. A whole group arrive wearing black dustbin liners that bear yellow horizontal hoops, like bees. The yellow stripes are done in adhesive tape, binding the plastic tight to their torsos, the same way you cover the plaster cast on a broken limb when you want to take a shower. In the case of the bees, however, I think moisture's going to be more of a problem *inside* those closely bound plastic bags. It's going to get a little humid in there.

Down in the rowdy area the wine is flowing. There's a muddy mix of people, some wearing plastic capes or other protective layers, but others too drunk and happy to care. They fall about joyously, and although I don't normally like crowds much, I almost wish I was down there drunk with them. More beer is what we need.

Paco is a tennis coach, and also a qualified instructor of a sport called paddle tennis (a cross between tennis and squash), which in Spain is played by rich, socially ambitious conservatives.

I wonder what his well-heeled students would make of seeing their tutor dressed as a red and green makeshift monster amid a throng of mud-caked drunken teenagers in Laza.

We wander behind the square, where a large field is in use as a parking lot (*nota bene*, Verín). A group of young people climb out of two cars, then pull out a number of thick stalks of *grelos*, each one at least ten feet in length. The *grelos* plant, if you leave it, just continues to grow upward, and can reach amazing heights. These are about the biggest I've ever seen, the stalks thicker than broom handles.

Puzzled, we head off down toward the bottom of the field, where a wooden cart is generating plenty of interest. Those watching are straight-faced, almost reverential, including the green monster and the rabbi, who swig their beer in confused silence. On the cart is a strange-looking wooden machine, and a number of bulging flour sacks. A man dressed in a brown corduroy suit and carrying a hooked stick is barking directions at a dozen men. After some elaborate preparations, they begin to drag the cart up a back lane toward the church, which sits high in the village, directly above the site of this evening's rowdy party.

We follow on, right behind the cart, which has some sort of siren within it that emits a loud drone, like the lowing of a massive mechanical cow. Eventually we reach the church steps. There is now a flurry of flashlights and a rumble of anticipation, as the cart attracts a small but excited crowd. It's like being at the stage door before a rock concert. Although we don't know it yet, the contents of those bulging sacks are one of the evening's main attractions.

We are at the high point of a narrow lane, and the dozen men puff and strain to get the cart lined up, before wooden chocks are kicked firm under its wheels. Over the cusp of the little hill is a descent of about twenty yards, the lane getting even narrower before opening onto the space where the mud fight took place this morning, which is now heaving with humanity, several ten-foot *grelos* stalks sticking up from within the crowds for no obvious reason. Paco wants to charge straight into the throng, but I advise caution, so we edge down as far as the point where the narrow lane opens onto the revels, and wait.

Huddled into the wall next to me is an old man. We cannot really hear each other, but we have a stab at conversing anyway. He is perhaps seventy and is trying to explain that in the past there used to be more space to run away, which initially I don't understand. As more and more people make their way down the narrow lane behind us I start to see what he means: we're trapped, along with everyone else.

Just in front of us is a clown. His head suddenly explodes in a puff of grey smoke, as a big handful of what looks like ash lands on the back of his head. People laugh, me included. *What's so funny?* says a man holding a plastic bag full of the ash,

102

before emptying a fistful right over me. The old gent next to me grins, and gets a faceful for his trouble. Ashman is no respecter of age.

The ash is bulked up with flour, turning it a mid-grey. More people with bags of the stuff appear, and make their way down the lane past us into the main area, tossing it widely and randomly in what turns out to be the dirty overture. Paco's devil skullcap was a wise choice. I've already lost my hat.

The evening's stars are next. Those bulging sacks on the cart contain moist soil and live ants, the big, juicy, biting kind, bred and nurtured especially for tonight's extravaganza. Apparently, the ants are sprinkled with vinegar just before the main event, to get them really angry. An army of ant scatterers emerges from behind us, each one with a bag of the anty soil, which they launch into the air above our heads. Screams go up as the sky fills with soil and very annoyed ants. At this point, and perhaps somewhat tardily, I decide to pull up the hood of my waterproof. Too late. The wet soil inveigles its way down into my inner vestments (T-shirt and golfing jacket, neither of which offers my neck any real protection). More and more ant throwers march past us. Everyone is maniacally scraping mud and insects from their hair and clothes, yelping and groaning with horror and hilarity in roughly equal measure. I untuck my T-shirt and shake free what I can.

'Come on!' Paco shouts, already fighting his way through the crowds ahead. But it's all right for him, he has the upper-body strength of a paddle tennis coach. I stay against the wall.

Right then a donkey rushes through the crowd, its back end missing Paco by inches. The animal is being led by some burly, no-nonsense men, and there is absolutely no room for either men or beast; it's like trying to get a live frog in the neck of a wine bottle. Yet they jog-drag their charge right into the fray with an air of heavy-handed madness. On the donkey sits a girl with either flowing blonde locks or a long wig (I was too amazed to take good note). Cheers go up as they arrive. It's a relief after the ants.

Following on is a boy with crazed eyes brandishing a chain saw, the blue smoke from its whining motor confirming that it is real. The chain, I suppose, has been removed, but just like Daddy in the bogeyman disguise, it's incredibly frightening. The red and green figure of Paco has disappeared.

The *Morena* now makes its entrance. Two men gallop about, shrouded in a thick brown cloth, mimicking the movements of a badly behaved cow. Up front they brandish a stylised wooden bovine head, complete with long horns. The *Morena* comes from the nearby hamlet of Cimadevila, whose inhabitants are the only ones permitted to dress up as the *Morena*. Playing fast and loose with its horns, the frisky cow accosts women, yanking up

104

their skirts and rearing up in front of them lewdly. Any man who intervenes to protect the honour of his lady gets beaten with ten-foot-long bramble branches – not *grelos* – which are carried by a troop of young lads who accompany the *Morena*, a sort of too-enthusiastic Praetorian guard. There is, of course, absolutely no room for any of this in the crowd, but somehow it all comes right in among us and continues, making the rounds to all corners of the throng.

The mayhem now intensifies. Those long bramble branches – *toxo* in Galician – are a spiky variety of gorse that hurts like hell if you get beaten on the head with it. And I *know* this. Several of the *toxo* carriers are bare-chested, and one of them is right down to his underpants. The cheering becomes ecstatic; it's as if the long, spiky *toxo* branches are old friends, and their arrival only intensifies the atmosphere. The *toxo* branches sway and dance in the air, joined by the enormous *grelos* sticks, which I think are mock-*toxo*, fancy-dress versions of the brambles.

The bath from this morning makes its entrance on wheels, now filled with the remaining ant dirt. Those closest to the bath fall into a frenzy, fighting and jostling with frenetic intensity to grab handfuls, which they launch skyward, even as more of the muck patters down on their own heads.

As if to attempt the impossible, the big wooden cart is itself dragged into the square. The mysterious structure mounted on it turns out to be some sort of large-wheeled device that throws flour out in a continuous, billowing cloud which extends high into the air, blinding everyone. The cries of joy are overwhelming. White-frosted heads dance and cavort, while revellers tug at their clothes, wincing as ants bite them in unreachable places. Somehow or other the flour cart does a full circuit, pulled along slowly by the men. The prickly *toxo* branches jump high in the air . . . Off to the left the orchestra plays on stoically . . . The shouting of the crowd is raucous, manic-hoarse, invigorating . . . Every species of filthy fun has been crammed into this little space.

Despite my pretty strong aversion to crowds, I lunge forward, suddenly feeling the urge to splurge, to let myself go, the same impulse (I now understand) that compels people at rock concerts to get up on stage and dive headfirst back into the audience. If I were to scream now I wouldn't hear it. God, I am enjoying myself, jumping up and down (I am afraid to say) like a headbanger. Nearby, three men from Galician TV (a different team from this morning) are creeping around in a nervous line, like elephants holding on to the tail of the one in front. They are not enjoying themselves, largely because they are very attractive targets, almost authority figures, and are getting pelted nonstop with flour, ants, mud, soppy rags, ash . . . Also, every time they try setting up to do any filming they get beaten to death by half-naked *toxo*-brandishing hooligans.

The TV presenter attempts a piece to the camera right next to me. As he gets the mike up to his mouth one of the youths with *toxo* whacks him so hard and so unremittingly with his prickly branch that other marauders actually pull him off the presenter, who is shielding his face in a pose that looks remarkably like that of a weeping saint. The TV men finally get their report, and the next day I will see myself on the small screen, covered in flour and mud and ants, grinning like a loon.

By the time I find Paco, my beard and hat are long gone, and so is his red skullcap. He is laughing uncontrollably. Outside a bar we have a few more beers, chasing them down with a green liquor that tastes like mouthwash. From time to time someone races by, throwing ant soil or ash or flour. By now we're almost blasé, pulling up our hoods and ducking as we dance out of the way along with everyone else, but mainly laughing. People all around us are nursing ant bites, but somehow we have both avoided them.

After making good use of the bar, we wander down a narrow side street for a breather. A man of about sixty, with a big billowing grey beard, staggers toward us, so stoned that it takes him several attempts to explain that he wants a light for the half-inch joint between his fingers, and several more attempts before he manages to put the thing between his lips and get it lit. We wander farther down the street. In the semi-darkness ahead is a large farm cart, its four high sides festooned with fern branches. Around it half a dozen *peliqueiros* loiter.

'*Qué cojones es esto . . . ?*' Paco whispers – *What the bollocks is this?* – squinting with disbelief at the high sides of the cart. Several men are busy hoisting great, double-handled plastic buckets up onto it. Steam rises from the buckets, and before long I catch my first salty whiff of tonight's evening meal.

'*¡Es la cachucha!*' I whisper back, almost retching at the stench, which is like old sweaty boots doused in molasses and axel grease. *It's the pig head!*

Once all the buckets are loaded, and there must be ten or fifteen, the cart is dragged right up into the thick of things, the *peliqueiros* forming a trotting guard to ease a way through the crowd.

'You hungry?' I ask Paco, as we follow the cart slowly back up the lane.

As it makes its appearance in the square a deafening roar goes up, followed immediately by chanting: *Cachucha! Cachucha! Cachucha!* By the time the cart comes to a stop, the tightly packed hordes that surround it sway and lean as if one single mass, and we are among them. Eager not to miss out on his pig's head, Paco has pushed ahead of me, and it's all I can do to maintain my position a few yards from the back of the cart, getting elbowed and kicked from all sides as drunk people in wrecked fancy dress strain like desperate animals to get close in, climbing up onto the shoulders of others, whooping and bawling and screaming: *Cachucha!*

Cachucha! We are all reaching upward, our begging, imploring hands stretched toward the man who has now leapt onto a platform on the cart, rousing the baying, hollering masses to yet greater delirium. Beneath our feet the floor is covered in crud. It's like walking on a big, uncooked pancake. Bottles lie everywhere. Our feet crunch on broken glass.

Finally, the man on the cart reaches into a bucket and pulls out an entire half head, bones and all. He holds it up triumphantly, like the severed head at a public execution. The wailing comes to a crazed peak. The odour of boiled pig is thick in the air, and the noise is unbelievable. The half-head drips with molten fat, and the *cachucha* man (who is in a dark suit with shirt and tie) winces at the heat as with both hands he rips it apart, yanking a chunkful of cheek from the pig's grinning profile, hot grease streaming over his hands and splashing out into the crowd. It reminds me of being in the front row of a boxing match and getting showered with sweat.

Paco just misses out, as some lucky soul makes off with the first bit. We all push closer in, barking and shouting at the *cachucha* man. *A orella!* someone next to me screams. *The ear!* A girl, not very tall, suddenly disappears underfoot; she just plummets down beside me and is gone. No one cares. We push harder still, as another head is torn apart and handed out, fat dripping everywhere as chunks of hot, wobbling pig are grabbed by their jubilant new owners and yanked through the air like fistfuls of pure gold. *Cachucha! Cachucha! Cachucha!*

Before long Paco gets his prize. With true gallantry he turns and offers it to me. But I refuse, and continue to edge forward, more elbows in my back, reaching up as high as I can, outstretched fingers wiggling to attract the attention of the *cachucha* man. Pride demands that I claim my own dinner tonight, and after a good bit of shoving and stretching, I have a piece of hot pig in my hand. Instinctively, I hold it close to my chest, greedy with meat lust, and make my way to a dark doorway. Paco is nowhere to be seen. I stand amid a pile of discarded cans and bottles, breathless, and suddenly ravenous.

What I have in my hand is a lump of cheek. Such is the stickiness of its slow-boiled outer skin that it is stuck firm to the palm of my hand. It stinks of swine, a primal, shudder-making stink, like the deep, guttural element of pork aromas stripped of their more delicate notes. But I have fought hard for this. I shove my mouth into the soft inner side of the fatty slab and gnaw at the flesh. It is intensely but not unpleasantly salty. Shreds of tender meat come away easily. Immediately there's grease all over my face. As I chew I inhale through my nose, and a slimy plug of fat courses halfway up my nostril. In my mouth the sensation is abhorrent yet bizarrely satisfying. The fat coats everything, inside and out. *Cachucha! Cachucha! Cachucha!*

The noise is receding as people stagger about, hunched over and concentrating on their chunk of head. I slurp-gnaw on my piece of jowl, warm grease dripping from my chin and down the front of my coat, which is already ingrained with soil, flour, and ash. *Cachucha! Cachucha!* God, this is wonderful. *Cachucha!* Dionysus, tonight you are in Laza.

Cachuuuuucha!

The last bus back to Verín is at half past four in the morning, although I suspect that for many people here it's gonna be a bus somewhat later in the day, if there's anyone sober enough to drive it. I finally find Paco, who has finished eating and is now laughing so much that it takes several more beers to quiet him down.

'That was amazing,' he says, his cheeks glistening.

We make our way up past the ravaged *cachucha* cart. The frenzy has now faded away. As we pass by they hand me a jaw. It's all there is left, they shout down to me. I take it. A full pig's jawbone, bigger than a size twelve boot, its inside dark and unknowable in the dim light of the square, but yielding up some strong-tasting bits of meat. I nibble at it, but the moment has gone.

Just then, the boy with the pale face and the blue overalls from this morning staggers by, rubber-legged and going absolutely nowhere on purpose. He sucks automatically on a teat-substitute bottle

111

of wine, a bilious wince-smile on his pale face announcing the ruby deluge to come. He's a walking vomit launcher, and I avoid eye contact just in case he's ready to blow. Young and defence-less now, he's beautifully wasted and incapable, his overalls darkened with mud, his eyes loose in their sockets. I want to put an arm around his shoulders and tell him how much I envy him tonight.

Three hooded TV men stomp past on their way to the parking lot. The presenter in particular is not looking happy. I want to remind him that he is getting paid to attend a Dionysian festival that's been celebrated for an unbroken thousand years . . . but I don't say anything. After all, he's just been whipped in the face with brambles by a teenager in his underpants.

When we get back to the manor house – a filthy, dishevelled ex-rabbi and a greasy green monster – the lady on reception looks at us sternly. She knows where we've been, but she says nothing, although her eyes follow us across the lobby. Dirty Day, I gather, does not earn universal approval in nearby Verín, which probably considers itself a cut above *cachucha* madness.

I get a similar reaction from Susana up in our room, who insists I take off my shoes before I enter, then refuses to let me contaminate my son until I am scrubbed clean.

Once in the bathroom I take stock. My hair is ash grey, other than on top, where it is flattened down with dried mud. There's flour and ash in the creases around my eyes, dirt and pig fat on my cheeks. My black waterproof looks as if it's been dragged through a sewer. Leaning over the bathtub, I ruffle the mud-compacted crown of my head. An ant falls into the tub. A big black ant, with a juicy thorax, which must have been caught fast in the mud as it dried on my scalp. It has been there at least an hour without so much as wiggling a leg. I give it a merciful squirt of water, and watch until it has disappeared down the plug hole. Then I take a long shower, as hot as I can stand, and wonder what on earth General Franco would have made of it all.

EAST OF EDEN

The year is 1992. Pablo Valledor is inseminating cows one morning in a field. A hog walks by, taking his attention. He stops what he's doing and asks himself: What's unusual about that pig? Is it in his eyes? (*No.*) Is it in his size? (*No.*) If you want to know why the pig looks just so, it's in his hips.

The pig sashays past with a comely shake of its rear end, which is, if not exactly alluring, then intriguing. Pablo is confused. Pigs just don't move that way. At the same time, he's started having flashbacks: a scene from a lecture hall in veterinary college, years ago, a young, impressionable Pablo taking notes . . . enormous floppy ears, extended back, long hind legs, the shifting back end of a Brazilian samba dancer . . . He's remembering a class on the Celtic pig.

The Galician Celtic, though, is extinct. Once dominant in Galicia, the breed is no more, as his college professors had explained with diagrams, old sepia photos, and population charts that looked like a graph of Enron's stock price. Pablo, standing at the business end of an

114

indignant Friesian, cannot quite believe what he is seeing.

'*Dios mio!*' he cries. 'My God, it's a dodo!' momentarily confusing Porcine Development and Husbandry, Year II with Darwinian Evolutionary Theory.

But there was no mistake that morning back in 1992. The Galician Celtic was alive. And it was shaking its ass at Pablo Valledor.

Our hero (Pablo, not the pig) was born and raised in Fonsagrada, 'land of the sacred fountain', a stopping-off point on the very oldest of the pilgrimage routes to Santiago. It is a remote part of northeastern Galicia, where oak and chestnut forests sweep across mountain valleys like thick, snugglesome eiderdowns; it feels like you've been dropped into a big leafy green paradise, even if you're doing cows from behind with a rubber plunger. Pablo, son of a ham curer, grew up with pig in his blood. And judging by the healthy curvature of his midsection, it's not just in the blood. When he saw those curiously moving hips, then, something must have told him that the Celtic pig had a tasty story to tell.

It turned out that some Celtics had survived. A few old-time farmers way up in the hills had kept their herds pure, and one or two enthusiasts had a stock of half a dozen or so. The Galician Celtic was technically extinct, down to just a handful of isolated swine. Yet . . .

A consortium of high-powered, multitalented Celtic supporters was assembled. A movie mogul (Julio Fernández, Spain's most successful film producer) put up the pig money; lawyers, accountants, a journalist, and Fonsagrada's ex-procurator all joined the cause. Their aim was to rescue the poor animal from terminal decline and restore to Galicia one of its greatest natural treasures.

I'm in the woods with Pablo to see the results. The Porco Celta Fonsagrada company doesn't do things by half measure. They get a forest, and they fill it with pigs.

Sun breaks through the canopy of oak and chestnut. Across pools of golden light long-bodied pigs stroll, nonchalantly on the forage.

'You see that? You *see*?'

Having manoeuvred ourselves squarely behind the rump of a big pink and black sow, we watch. The Celtic pig has one vertebra more than the European white breed, and its longer back requires longer legs for support. These are lither than a normal pig's legs, and its hind quarters are rather like those of an *ibérico*, the exclusive pure-breed pig, from which the finest ham in the world is produced. All of which makes it necessary for the Celtic to adopt a walk that Pablo, using veterinary terminology, describes as 'like a girl insinuating'. As the sow walks away from us, it does indeed look like Jayne Mansfield mincing off, although Jayne's voluptuous back end would not normally have been dappled with shitty mud.

Pablo and friends have created a Galician version of a *dehesa*, the ancient wooded habitat in the southwest of Spain and home of the renowned *ibérico* pigs – also known as *pata negras*, or 'black hoofs'. During the winter months, these aristocrats of the porcine world eat almost nothing but acorns, principally the sweet, oil-packed fruits of a rare subspecies of the evergreen oak. They gorge on up to twenty pounds of these acorns per day, piling on an incredible one hundred sixty pounds or more in just a few months, much of that extra bulk in the form of the succulent, oil-rich fat that sets *ibérico* ham apart from all other hams on the planet.

Incidentally, whereas Susana quite literally cannot stomach most meat, she somehow manages to make an exception when it's *ibérico* ham at 50 quid per pound. She's not a vegetarian at all, she's out to bankrupt me. Nico loves the stuff too, so now and then I take out a bank loan and buy an entire leg of pure *ibérico* acorn-fed ham from Manuel Maldonado, one of Spain's best producers. It sits on its slicing rack in the kitchen, and each time we pass, we hack a slice off with the carving knife. It costs a fortune, but then again we don't go out much.

Unlike the dry, hot *dehesa* of Extremadura, where our Maldonado hams come from, the Galician *dehesa* does not have the evergreen oak and its oily acorns. The animals, though, hang out in the shade and forage just the same, for common acorns, chestnuts, and whatever else grows wild there. It's idyllic. It's peaceful. The chow's good. Suddenly, I long to be a pig.

Celtics have always roamed free. Three-quarters of Galicia is covered in trees. There's a lot of forest to go roaming around. So what happened? Why did the breed die out so abruptly? The answer: poverty, a dictator, and the internal combustion engine.

The Celtic was traditionally *the* Galician pig. Every rural family had a *house pig*, and it would have been a Celtic. There were no other breeds. And it was a truly excellent breed. Its deep pink, flavoursome meat is marbled with intramuscular fat, similar to the *ibérico*, and *un*like the meat of normal white-breed pigs, which tends to be dry because whatever fattiness the animal's ancestors once had has been bred out of it over the years. Celtic pigs were, in effect, Galician black hoofs. Their hams were exported to Madrid, where they were considered high-quality stuff, competing with the most prestigious hams from the south-west. In rural Galicia, selling your home-reared ham was a crucial source of income for the poorest families, who would often have to make do with the lesser cuts for themselves. This perhaps explains why *cachucha*, the head, is still eaten here; it symbolises a shared heritage of rural poverty.

Pablo's father was the last *jamonero* to cure hams

in the Fonsagrada area and sell them down in Madrid. You can still see his old premises in Fonsagrada-town, the outer walls of the building body-pierced with iron rings where peasants would tether their donkey and cow carts while they off-loaded the legs of their freshly slaughtered house pig.

The traditional way of keeping hogs was, in today's language, high-end organic. They were allowed to slope around at home like bored teenagers, kicking their heels and snaffling whatever food was thrown at them. They ate wheat, corn, surplus potatoes, cabbage, beets, and turnips, and would take themselves off to the nearest bit of forest to pig out on acorns, chestnuts, and wild mushrooms. While the humans led a pretty stark existence, especially in this part of Galicia, the pigs had a whale of a time, wandering free, eating whatever took their fancy.

What happened next can be blamed, like so much else, on General Franco. After World War II, while Marshall Plan money poured into Europe from the United States, stimulating economic recovery throughout the war-torn continent, Spain was left with no American dollars, a second-rate, quasi-fascist dictator, and a crappy economy made crappier still by Franco's policy of economic self-reliance, or *autarky* (translation: We're poor and we're isolated, but we're Spanish!). At this point European white-breed pigs arrived in Galicia, breeds that had already undergone genetic selection to produce leaner, fast-growing animals. The new imported breeds yielded saleable hams more quickly. At this time, the benefit of fat (especially intramuscular fat) for the quality of the meat was little understood. To the region's desperately poor farmers, replacing their old Celtics with white breeds seemed like good economic sense. And so the change began.

Autarky was abandoned in 1959, after the Generalissimo was finally persuaded that it didn't work, and the Spanish economy began its slow crawl into the twentieth century. Only then did places like Fonsagrada start to get proper roads. And you can't let your hogs roam free where there's traffic. The old free-range system of pig rearing was replaced by the use of enclosed sties and grain-based feed, and the chestnuts lay rotting on the forest floor.

The Galician pig became a miscegenated animal, mixed and matched for meat bulk and speed of growth. No pedigree. No class. Nothing special. The Celtics disappeared, along with the traditional system of feeding and fattening. Galician ham lost its prestige, and the export trade died.

Pablo and I wander through the forest, eventually finding ourselves on a stretch of steeply inclined meadow. A pack of long-torsoed hogs burst through the undergrowth just above us and start jogging down the slope pretty much in our direction. And these beasts have long tusks. Earlier today I examined a row of salted Celtic heads, cleft right down the middle and revealing some very sharp jaws indeed. They could definitely do you some damage, Pablo had said, holding up a salt-encrusted demi-noggin and grinning at the big, pointed teeth, which were the size of a bull crab's claws.

The animals rush past, and I can see the yellow glint of those killer mandibles beneath glistening snouts. Somehow I survive. As they speed down the slope I notice that every hog is tattooed with an ID number on its dish-towel-sized ear. Throughout its life and afterward, everything about these Celtics is monitored: bone growth, weight, muscle development, fat reserves, and finally taste. If a pig is adjudged to be great, Mummy keeps her rent-controlled apartment in the maternity barn, and Daddy is invited to continue getting all hot and lovin' with a semen pot.

It's a form of gastro-porcine eugenics (or is it porcine gastrogenics?). Rather than searching for high-yield, fast-growing animals, though, the aim of this form of selection is to produce the best possible example of a slow-growing, gourmet Celtic. And all the piggeryporkery is working.

Breeding for perfection is, I should imagine, rather like playing God on the fifth day: the Almighty, desperately overextended, sets up a committee to design a really scrumptious, all-purpose animal. Can you imagine the fun they'd have? A beef-flavoured chicken? No, no; a chicken with tarragon stalks instead of breastbones. Yes! A cow that gives coconut milk . . . a duck that lays pan-fried foie gras . . . a rabbit that shits peanut brittle . . . an *ibérico* pig that tastes like, well, like *ibérico* (they got that one right).

'And what about Galicia?' someone says, looking down at a much-scribbled plan of the Western European land mass. 'Can they have *ibéricos* too?'

'No, there's some different migratory flows planned for up there. And He's made Galicia kind of Atlanticky. Send Celtics.'

'What're they like?'

'Celtics? They're delicious. Got all that infiltrated fat in the meat too, just like *ibéricos*.'

'Lucky bastards!'

The Celtic pig is not directly related to the *ibérico* pig at all. It shares a line of descent with the common European breeds. What sets it apart is that the Celtic in Galicia, like the *ibérico* in the south, has not suffered any concerted attempt at genetic selection. Also, most intensively bred pigs in production today are slaughtered at between three and five months old, before the muscle tissue has had time to develop. Young pork is pallid, since younger animals have lower levels of myoglobin (the protein that lends red meat its attractive hue). By contrast, Galician Celtics on the Fonsagrada program are slaughtered big and fat and mature, just like *ibéricos*. They look obese, almost ready to burst, again, just like *ibéricos* do in their latter stages. *Fat* pigs. Pigs are supposed to be fat. These are pigs as Nature intended. If you ever happen to see a pig in a painting from the Middle Ages, it will immediately strike you: they're like zeppelins.

The Fonsagrada Celtics, in addition to their gorge-fest during the chestnut and acorn season, have a corn plantation for their exclusive trampling and munching; it's like keeping a bull and laying on a china shop for its amusement. Thick, leafy vegetation covers the floor of the adjoining meadow, all intended for the pigs. If that's not enough, there's grain feed available at low-slung tapas bars north and south. To cap it all they have their own mud baths, complete with a concierge pig keeper, who makes sure they are all in good health and spirits. His name is Roberto. Is there anything else they could have done for these lucky, lucky hogs? Massages? Cuban cigars? Compare that to an intensively reared industrial porker: suckled from a sow so tightly caged that she cannot turn her head to see her own offspring; a few miserable months in a light-deprived pig pound, eating protein-enriched grain mix; then the squealing horror of the stun-gun parade.

Pigs are sensitive creatures. Stress out a pig prior to slaughter and you increase the levels of glucose and lactic acid in the flesh. Postmortem this will produce an excessive rise in acidity, leading to a condition called PSE (pale, soft, exudative). Weeping, off-white pork. Sound familiar? Stressing your hog is like basting him in rancid vinegar. Be nice, it'll taste better. The Celtic princes of Fonsagrada are transported to the slaughterhouse a day prior to the event, allowed a restful night, then killed quietly and quickly, one at a time, in a specially designed carbon-monoxide chamber. They die without knowing anything about it. There's nothing touchy-feely or sentimental in this. It's all about the taste.

If you *do* like to get all touchy-feely about your meat, you need *porco leasing*! You can adopt one of Pablo's suckling pigs from an Internet photo album. Over the course of its life you can pay it personal visits, to check on the development of all that scrumptious intramuscular fat. I wouldn't get to know its adoring smile, though, because the first delivery you'll take, a couple of months after slaughter, will include its salt-cured face, split into two manageable pieces, just right for the *cocido* pot. Other bits are dispatched as soon as they're cured, the last delivery being that of the hams, salted briefly then hung up to dry-cure in mountain air until the meat inside has taken on a dark, mature sheen, and is ready to eat in tissue-thin slices. By the time you tuck into your Celtic ham, three to four years will have passed since the animal was born. By contrast, the pork you buy down at the supermarket goes from neonate to dinner plate in a matter of weeks.

Pablo explains all this as he drives me with verve through some curvaceous valleys on the way to our next stop, swinging the car around bend after precipitous bend as if to make the point that he can't be expected to show as much concern for our own lives as he does for those of his pigs. I know he's a vet, I tell myself, but I wonder if he's ever had a mammal defecate on his passenger seat. We're trying to rent that wood over there, he says, pointing at the valley side opposite, which over-flows with dark, luscious oaks, stretching way into the distance.

Many of the forests in the area are owned communally by villagers, or owned in a sort of semi-proprietorial arrangement by which you retain rights as long as you stay in the village. Sometimes the rights of specific trees belong to specific villagers and have labels nailed to them, a system that harks back to the days before cheap wood imports, when a mature chestnut could yield you a small fortune. Imagine, then, the situation when a company part-owned by a multimillion-aire cinema mogul arrives in a village of Galician peasants and asks: Whose is this forest?

Mine! shouts the entire population, man, woman, and dog. If Galicians are noncommittal and evasive in normal conversation, can you imagine what they're like when it comes to selling land? No, you can't. Whatever you are imagining, the truth is far, far worse than that. Buying land off a Galician is like trying to buy air off a will-o'-the-wisp.

We swing by a hamlet called Liñares de Vilafurada, home to José Rancaño Fernández, one of the members of the Celtic company and, as the retired procurator of Fonsagrada, just the kind of well-connected legal brain you need to get all torty with a bunch of tree-hugging locals.

Don José is what one might describe as a member of the deep-rural gentry. There is a soft-spoken modesty to him, something paternalistic and gentle.

'Let's show him around!' Pablo says, a close friend of the family, as he sprints up the exterior stone staircase of José's house.

The home in question is hacienda-like in layout, built around a large stone-paved courtyard. The walls of the house are three feet thick, and the present construction dates back to 1802, although there's also a new part (1828). Having scaled the stairs, we enter the building and make our way down a corridor. At the end a door leads us into the choir gallery of a chapel that serves the parish of Liñares. Beneath us is the nave, which dominates the entire end of the chapel and boasts a carved wooden altarpiece grand enough for a far bigger church; the altar table actually touches the walls at each side, and in front of the altar there's room to squash about a dozen souls on a couple of benches. Off to one side is a walk-in cupboard that serves as a confessional; if the priest happens to be a big eater, then it's a squeeze-in-and-leave-the-door-ajar cupboard, a confessional situation awkward enough to stop absolutely any teenaged boy from owning up to it. The most amazing thing about this gem of a chapel, however, is that its polished plaster walls are covered floor to ceiling in a sumptuous trompe l'oeil of orange-veined marble. It's like having a jewel-box Florentine cathedral in your spare room.

Don José explains that the whole house was tromped in 1828 by a gang of travelling Portuguese artisans. Each room is different, and each one, with only the slightest squint, could be in Versailles. The floors and ceilings themselves are expanses of beautiful, rich chestnut; the one exception is a bedroom floor done in the less prized red pine – for which Don José almost apologises. I look down at it with utter disdain: *red pine*.

Downstairs there is an old stone-floored kitchen, blackened with two centuries of soot, and in the middle the *lareira*, an open-hearth fire, above which the remains of a side of bacon hangs. If Don Quixote were to rattle through in his armour at this moment, it would not be much of a surprise.

We retire to a second, modern kitchen, and sit around a massive wood-burning range, where José's wife is tending a big pot of greens that bubbles merrily. The standard arrangement in Galician country kitchens is to set the range within a big, table-like working top surface, normally stone, and build cupboards underneath. Benches are placed around three sides, making a cozy dinner table for a dozen. The only problem with these table-cum-stoves is that once you're sitting there all snug and warm, chatting and nibbling at whatever happens to be available, you never want to leave.

We get ourselves ensconced around the range table. The Fonsagrada area is noted for its hospitality. Not many people would have passed through villages like Liñares in the old days, and any guest would have been given the full treatment. Don José explains all this as his wife sets a plate of home-produced chorizos down before us. Pablo, not one for reticence in the matter of pork, dives in. A brick of boiled side bacon arrives. It is strong and hoggy to the taste, and I carve off thin slivers and eat them with bread, savouring the intense sweetness of the chewy, almost glutinous fat. My bacon slivers earn general derision; Pablo is hacking off great lumps as he talks about Celtics and forests and this and that, and eventually Don José instructs me to cut bigger pieces. Now that's the kind of hospitality I can live with.

Conversation around the range centres on Celtic pork. Business is good, and there are plans for more forests, more animals. High-end butchers throughout Galicia are starting to stock the meat, and restaurants are getting in on the act. There are now over two hundred breeders of the Celtic registered with ASOPORCEL, the officially recognised breeders' association. Meanwhile, the dry-cured ham is selling for about the same whopping price as top-quality *ibérico*, and El Corte Inglés ('The English Cut'), Spain's best-known chain of department stores, is getting interested.

At the moment Celtic pork is not available in the United States, where for years Spanish pork was banned. But things are changing fast. The first producer of *ibérico* ham finally got an import license in 2007, and these days you can walk into Mario Batali's Bar Jamón in Manhattan and get yourself a tapa of the hallowed stuff, at a hallowed price. How long before we see a Galician Celtic ham on the counter, snuggling up close to the almighty black leg?

Exports or not, this is a gourmet revolution, right here in Don José's kitchen, a revolution born of an animal that, according to the livestock census, was extinct. I hack some more bacon off the lump in front of me, and savour the warm fat of the miracle.

José's son, who still lives in the family house, provides us with tumblers full of red wine. I take perhaps three sips, and the tumbler is immediately topped up. He has a dishevelled look, baggy trousers that seem not to be zipped up at the front, and an old jersey that hangs off him like a second skin he's almost ready to moult. He moves slowly, cigarette permanently in his mouth, hair savagely tousled, and talks with a ruminative lilt, as if each phrase rumbles out of him with an immutable inertia. He is in his middle years, and he lives and works here in the family home that he will one day inherit.

It takes me a while to grasp what is odd about him. Then it hits me: he isn't fidgeting and fussing, and there's no cell phone or BlackBerry constantly

129

twirling in his fingers. He's *relaxed*. He is ultra-relaxed, rustic-relaxed. It must be genetic because he shares this quality with his father, an aura of calmness and peace. That's it: I envisage a breeding program, just like the one for the Celtics, a program to produce less anxious, less e-mailed-out human beings. We could repopulate the big cities, barrio by barrio, street by street . . .

A large wedge of hard, cured goat's cheese is brought and set on the table. Meanwhile, José's wife takes a fist-sized piece of belly fat, dices it into a frying pan, and lets it melt partially, before adding a tablespoon of paprika. This is a *refrito*, one of the staples of Spanish cooking. Only in this case it's Galician style. A *refrito* would normally start with olive oil, with perhaps a little chopped garlic or onion lightly fried in it, then the paprika (and anything else you have to hand). You toss the lot into your stew toward the end, adding colour, the flavour of freshly toasted garlic, plus a silky smoothness and depth.

Our Galician *refrito* goes into the big pot of greens. Are they for us? I wonder, as the clock ticks on. Time is flexible here; they all tell me this, as the talk goes on regardless. More bread is called for. More wine is poured. The clock ticks.

I get home late. In my arms are two smoked Celtic tongues, a block of side bacon complete with bones, a chorizo as big as a dumbbell, and an array of more modest-sized sausages. Technically,

I could claim all these items as eaten, striking them from my list. But the challenge I have set myself is a geographical as well as a culinary one. I want to go out and find these things, to eat them in situ. In Liñares I found bacon in the cozy kitchen of a hacienda with its own miniature cathedral. So that is what I tick off. The running count stands thus:

shoulder ham
loin
neck and shoulder meat
rib meat
bone marrow
vertebrae
head
side bacon

Not bad, I tell myself, as I dump my armful of Celtic products on the kitchen table. Susana appears at the door, hovering suspiciously, and casting disapproving glances in my direction. She might eat *ibérico* ham, but Celtic tongue is another matter.

I take a breath, and reach for some bread.

WHY FOOD?

Barcelona airport. The man ahead of me waiting to board the plane sports a smart twill jacket and a silk tie. He is also wearing cuff links. Now, cuff links in Spain are reserved mainly for weddings, and this guy is not carrying any confetti. His skin is thin and uniformly tanned, like a chicken that's been left to slow-roast all morning. He could be a well-maintained sixty-five or a fabulously lithe seventy-five.

He turns to talk to me. The flight is to London, where I'm heading for a brief visit. So, it's fifty-fifty that this well-dressed gent is English, a fact that his plummy accent soon confirms. George Bernard Shaw said, 'It is impossible for an Englishman to open his mouth without making some other Englishman hate or despise him.' He was right.

For the purposes of prejudice and mutual loathing, the English group themselves according to a North-South divide, or what is more accurate, a North versus South divide. We from the North pride ourselves on being straight-talking, down-to-earth types, toughened up by a history of industrial toil. The Southerners, meanwhile, merely profited from all this industry by being exploitative absentee landlords and ruthless industrial capitalists, busying themselves all the while with Italian opera and French wines.

When it comes to identifying from which side of the divide someone hails, nothing serves so well as the way one talks, hence Shaw's comment. The man before me in the queue has a Southern accent, one with very strong hints of an affluent, upper-class background. I, on the other hand, have a Northern accent, that suggests more or less the opposite.

In Spain, Galicians are the Northerners. And their particular stereotype is one of old-fashioned rural ways, a certain simplicity and naivete of character, even a sort of reserved docility. Their rather charming, melodious accent doesn't help, and neither does the reputation for being from a poor, damp, underdeveloped corner of the country. Until recently, Spanish children used to shout out *Last one's a Galician!* to start a race.

Twill-man has a villa near Málaga in Andalucia, where he has lived for fifteen years. He falls effortlessly into a conversation about the niggles and deficiencies of his Andalucian life: unreliable plumbers, where you can get fish and chips, the price of everything. The English *love* to talk about the price of things. They sell their home in the UK, cash in their life insurance, and buy a villa on the south coast of Spain . . . but what really moves them is how much they're going to save on marmalade and teabags.

If you live abroad you have two choices: either avoid expats altogether, or accept that most of what you talk about will be expat issues, including those interminable comparisons with home. Sometimes I pretend to be Spanish for the entire duration of a flight; I just don't want to know how much better sewage provision is in Wolverhampton than Torremelinos.

One might wonder why certain expats are just that, *ex-patria*, because they often seem to adore the homeland so profoundly that it is not clear just why they ever left. They carry around an idealised image, framed by a million minor frustrations they've encountered during their years among the perfidious foreigner. The delights of home are never stronger than when you're not there.

This is exactly what happens with Galicians, long accustomed to economic migration. Thirty years in Buenos Aires or Geneva or London, working like slaves in hotels or on building sites, and suffering terribly from *morriña*, that uniquely Galician brand of homesickness. Then, when they eventually return, they moan like hell.

The oven-roasted gent queuing with me is effortlessly condescending, his eyes looking over my head when he talks, as if he is speaking to himself, enclosed in a series of private satisfactions, and only sharing his thoughts with me on a whim.

'Oh God!' he says, flicking a well-manicured hand in derision as he launches into an attack on the Spanish postal service. 'The *whatchamacallit . . .*' he calls it, struggling for the word *correos*. A minute later he's berating the Spanish for their driving (which is fair enough), only when he tries to say the Spanish name of the road on which his last near-death experience took place, the A-45, he stumbles over 'forty-five'. He cannot, in fact, speak Spanish, the language of the country that has been his home for the last fifteen years.

Linguistically speaking (which is the best way), living on Spain's southeast coastline must be a curious experience. In addition to the millions of British holiday makers that Spain welcomes nervously each summer, well over half a million Britons have taken up permanent residence there. For these English-speaking émigrés, ensconced in their golfing homes, gated communities, and poolside apartments, the only foreign language they are likely to hear is the occasional grunt from German neighbours, and in any case Gunter will speak his own brand of humourless, declarative English (and will, just occasionally, pull you up on your grammar). Some sort of English will be spoken in local bars and businesses, courts, schools, council buildings, and on local TV channels. The boy who cleans the pool will speak it, as will the mechanic who changes your oil. Regularly, English-speaking retirees are rushed to local hospitals and cannot explain in Spanish what's wrong with them, but it matters not; the doctors all speak English.

If you want to use a language other than English, choose a part of Spain that the expats forgot, or where they came once and it rained. In Galicia you will need to say things in another language. And it's no good just speaking in VERY LOUD, VERY SLOW ENGLISH; there are no Anglophone bread sellers and bus drivers here. As for understanding what is said back to you, that is to some extent an expendable skill, and you very quickly learn how to pretend. It is remarkably easy.

A Quick Guide to Pretending to Speak a Foreign Language

People don't begin conversations randomly. There are certain ground rules: you don't talk to your hairdresser about politics, and you don't talk to your mother about fetishism. As the foreigner, people will only talk to you about three things:

1. How long you have been here.
2. Whether you like it here.
3. The food here.

Susana and I have spent the best part of twenty years yo-yoing back and forth between Galicia and England, living here for a while, then over there for a bit, as the mood took us. And in all that time of coming to Galicia, no one has ever asked me what interesting films I've seen lately. The only exception is my sister-in-law, but she reads a lot of Raymond Carver and can hardly be held up as typical.

People do not *consciously* behave differently when there's a foreigner in the conversation. Yet they do. 'Foreigner talk' has been studied in great depth by linguists, so we know a lot about it. No one will expect you to introduce a new topic of conversation, nor to take as many speaking turns as other speakers. Being a foreigner essentially means you are expected to do a lot more listening. This certainly came as a shock to me, because I'm an argumentative loudmouth by nature. Yet in the deafening, polyphonic shouting matches that are Spanish (and Galician) conversations, unless you have the confidence to verbally slap people about, interrupting, ignoring, and overpowering the opposition (who will all be speaking at the same time), you'll spend a lot of time with your mouth shut. Even if your mouth is open and moving, nobody is likely to be listening to what's coming out of it.

As a foreigner your primary speaking task will involve weaving complex arabesques on the three seemingly uncomplicated topics above. And your progress will depend particularly on your opinions about the local food. Everyone in the world enjoys talking about their own cuisine. And when it comes to Galicia, talking about food is an obsessional, never-ending act. If you can join in, so much the better. But be polite. Levelling criticisms against the local food anywhere is a high-wire act, suitable only for the very, very proficient. I can get away with it here because people know that I have occasionally wept over a slice of tortilla, and that when I cut myself shaving, Galician pork fat drips down my chin.

So much for your speaking skills. Understanding what is said back to you is a little more tricky. The rules for listening are simple: forget grammar, forget conjugation, forget everything from the language classes you took prior to setting out. Most people don't speak like they do in Berlitz, wherever that is. Just listen out for the nouns, a verb here and there if you can manage it. Don't bother waiting around for a whole sentence; just grab a few words as they rush past you. Forget tense. Just forget tense altogether. Pronouns? Even if you hear one, it will have dissolved into thin air before you've worked out what it refers to, by which time the rest of the phrase will have disappeared after it. Consider, for example, the Spanish pronoun *se*. It can mean:

oneself
himself
herself
itself
yourself
yourselves
themselves

to him
to her
to it
to you
to them

It also approximates 'it' in phrases like 'it is known' (*se sabe que*) and 'one' in expressions like 'one never knows' (*nunca se sabe*). On top of all that, the word *sé*, which sounds just the same but with a dash of stress, means 'I know'. I bet you don't, though.

You're never going to catch all those *se*'s flying past you, however hard you listen to the sentence. For quite a long time you will not understand a whole sentence. Whole sentences are not going to be your communicative bread and butter at all. You'll feel like a kid. The difference is that, whereas a gurgling, diaper-wetting kid quickly becomes fluent in any language that's thrown at him, you won't. Get used to it, you're always going to be a bit of a baby when you open your mouth.

Many of the expat's feelings of homesickness and frustration come, I suspect, not from the obvious culture shocks of confusing bureaucracy, unfamiliar food, or changes in daily routines, but from an insidious feeling of powerlessness, which is partly the consequence of not being able to express yourself properly. It's a kind of powerlessness that one doesn't necessarily recognise or understand, but which at times is like a blurry dissatisfaction with things, as if a patina of superficiality has been draped across one's life, a drag of depressing simplicity. One antidote is to seek out expat friends, but in that case you're probably going to learn an awful lot about Wolverhampton's waste disposal system.

Whatever your nationality, if you live abroad you will also become a representative of your country of origin. And that can occasionally be problematic, because there's always going to be something that you have to apologise for, some national indiscretion that it falls to you to excuse: whaling (Japan and Norway), nuclear testing in the South Pacific (France), KFC Mashed Potato Bowls (USA).

If you're in Spain and you're British, it's Gibraltar, that silly lump of rock sticking up just off the south coast of Spain. Gibraltar is a British colony, and this fact always puts me in an awkward position. Paco is forever baiting me about Gibraltar, although if he wants an argument he's come to the wrong person, because I think I can reasonably claim to be the world's foremost expert on how the British should talk about the issue to a Spaniard:

DO SAY: It's a regrettable vestige of colonial times.
DON'T SAY: We got it legally at the treaty of Utrecht. Hands off.

DO SAY: The problem is how to convince the Gibraltarians to become Spanish.

140

DON'T SAY: The problem is the Gibraltarians do not want to become Spanish.

DO SAY: You know, it's a magnet for crime and money laundering.
DON'T SAY: It is one of the world's leading offshore financial centres.

DO SAY: The return of this British colony to Spain is long overdue; colonialism is a disgrace in any form.
DON'T SAY: Las Islas Canarias, las Islas Baleares, Ceuta, Melilla, las Islas Chafarrinas, el Peñón de Alhucemas, el Peñón de Vélez de la Gomera, la Isla de Perejil (Spain's remaining colonial territories).

If all else fails, just smile and say you like the food.

BLACK CAT

Imagine the scene. Ferran Adrià, the world's greatest chef, sits with a couple of his sous chefs at a white-clothed table in an anteroom just off the main kitchen of El Bulli, the world's greatest restaurant, a place where the culinary arts have been elevated to the status of molecular alchemy. Before them on the impeccable linen is an egg. 'But what else?' the world's greatest living chef might say. 'What else is there?'

'The French,' notes one of his assistants, 'have three hundred ways of cooking an egg'.

'Exactly,' the great man replies. 'They have them. Already. But what else can there be? Is there nothing more? What *might* an egg be?'

What might Adrià do with an egg? What transformations, what morphings might occur to him, as he takes the brown-speckled object in the palm of his hand, feeling its weight, observing its contours, the tips of his fingers gently pressing its matte exterior and seeming almost to commune with its inner richness?

Suddenly he stops. By degrees the tension in his limbs comes to charge the space around him with the electricity of wild creativity. His assistants freeze also . . .

'We make a malleable laminate from the whites,' he begins, now turning the egg in his fingers as if it were an enormous diamond, and he the thief who has just plucked it from under the nose of its rightful owner, 'and from that we make ravioli.'

The words spin from the wizard's lips like the sweet ectoplasm of a fantastical netherworld, a place of gastronomical serendipity, of magic, the place they call El Bulli, the world's greatest restaurant.

'We make ravioli, and we fill it with –'

'The yolk!' someone whispers, involuntarily.

A moment of quiet confusion follows. Adrià shakes his head. No one knows what to say. Then, after a long, Buddha-like breath, the great chef speaks:

'We fill the ravioli with . . . pasta.'

'Pasta sauce!' another of the assistants mumbles in awe.

The chef's head shakes again, tolerant, forgiving. 'No, Josep. With *pasta*.'

By the end of the session, plans for the simple egg are many and various, among them a rosary of roast yolk beads on egg-white gossamer, and dippy fingers of baked egg with a chicken schmaltz dip. 'Which comes first?' diners are playfully but firmly requested to answer before they tuck in. Finally, and most gloriously, there will be a boiled egg with an unblemished, uncracked shell, yet when the customer breaks into it he discovers that inside is a perfectly soft boiled egg; only, the egg is *from another shell*, extracted raw (it is supposed) and translated to its new home before cooking, although no one knows how. A member of the service brigade will be stationed close to each customer's shoulder to remind him of the fact in reverent tones as the shell is broken and the soft impostor flesh of the egg devoured with buttered toast. In a matter of weeks, Adrià's *huevo trasladado* ('removed egg') becomes a sensation throughout Europe.

Seeking to upstage the Master's miraculous egg, ambitious chefs across the continent push the boundaries of experimental cuisine in every conceivable direction. There are those who blind-fold their customers throughout the entire meal. At a restaurant on the French border, it is said, diners' tongues and lips are paralysed with Botox injections, and droplets of puréed food are allowed to fall gently into their immobile mouths at chef's command. In Lyon, they say, there is an eatery that remains bolted shut at all times; those lucky enough to get a reservation anxiously await a text message that contains merely a list of nouns and adjectives on which to feast their higher culinary imaginations . . .

What does all this have to do with Galicia, miles away from our imaginary scene in El Bulli, on the opposite side of the Iberian Peninsula, where rustic is still revered, and 'experimental' no more than a synonym for 'small portions'? Well, several centuries ago something exquisitely experimental occurred in a modest farmhouse kitchen here. It may have happened simultaneously in several houses, in any number. We will never know. But certainly it happened. I am in Santiago de Compostela to taste the results.

I moved to Santiago de Compostela straight after graduating from college in England. By that time I had already met Susana, and the idea was to stay a year, although one led to two, etc. I shared a flat there with five girls, and wasn't allowed to answer the telephone in case any of their God-fearing parents happened to be calling. For the two years I was in the flat I didn't once pick up the phone. Even if I was at home on my own, I just had to let it ring and ring. That kind of thing colours a person.

Santiago is the third holiest place of pilgrimage in the Christian world, after Jerusalem and Rome. It was one of Europe's first tourist centres back in medieval times. The city is built on the shrine of the Apostle James (James the Great, not the Lesser; there were two Jameses), who travelled through Spain preaching the gospel and created quite a stir with a series of crowd-pleasing miracles. On returning to Judea, he was beheaded by Herod, which wasn't so great. Myth has it that a host of angels then took his body to Spain in a rudderless stone boat that landed in the Galician village of Iría Flavia, later renamed Padrón (*pedrón* means 'big stone' in Spanish). Foodie trivia: Padrón is famous for a variety of tiny green peppers grown there that are generally sweet and innocuous; they lull you into a false sense of security as you pop them in your mouth one after the other, until a hot one comes along and gives you a nosebleed.

Anyway, eight hundred years after the body of James arrived in pepperland, he appeared on horseback at the battle of Clavijo, sword unsheathed, and helped the Christian forces defeat the Muslim invaders. A cult grew up around James the Moor-slayer, and although the name James is often rendered as Jacobo in Spanish, the alternate form, Iago, was normally used to refer to the saint. Iago's remains came to form the basis of a shrine, which was later removed to the place that would bear his name: Saint Iago. The military order of the Knights of Saint James was established at Santiago, and by the time the Moors were finally expelled from Catholic Spain, in 1492, James was the country's patron saint, a job that he has kept ever since. His remains allegedly sit in a bejewelled casket beneath the cathedral's altar (I use the word 'allegedly' in the sense of 'but it is not true').

There are a great many altarpieces in Galician churches depicting Saint James Matamoros, bedecked in saintly battle dress, astride a white charger and driving his sword into the heart of a grovelling blackamoor – invariably a weedy, boss-eyed coward dressed in what looks like a dirty sack with half-hearted decorative work on the hem. In some of the depictions there is a big paint splash of red blood daubed around the contorted mouth of the filthy invader, his legs already bandy and useless beneath him, humbled, it appears, by the very sight of the big red cross on the saint's chest. These days the Moor-slaying is generally played down.

Pilgrims arrive in Santiago all year long, many of them having come on foot, following El Camino de Santiago, the Road to Santiago, the thousand-year-old route of penitence devised at the time of medieval pilgrimage tourism, and still popular among the world's Catholics and masochists. There are a variety of medieval routes into Santiago, the best-known of them taking you right across northern Spain from the French border. If you need even more penitence than that, there's a route that starts up in Amsterdam (where you can sin right up till the moment you set out). And just below Amsterdam, in Flanders, a medieval tradition exists to this day by which one convicted felon per year is allowed to walk all the way to Santiago carrying a heavy backpack (and accompanied by a prison warden); when he arrives, his jail term is rescinded. Today I'm back in Santiago for a pig-based pilgrimage of my own.

The city's full name, Santiago de Compostela, refers to the miraculous star (*stella*) that shone above the field (*campo*) where the shrine lay; hence, 'Saint James of the field of the star'. This etymology is only one of several possible ones, but then again we are in Galicia, and no one would want things to be too clear-cut. Santiago's cathedral is a spectacular twelfth-century Romanesque monument, onto which a huge Baroque facade was tacked on later, and which is undeniably a fine example of a huge facade. The original western entrance, the 'Portico of Glory', sits within this newer, outer wall. A breathtaking granite-carved panoply of life-sized figures, from apostles to musicians, the portico is widely considered to be one of the greatest examples of medieval religious iconography in Europe. Also, and rather unusually, the master mason who designed it, Maestro Mateo, depicted himself within his own masterpiece, kneeling humbly at ground level. By tradition people bump foreheads with the Maestro in the hope that some of his genius will rub off on them.

Mateo's work, alas, is not as vivid as it once was, since parts of the original coloured paintwork are gone, after a team from London's Victoria and Albert Museum came in the nineteenth century to take plaster casts, and succeeded in taking away some of the paint as well. It makes one proud to be British. Incidentally, in the nearby twelfth-century church of Santa María Salomé you can see what is probably the earliest sculpture of an angel wearing glasses. Worth knowing if you play Trivial Pursuit Deluxe Catholic Edition.

Santiago's cathedral is famous for its *botafumeiro*, a gigantic, silver-plated incense burner, said to be the biggest in the world. Weighing in at 180 pounds, it hovers just above the transept floor, on thick ropes attached to a pulley mechanism way up in the dome of the roof. A team of eight red-robed men shovel burning coals and incense into it, then set to work, yanking mightily on the ropes until the *botafumeiro* begins to swing through the air, gaining height all the time, until finally it is sweeping north and south across the great transept at a tremendous speed, almost touching the ceiling on both sides, belching out its fragrant smoke as it goes. It scares the shit out of you, which is an old Catholic trick. Pure theatre, and a big draw at Corpus Christi.

In 1499, Catherine of Aragon stopped off in Santiago to see the spectacle on her way to England to marry King Henry VIII; the messy divorce that followed led to the English Reformation, centuries of anti-Catholic persecution, and generally a whole lot of pan-European unpleasantness. If only Catherine had read the signs: during her prenuptial visit to the cathedral, the *botafumeiro* became detached from its ropes and crashed through the window of the north transept. How different modern Europe might look today if Catherine, having watched the giant incense burner flying out the window, had decided to stay home and marry one of those nice Hapsburg boys from Madrid.

149

Royal divination aside, we might remember that one of the reasons for the use of incense in medieval times was to rid the place of the terrible stench of ordinary folk. A cathedralful of unwashed penitents just in from a three-month, bath-free walk across Europe in the heat of summer was, in olfactory terms, a serious issue, and the ecclesiastical authorities were certainly tackling the problem head-on when they ordered the biggest air freshener in Christendom.

Pilgrims were supposed to arrive in Santiago relatively clean, since the last stop-off before the trek into town is on a hill called Lavacolla, these days the location for the city's airport. Lavacolla translates as 'wash your tail', with 'tail' here meaning 'butt'. If the masses were arriving at the cathedral after their wash, yet still there was need for a forty mile-per-hour incense delivery system, one can only imagine how fragrant their tails had been a few miles farther back, where the time-honoured tradition of offering pilgrims hospitality along the Road to Santiago was probably replaced by one of fighting them off with a big stick.

Santiago's cathedral was built on a granite hillside, and around it grew the city. Hewn of the same granite as the hill itself, a sort of twinkle-grey-yellow colour that mopes when wet, the place seems almost to have been scraped and chiselled from a single mass of rock. Vast monasteries and churches vie for space amid an implausible crowding of monuments, an array of truly enormous square edifices

150

set so close to one another that the city, viewed from certain angles, looks like a drinks party for a group of very important buildings held in a place not quite big enough for the occasion. There's a kind of understated magic here, a quiet other-worldliness that is no doubt partly a result of there being not one inch of asphalt in the place; it's stone all the way, narrow and crooked streets and alleys untouched for five or six hundred years. Other than by the rain, which touches them a lot.

Apart from a cluster of trinket shops and some traditional *plateros* (silversmiths) up by the cathedral, the medieval part of town is surprisingly low-key in its pandering to tourists. Wandering along its two principal shopping streets – medieval malls, with colonnaded granite arcades on both sides to protect shoppers from Galicia's incessant rain – you could almost forget that the last few hundred years had happened. People still live here, lots of them, in the higgledypiggledy buildings that cower everywhere in the shadows of grander ecclesiastical piles. Local residents pick their way with bags of groceries through the hordes of daily tourists; vans make deliveries; the occasional dog sidles past, on the sniff for discarded tuna pasties. Old women dressed in black and grey move slowly along, like extras from a Fellini film. And the most elderly of these women were youngsters when Spain tore itself apart in a horrific civil war, brother against brother, to be followed by Franco's brutal military dictatorship, four decades of torture, execution, and political oppression. They hobble down the rain-worn stone streets, stoic and taciturn, and when they need to go to the bank or a shop, and there's a queue, they hobble right to the front, stoic and taciturn, dithering with their purse, as if they hardly know where they are, and innocently push you all back a place.

At the end of one of the main streets I come to a *pastelería*. A Spanish street without a cake shop, or at least a bakery, is like a vertebrate without bones; it would stagger to an unseemly death in a matter of minutes. It's a cliché to say it, perhaps, but here, as in many parts of southern Europe, people buy fresh bread every day. You don't need a cute, old-fashioned bread shop, either. If a convenience store happens to be your only handy shop, then you will buy your fresh stick of bread there, every day. This particular shop is also selling cakes, because Spaniards don't make cakes – ever. They buy them. If you do happen to bake a cake in Spain, a chocolate cake, say, even a plain Victoria sandwich (which, I remind you, has just four ingredients, and which you really have to try hard to mess up), people will consider you a marvel of Nature, nibbling their slice of sponge-cake and gasping with wonder. Susana thinks it has to do with the Catholic/ Protestant distinction – that Protestants somehow enjoy following the strictures of a recipe, the specific quantities and timings and temperatures that baking demands, whereas Catholics prefer an element of chaos and inexactitude in life. The industrial revolution was largely a Protestant affair, she notes, as were many of its great engineers. And its cake makers. On baking day the conversation in our house is a lot of fun.

A little farther on is an old-fashioned food store, an *ultramarinos* (*ultramar* means 'overseas'), a place that in the past would have sold stuff from far and wide, a general store. It is incredibly small, yet sells everything you could possibly imagine you might ever need. Pride of place in the window display is a selection of dome-shaped cheeses called 'little tits' – *tetillas* – although they look sizeable to me. This brings to mind the fact that in the past, robust women from Galician villages were the favoured wet nurses of Madrid's rich, so the issue of breast size is perhaps more complex than I know. In any case, the cheesy bosoms (also known as *perillas* – 'little pears') contain a mild, lightly cured, and somewhat creamy cheese, not particularly interesting on its own, but when eaten with slices of *membrillo* – a sweet quince preserve – it is gorgeous. In some places, an entire cheese and a big dish of *membrillo* is served as a pudding, along with a knife, and you simply eat as much as you want. Not in Santiago, though; too many greedy students and backpackers on a budget. Foodie trivia: in neighbouring Portugal, the same jamlike quince preserve is called *marmelada*, from which our own word 'marmalade' derives.

The shop that sells everything used to have a small sign in the bottom corner of the window: WE SPEAK IN SIGN LANGUAGE. Inside there is hardly room to turn around, and its wares are mostly on open view, easily pointed at by the customer. I can think of no shop in the world that has less need to offer language facilities of any kind. Perhaps it was a Galician joke. I look for the notice now, but it is no longer there. There is, however, a sign announcing that English is spoken within. I consider taking up the challenge and asking, in English, for a quarter bushel of pine nuts. At the last moment I chicken out and ask in Spanish, just a bagful. The lady in the shop tells me that, no, she has no pine nuts. No one has pine nuts anymore.

I get to the corner of Calle Franco (not named after the dictator) and see that the hot chestnut seller is there as usual, doing brisk business. He'll be switching to ice cream sometime soon, about the time the first buds open. There's a multilingual hum in the air as groups of visitors drift past me, making their way across from the Alameda park, its walkways lined with almond trees. One hears a great deal of English on the streets of Santiago, plus German, French, Dutch, and Japanese. And almost all these foreign speakers wear anoraks. Calle Franco, a narrow, winding pedestrian street, looks as if an orange, blue, and green waterproof snake is slithering lethargically along it. Pilgrims wear anoraks here because they have been warned: this is not the Spain you know. Today there's a cloyingness in the air, and the city is like a stone-cold sauna. In Galicia it can be rainy yet stickily hot; it can be blindingly sunny yet as cold as the Arctic. It might rain every day for a month, yet one spring morning you will awake to a blazing bright warm day. Don't be fooled; take your brolly. Galician weather is unpredictable, unknowable. There are so many microclimates here that it sometimes seems that every person has his own. Mine is wet. Poets of the region have said 'Galicia: where rain is art'. I think this is what's called identifying the Unique Selling Point.

Santiago is the home of one of Europe's great universities. Thirty thousand students live here, mainly in the new town, a constant twelve stories of apartment buildings thrown up cheaply in the sixties and seventies, and lending the streets an almost Eastern European atmosphere, drab and monotonous (the main square in the new part of town is popularly known as Red Square). You can see the beginnings of the modern sprawl from the top of Calle Franco, which by way of contrast is a crooked medieval street crammed full of pokey bars and taverns, very much a place for students as well as tourists, and the city's principal booze route since anyone was sober enough to remember. It's about ten feet wide, paved in slabs of well-worn granite, and all the way down it are places that in one guise or another have been serving boiled octopus and dry-cured ham and various kinds of *empanadas* (flat savoury pasties) to students and pilgrims for well over half a millennium.

I walk down Franco, edging my way past gaggles of young backpackers, scallop shells dangling from their packs (the shell is the old pilgrim badge, the sign of Saint James). The street follows a gentle descent, which has been used to great effect over the centuries by carousing students, who wisely start at the top and let gravity lead them along on wine-wobbly legs. I remember being initiated into an old student tradition here known as the Paris-Dakar by our friend Carlos, a brilliant linguist who cannot hold his drink. I first met him when he was still a student of English philology at the university, at which point he already had an English vocabulary twice the size of mine and far better diction. On that occasion he had succeeded in mistaking a tube of Super Glue for the eye ointment he was taking and had stuck his eye shut. Throughout the evening he slowly pried the eyelids apart, in considerable discomfort, but too embarrassed to go to the doctor. Anyway, at the top of Franco is a bar called Paris, and toward the bottom one called Dakar. Between them are perhaps thirty bars. You have probably guessed the rest. By the time we had done the Paris-Dakar that night, nearly twenty years ago, we were staggering, and those narrow alleys had turned into confusing, echoey stone tunnels from which there seemed to be no escape; when a street-cleaning wagon roared toward us, headlights ablaze, we thought it was a monster, and ran.

I can no longer drink thirty wines. Calle Franco has not changed much, although one or two of the oldest, darkest bars have been replaced by slick seafood restaurants. One of them even has a greeter in a brown velvet jacket standing outside, which is somehow risibly un-Galician. Even he looks embarrassed. Locals cast him questioning glances. *I know*, his eyes say back, *I know . . .*

Today I ignore the charms of the greeter. I am heading back to an old haunt of mine, O Gato Negro, the Black Cat. It's not on Calle Franco. It's not on a street at all. Not even on a corner. It's on a doglegged slip of a lane that leads from a small square to another street, the name of which no one ever (and I mean ever) remembers. The Black Cat is near the edge of a corner; it has not, I imagine, appeared on any map. But then again you never need to give directions. Everyone knows where it is.

It's a small tavern. You might almost call it a hovel without being insulting, a place where animals would have been kept. And it is one of the oldest and best-known places in Santiago. Every time I return, pilgrim-like, I worry that perhaps it has finally closed down. It certainly doesn't seem to have changed much in the past hundred years, yet people often speculate as to its chances of surviving much longer, as if it's a feisty but ageing maiden aunt. No doubt in twenty or thirty years' time some other insignificant foreigner will write about the Black Cat, equally worried about whether the owners will carry on the family tradition for another generation. Each time I go back to Santiago I expect to see that it has been transformed into a wine bar called the Black Cat, in which the uneven, sawdust-sprinkled stone floor has been scrubbed clean of its homely grime, and the rude, old-fashioned ceramic wine cups are full of sparkling Cava. Today, however, it is still the way it's always been, although I suspect that it has had several coats of paint since I first went there. The woodwork is currently bright green, the bumps and holes in it gummed up with layer upon layer of paint; the door and window frames look as if they've been moulded from green plasticine.

My old friend Pepe, whom I haven't seen since he went off to work as a wandering stonemason in the South, first brought me here. His dad was one of the Black Cat's longest-standing customers, and part of a *peña*, a sort of informal group of friends who meet in the same place regularly, often keeping up the tradition for year after year. That *peña*, I remember, used to sit at a table in the back room. Everyone else was supposed to know not to sit there at the time the *peña* normally arrived, and you were supposed to know what time that was.

When I lived in Santiago, the old lady at the

Black Cat would call me 'my little king'. I guess she did that with any fresh-faced young man who ate there regularly, although I still like to think I was the only one. I would always have *caldo*. For a start, a big bowl of the hot broth was about thirty cents. At that time, if I remember, a packet of Ducados cigarettes didn't cost much more. If you liked broth and Ducados cigarettes (made with old-fashioned 'black' tobacco) then in Santiago you could live like a little king, and for a lot less. Black tobacco is one of the many traditions that is slowly losing ground in modern Spain. When you light up, the taste is so strong – burnt rubber, carpet cleaner, Satan's halitosis – it's as if someone has punched you hard in the throat. Back when I was a student in Cambridge I used to carry a pack with me. If one of the tramps that shuffled around the city centre tried to bum a cigarette, I'd pull out my pack of Ducados. They soon got to know me.

Today the Black Cat is heaving with life. There are students, tourists, men in overalls, people in smart office suits. Once inside you realise that the space you have squeezed into is the size of you minus your arms. There is nowhere for your elbows to go. The noise is intense. Plates of food float high above the noise, a constant stream of fried sardines, disks of paprika-dusted octopus, griddled langoustines, country cheese so soft it oozes like molten glass . . . plus about a dozen other things, more or less a complete list of traditional Galician bar cuisine, the world's greatest fast food.

As with all taverns of this kind, the atmosphere borders on chaotic. You have to shout to tell the barman what you want, and you are never quite sure whether the message has got through. The floor is sprinkled not only with sawdust, but also toothpicks, cigarette butts, and discarded paper serviettes. As soon as a six-inch gap opens up at the bar you dive forward and claim it with one hand, then shimmy your way in until you have staked your claim with an elbow. Finally I get close enough to catch the barman's attention, and yell at him. Today, for the purposes of research, I have ordered *chicharrones*.

The word *chicharrones* comes from *chicha*, which has a variety of meanings in Spanish, among them the slightly disparaging sense of 'ordinary meat' (i.e., meat that's nothing special) and a general term for a variety of maize-based liquors, from which we get the wonderful expression *No es ni chicha ni limonada* ('It's neither liquor nor lemonade') – neither one thing nor the other. With so much understatement and indecisiveness going on, it comes as no surprise that *chicharrones* are a Galician speciality. If you come from anywhere else in the Spanish-speaking world where *chicharrones* are eaten, you'll probably be thinking cracklings. But not here. Galician *chicharrones* are something quite different, and unique to this part of the world.

A plateful of *chicharrones* looks as if someone has run over a hedgehog then tried his best to reassemble it. They are in fact made from pork meat. Our organic butcher in Coruña uses shoulder ham and belly pork, but you can use whatever off-cuts you have at hand; a pork butcher in Santiago that I know also uses face meat. Whatever else goes in the pan, some part of the belly is probably going to follow, because you really need a good bit of fat for this recipe.

To make *chicharrones*, you chunk the meat, add as much extra pork fat as is necessary, and slow-stew it in a pan with a little water until the meat, by now luxuriating in the melted fat, falls apart. The meat is then teased into fine, loose strands with a fork. And that's it. Soft, tender, stringy pork.

Each strand of pork is protected in a layer of grease, but the succulence of the meat reduces over time. What starts off as pink and soft, turns, after a few days in the window display, into a crusty, dried-out lump, and begins to resemble an unkempt toupee. Be vigilant; take a look behind the bar before ordering. There's nothing worse than dehydrated *chicharrones*; they taste like the bristles scraped from the skin of the hoary old beast itself.

One intriguing way of cooking *chicharrones* is to mix them with sugar and bake them in a pie. I heard of this recipe from someone who was reminiscing about the sweet, meaty pie that her grandmother used to make using *chicharrones*.

161

Everyone here seems to have had a grandmother who was a great cook. Alas, many of those grandmothers are no longer around, and I never did track down a sweet belly pork pie.

Today, my savoury *chicharrones* are fresh and unsweetened. The meat is light and soft, and each little meaty thread carries enough cold fat to make it moist and tender, just enough to leave that comforting film on the roof of your mouth. It is not unlike eating a stringy meat pâté, since you can scoop up a little with a lump of bread and mould the two together. This kind of food, it has to be said, is not going to help you with your calorie-controlled diet. Go to any village in Galicia and see for yourself; not a lot of skinny folk about. Spain may be known for its life-enhancing Mediterranean diet, but Galicia is on the Atlantic, and Santiago de Compostela is almost exactly as far away from the Mediterranean as it is from Munich.

But what does any of this have to do with Ferran Adrià, the world's greatest living chef, and his avant-garde restaurant, El Bulli? Well, several hundred years ago, somewhere in Galicia, a family pig was slaughtered. Imagine the scene: it is probably November or December, because unless you are very rich you'll just have the one pig each year, and early winter is when you'll kill it. A potful of pork oddments is being cooked up, and the sweet smell weighs heavy on the air. The lady of the house is just about to pour off the fat – to be used for hearty breakfasts of rye bread scraped with pig lard – when she stops. Like the great Catalan chef, she is not satisfied with plain old pork. There must be something else, she thinks, a means of making the meat more interesting. Perhaps one of her children is a reluctant eater, or perhaps she is just sick of pork lumps.

Whatever the reason, she wants more from life, more from her food. Unlike Mr Adrià, though, she has no cupboard full of exotic spices, no rabbit brain mousse or carpaccio of performing seal with which to adorn her recipes. All she has is her pot. So, she leaves it right where it is, on the *lareira* – the floor-level stone hearth where she cooks – to see what will happen. An hour later, when the meat has almost disintegrated into its own fat, she begins to pick at it with a fork, cajoling the flesh until it comes apart and yields up its fibers, pink and succulent and surprisingly appetising to the eye. On she goes, picking and separating until all that's left is a tangle of pork threads. Though she doesn't know it, she's at the cutting edge.

'What the hell is this?' her husband asks, as the mystery dish is set before the family. On it there seems to be fried rat tails.

'Have a taste!' she says nervously.

On closer inspection, it seems that it might be a mound of wet donkey mane.

'Is it boiled tree bark?' a boy asks. 'I've had that. It's disgusting.'

'No,' his brother says, 'it's squashed hedgehog. Yum-yum.'

He grabs a fork, his mouth watering.

'No, it's the *chichas*!' Mum cries, unable to contain herself any longer.

'The . . . *chichas*?' they say, all at once, looking first at the plate and then at the woman, who must surely be a witch.

Then one of the boys, as if to satisfy himself that it is not hedgehog after all, slowly reaches out and takes a single strand. Everyone stops bickering and watches as he brings the thread of soft meat to his mouth and pops it in . . .

Chicharrones, then, were born of experimentation and caprice. Of a need for fancy. And just like the world-famed dishes coming daily from the kitchen of El Bulli way over on the Mediterranean coast, there is no good reason for making Galician *chicharrones* at all. The meat would keep far better whole, since the fine strings swiftly turn from succulent pink to dried-out, semi-translucent brown. In purely gastronomic terms, doing this to pork is pure style, a style devised by someone who had only a pan and a fork at her disposal. If Ferran Adrià had done it first, he would have called it Hog Vermicelli, and the small scattering of pork bits on your plate would come in a suspension of monkey spittle topped off with a single daisy leaf.

In Galicia it comes in a lump, with a hunk of bread. No one here got a Michelin star for *chicharrones*. But it's hard to imagine how the world's greatest chef could have improved them.

ENCOUNTERS WITH EMINENT GALICIANS I: DAÑA VICTORIA OF LÁNCARA

Now, if you are in the hamlet of Lower Armea and want to get to Upper Armea, you probably would not expect to have to stop nine times for directions on the way. The two Armeas are, admittedly, about five miles apart. But still . . .

A farmer points me in the right direction, stressing that I'll need to ask again; two old ladies out for a walk shriek, saying it's miles away; a gap-toothed woman in mud-caked slippers emerges from a seemingly abandoned farm and laughs when I say I'm lost, recognising that if I've wound up on her doorstep then I almost certainly am; the short-order chef in a roadside cafeteria tells me I am almost there; a retired couple say I have gone just slightly too far; a plumber in Upper Armea itself is curious to know why I've come at all; a farmer guesses why I'm here, but his two very aggressive dogs make me cower until I am ashamed of myself, and I don't really hear his instructions; a farmer's wife across the way points me back the *other* way; an elderly Portuguese lady called Dosinda stands with me in the rain for twenty-five minutes (count 'em) and tells me the story of her long life . . .

A girl working in a local café admitted to me that even she sometimes gets lost on the backroads here. That's how it is in the municipality of Láncara, on the bottom edge of Galicia's central plateau, a relatively flat, rural landscape where these days not a great deal happens, a place, indeed, notable for those who left rather than those still here.

I drive down a dark, tree-covered lane that succeeds in being both very muddy and almost strikingly uninspiring. Someone is mucking out his ground floor as I pass. At the door of the last building along, I knock.

Victoria appears not at the door but at a window close to it. If you can believe the papers, she's seventy-eight years old, although she could pass for a lot less than that, strawberry blonde hair in loose curls and small eyes that twinkle in a lively but no-nonsense way. She's not the only one with eyes like that, either. You've seen those eyes before . . .

For quite a while we talk through the half-opened window, which has a steel grill affixed on the outside. I apologise for coming unannounced, and for being like all the others who are bothering her at the moment, what with her cousin sick and all.

'There's nothing more to say!' she explains patiently, an almost sympathetic smile, 'and I'm not properly dressed! We were late getting up today.'

Behind her, a man hangs about in the shadows smoking. From time to time he hushes a yelping puppy called Perla. He also chips into the conversation, which is disconcerting because I cannot see his face. Meanwhile, I pull the hood of my waterproof further forward over my brow as the rain comes down harder.

'Oh, come on, Julio,' she says to her husband at last. 'Let's get the poor *chico* inside. He's getting soaked.'

So Victoria López Castro invites a stranger into her warm, dry kitchen. She probably finds herself doing this quite often, every time something happens in Cuba, every time her cousin Fidel is in the news.

When it comes to her eyes, though, they're Raúl's, eerily so, once you see the similarity. She's also got that full-faced, cheeky grin that Raúl Castro occasionally lets slip, so unlike his po-faced older brother.

The Castro family is without much doubt the most famous family of Galician emigrants. Fidel and Raúl's father was born here in Láncara, and emigrated to Cuba. His sons have not forgotten their roots; Raúl stopped off in the village two years ago, and although Fidel hasn't been back since 1992, when Galicia's then president, the

167

archconservative Manuel Fraga, invited him, there's been plenty of contact with Havana.

In 1853 the Spanish government officially sanctioned emigration for the first time, legalising what until that point had been a furtive process. Cuba, then a Spanish colony, immediately became the most popular destination, along with the recently independent South American republics of Mexico, Argentina, Uruguay, and Chile. Although any Spaniard could pack up and go, none went in such numbers as those from Galicia, one of the poorest regions of Spain, and which had two transatlantic ports at its disposal: 122,875 Galicians emigrated between 1860 and 1880, from a home population at the time of somewhere around a million and a half.

Young, single men from villages formed the bulk of those leaving. Rosalía de Castro, Galicia's best-known poet, gave this stark description of her homeland in those times:

'THE WIDOWS OF THE LIVING
AND THE WIDOWS OF THE DEAD'

This one goes and that one goes
and all, all of them go.
Galicia, you find yourself without men
to work your land.
In exchange you have orphan boys and
orphan girls

and fields of solitude,
and mothers without sons
and sons without fathers.
And you have hearts that suffer
long, mortal absences
that no one will console.
    from *Follas novas*, 1880. My translation.

The Galician character is shaped to a great degree by emigration, by the complex emotions that emigration gives rise to. *Morriña*, that typically Galician brand of home-yearning, is perhaps easier to understand when you think of those country folk, who had probably never been far from their village before, yet suddenly, having staked their future on third-class transit to the New World, found themselves alone on the banks of Manhattan's East River, staring openmouthed at the Brooklyn Bridge, and not blinking much.

Although the majority of these emigrants were from the countryside, they generally headed for the big cities, working in service industries and construction. They hardly ever chose agriculture. I don't blame them. It's all very well Rosalía bemoaning the farmland that no one was there to work, but if you had escaped rural poverty for the chance of a better life, would you go looking for someone else's potato farm to toil on?

'Have you seen *the house*?' Victoria says, settling down at the kitchen table.

'Not yet,' I tell her.

Angel Castro, Fidel Castro's father (hence, Victoria's uncle), was born in a single room above some cow stables a few miles away, not far from Lower Armea, which I had mistaken for Upper Armea. (There is no sign announcing Lower Armea, and the sign to Upper Armea just says Armea; I consider myself vindicated.) Angel was tall, intensely intelligent, and serious-faced (remind you of anyone?). But whatever your talents, without money or substantial amounts of land, your life in late-nineteenth-century Láncara was going to involve day labouring, and the prospect of doing nothing else but labouring for the rest of your days.

The Castros recognised that Angel was special, and somehow managed to get him to Madrid, where kindly relatives steered him through an education of sorts. Seeking adventure, he joined up to fight in the Spanish-American War, and sailed off to Cuba. El Desastre ('the Disaster'), it was called, the war that stripped Spain of her last colonies (Cuba, Puerto Rico, and the Philippines) and threw the country into a period of depressed self-examination, rather like the depression that hit Great Britain after the Suez Crisis in 1956, the kind of psychological malaise that hits any country once it realises that it is no longer a main player in the great geopolitical game. There should be Prozac for nation-states in decline; it would prevent all sorts of minor territorial skirmishes.

Despite Spain's losing the war, Angel liked Cuba. After the disaster he returned to the island with his brother Gonzalo. And they were not alone. By this time bigger, faster passenger steamers were lining up to take Galicians across the *charco* (pond), satisfying the growing clamour for a better life. From 1880 to 1930 the exodus from Galicia was huge. It reached a peak in 1912, when 203,542 people left, with 165,010 following on in 1913. By 1930, there would be 600,000 Galicians and their descendants living in Buenos Aires alone. Gonzalo Castro would himself settle there, by which time Buenos Aires was getting a new nickname: Galicia's fifth province. And in South America generally, those from any part of Spain were referred to simply *as gallegos* (Galicians), such was the concentration of Galicians among the burgeoning Spanish emigrant population.

Meanwhile, in Cuba, Angel Castro set to work, opening a restaurant called EI Progreso ('Progress'), then buying a share of a mine called EI Deseo ('Desire'). On the way he married a wealthy young woman from Havana (two kids, but the marriage ended). He moved into the wood-cutting business, and from there into sugar cane plantations and lucrative trade with the *yankis*.

'When he came back to visit,' Victoria says, recalling the stories that her own mother had told her, 'he was already a big shot, and he was only thirty. He brought clothes and money, and he

171

treated my mother with great kindness. People begged him to be taken to Cuba. They *begged* him. That's what it was like here.'

Angel was by now confident in the ways of the world. During his stay in Galicia he lodged in a tavern, sitting up with the owner for two days and two nights playing cards, eventually winning the tavern and all its contents off the exhausted owner (he never enforced the payment of the debt).

Back in Cuba he married for a second time. Lina Ruz, a young plantation worker, bore him seven more children, among them Fidel and Raúl. By this time Angel's *colonia*, his 'colony' or estate, stretched out across the island's old eastern province: 23,000 acres of sugar plantations, plus a school, a cockpit, a movie theatre, and a drugstore for his hundreds of workers, many of them immigrants themselves. There was even a train to get them around. The Kaiser of Cuba, they called him, such was his prominence on the island.

Angel Castro died in October 1956, while his sons Fidel and Raúl were exiled in Mexico (along with Che Guevara), just six weeks before their armed landing in Cuba, which would trigger the Cuban revolution. Three years later the revolutionary government was declared. Private property was expropriated, including the vast estate of the Castros. Many of the Galicians who had gone to Cuba to escape poverty now abandoned the island and returned home penniless, carrying no more than the suitcase with

172

which they had set out many years before. I wonder what Angel's opinion would have been.

There in Victoria's kitchen, Julio slips some more wood into the range and lights another cigarette. We've moved on from the father to the son.

'What is there left to say?' she repeats for a third time. 'Nothing! It's all been said about Fidel.'

She adores him, though. It's obvious. You can see it just in the way she talks about him. She is his favourite cousin, she tells me, and vice versa.

'We just got on,' she says, 'the first time we met.'

They were linked, perhaps, not just by family ties, but because she hailed from the Castros' ancestral home. Indeed, these days she's the last of the Castros in Láncara, Fidel's last remaining Galician relative on Galician soil. If anyone wants to talk about Fidel's roots, they call Victoria. Someone rings from a TV network as we talk. She tells Julio to pretend she's out. I feel honoured to be sitting in the kitchen, because I got her name from the newspaper and just turned up, asking around for her house once I was here. I did have to stand in the rain for a little while, though.

Fidel Castro, who handed power over to his brother Raúl not long before my visit to Láncara, is no longer of much interest to me. I can read the story of how the son of a Galician emigrant became the world's most conspicuous communist leader anywhere. What I cannot quite grasp is why Victoria lives here at the end of a dark, muddy lane in what the most gracious visitor would have to call a pokey hamlet. Why shouldn't she? you ask. Well, for one thing she had options . . .

Galician mass emigration came to an end in the 1930s, curtailed by economic crisis in the Americas, the Spanish Civil War (1936–39), then the Second World War. Afterward, as the rest of postwar Europe was undergoing reconstruction and rebuilding, with booming economies and rapidly climbing standards of living, fascist Spain festered, and Galicia remained a patchwork of hamlets where people still ploughed with their solitary cow. General Franco was in power, political freedom had disappeared, and life was as bleak as it had been a century earlier. *Sod that*, came the cry from the villages.

Between the early fifties and the early seventies another wave of emigration took place, many choosing Venezuela this time, but with increasing numbers favouring the rich economies of Europe, from the factories of West Germany to the luxury hotels of London and Paris. This time around a lot of women went as well, some of them alone, bent on adventure, seizing their opportunity to see something of the world.

'It was about time!' Victoria says, beaming at me, as if that sudden decision she made in 1962 is still a sweet, thrilling memory. After years looking after her mother and everyone else, she decided it was her turn.

'Just like that!' she says, flicking her fingers as if her choice of Switzerland was a sort of conjuring trick. 'Apart from anything else, it was my chance to earn some money!' she explains with a cheeky laugh. 'What could you do here? Nothing! There was no chance of anything here. It's difficult to imagine, now.'

So off she went, from Láncara to Zurich, a young woman on her own who spoke no foreign languages and had no idea what to expect. She was there twenty years, and she tried her hand at every kind of work available, most notably in a munitions factory, where she saw fellow workers have their hands and arms blown clean off.

'Every time I dropped my work tray I just froze,' she tells me, her face screwed up in what is, I can only assume, a mime of someone who's just dropped their live munitions on the floor right in front of them.

She loved the city of Zurich, although loving a city like Zurich is not hard to do, with its beautiful balance and scale, its muted elegance, that low-key good humour of the Swiss that pervades the place. To Victoria, Switzerland was a sort of tingling, magical paradise, full of luxury and possibility.

Twenty years later, in 1982, she came home. It was typical of those who emigrated in the 1950s onward to return home. Victoria came back to a Spain that was finally rid of its military dictator. Democracy had been established (first general elections, 1977), and within a generation of the death of General Franco, Spain's economy would be the ninth largest in the world, fuelled by the tourist trade, a rapidly expanding industrial base, and massive cash injections from the European Union. Like so many more returning Galicians, Victoria also had enough money to put rural poverty firmly behind her. She bought a new flat in the nearby town of Sarria and filled it with new furniture, and she invested in a holiday home down on Spain's southern coast. Suddenly, she was a property owner.

Then Fidel rang.

'Come to Cuba!' he shouted down a crackly line.

She went. And she lived like a communist princess, the guest of her famous cousin. There was an instant rapport between them, two cousins who until then had never met. They became close, and he bestowed on her a personal chauffeur, a cook, and a fine house in Havana.

'And when the cook was ill,' she tells me, 'the chauffeur would call, a tray in his hands. 'This is from the kitchens of the Revolutionary Palace,' he would say!'

A year went by, a year in which she lived a life of unusual privilege, the pampered guest of a communist dictator.

'He told me I should stay there permanently,' she says, not without a touch of pride. 'He tried hard to convince me, saying I could have the house, the driver . . . But I didn't.'

'*Why not!*' I say, my jaw dropping almost as far as the kitchen table.

She shrugs. 'I'd bought property back in Spain, you see,' she says. 'Even the furniture.'

Reluctantly, then, she left Havana and returned home, just as she had left Zurich reluctantly. Once back on familiar ground she decided against life on the sun-kissed south of Spain, where she had a brand-new apartment. She *also* decided not to take up residence in her new flat in the town of Sarria.

'When you get to my age you have to make an effort,' she says, having brushed her hair and put on a little lipstick. *If* I get to your age, I say to myself, thinking about my pork-rich diet, as I watch her scamper up the stairs to the terrace like a teenager.

'I used to be quite pretty, but, you know, these days I have to try a little harder.'

We take a few photographs. She's naturally photogenic, and has had a lot of practice. Last week she posed for the newspaper *La Voz de Galicia*, holding a four-foot poster of her favourite cousin in front of her. Now she's posing for me.

The terrace overlooks the green fields that fall gently away from the hamlet of Upper Armea. It was to here that Victoria decided to return, to the place her mother had always lived. She built herself a modern home on the remains of an old stable block belonging to the family. This was where she would settle, whatever Fidel had to say on the matter.

Julio stands next to her. Right over his shoulder, in the distance, you can see the hamlet where he was born. Another 'emigrant,' he spent half a century in Barcelona (another popular destination for Galicians), five hundred miles to the east. After he was widowed he came home and started seeing Victoria. Several years of living together followed, but they finally tied the knot last December, she for the first time at almost eighty.

Returning to the kitchen, we sit at the table, the very table where all sorts of members of the Castro regime have dined over the years, from Conchita (Fidel's old secretary – herself a Galician) to bodyguards and police and diplomatic staff, including the Cuban consul in Galicia, who is a regular visitor.

We continue talking about various members of the Castro family: who went where, what happened to them. But I am still thinking about that decision to leave Havana. I mention that it seems to me a strange feature of recent Galician emigration that so many returned to relatively humble surroundings, however splendid the life abroad had been.

'Look at me,' Victoria says. 'I came back here. This is where I'll die.'

It is an obstinate kind of returning, to places with little more than memories to offer, places with ageing, dwindling populations and no obvious future. It's the *morriña*, they say, the 'home yearning' that draws them back. Perhaps in the case of Galicians it's the long history of economic emigration itself that strengthens the resolve to make that final move home, a desire that the last chapter of your life should be written by you, not dictated by economic imperative.

Returning home is testament to the strength and complexity of the feeling of belonging, belonging to the land of one's forebears. I think there's also a more elemental feeling involved, that of wanting to be *home again* after the welter of emotions that living abroad forces upon you. And it doesn't matter what kind of life you've made for yourself away from home, how integrated you have become, how content you are in your foreign land. You'll never entirely escape those subtle, inexpressible feelings of loss that assail you when you least expect them, fleeting memories of a place that formed and nurtured you, but which you can no longer touch or see. Home is a part – perhaps the greatest part – of what it means to be you, but for the emigrant, that part of him has been suspended, put on hold, blocked out. This, I think, is what people are chasing when they return, the distant promise of wholeness. As to whether they find it, perhaps one day I'll find out.

As for Doña Victoria, the *morriña* must have been pretty intense. If you can turn your nose up at Havana's Revolutionary Palace, that's some homesickness you've got in your belly.

I have pork cutlets and a jug of local white wine in Casa Meleiro, a solid-looking manor house and restaurant on the main road in Láncara. Afterward, I get talking to the elderly owner, José. He also emigrated to Cuba in the 1940s, although, quite amazingly, he didn't seek out Angel Castro when he got there. However, he heard all about the Castro boys when the two of them seized power in 1959.

'I was working for a rich cardiologist,' he tells me. 'He was a millionaire. A multimillionaire. Famous in Cuba and beyond. Like all the rich folk, he escaped to Miami. I followed him.'

A year later José returned to Láncara, tired of being in a non-Spanish-speaking country, to live fifty yards away from the ancestral home of Cuba's new firebrand leader, whom he had never met.

There's a large photograph on the wall of the bar.

'Is that you?' I ask him.

'Yes!' he says.

Half a dozen men in suits stand proudly. They were on a cultural trip to Cuba, one of several semi-official visits by prominent Láncarans over the years, which the Castros were glad to receive (but not pay for). In the photo, amid the suits, stands Fidel, tall and erect in green fatigues.

'That was in 2001. He invited us to the palace

for dinner, cooking and serving the food himself. We were there till four in the morning.'

'I bet he was doing most of the talking,' I venture.

Castro, of course, is famed for his seven-hour political speeches.

José laughs. He doesn't deny it, though.

I cross the road. The Castro family dwelling, now abandoned, is essentially cow stables, its walls constructed of oddments of red-brown stone, from two-foot boulders to slivers of rock no thicker than your finger, all built up in swirling free form, so that from a distance the place looks as if it's been made from slices of mixed-nut praline. The sloping roofs go high enough to accommodate an upper floor, where a tiny window peeks out from beneath the tiles of the roof. Here it was that Angel Castro grew up, right above the cows. Consider, then, what his son Fidel was able to say of his own childhood in Cuba, just one generation later:

'The family I was born into were landowners in comfortable circumstances. We were thought of as rich, and people treated us as such . . . I got endless attention from everyone, they flattered me and treated me differently from the other boys I played with. These children were often barefoot, whereas we wore shoes; they often went hungry, whereas at our house the struggle was to get us to eat.'

★　★　★

Estimates vary, but from the 1860s until the early 1970s, somewhere in the region of two million Galicians emigrated. The Galician diaspora is one of a kind. Even today, Galician communities abroad maintain a strong cultural identity. Hundreds of official Galician centres, associations, and other groups exist around the world, especially in South America; in Buenos Aires alone there are around three hundred such societies.

After the death of Franco, when Galicia became a semi-autonomous region, it was decided that members of the diaspora should be granted the right to vote not only in Galician elections but in the Spanish general election. Remarkably, this arrangement extends also to children and grandchildren of emigrants, even if these descendants hold a different nationality and have never set foot in Europe. Currently a third of a million such 'Galician' voters are registered, well over 13 per cent of the total Galician electorate. Incredible as it seems, the postal votes of a bunch of second-generation Americans in Des Moines might just swing the Spanish general election. Check your family tree, it could be you.

If any of these many, many exiles do want to come back to the old place, Galicia's government has a dedicated ministry that coordinates the process, offering financial and other practical assistance. Once a Galician, it seems, always a Galician.

I look at the Castro cowshed in Láncara. There's a carved commemorative stone set into the wall:

In this house in 1875 was born Angel
Castro Argiz,
a Galician who emigrated to Cuba,
where he planted trees that still flourish

Flourish? I suppose it depends on your point of view. But let's put it another way. If Spain had not been in the grip of Franco's military dictatorship in the 1950s, perhaps Angel might have been tempted to return home and build himself a nice, comfortable retirement house here in Láncara. As it was, he stuck around in Cuba, which gave his sons the opportunity to create a military dictatorship of their very own.

THE ORDER OF THE PORK STEW

The problem with Carnival, that great wave of eating, drinking, and merrymaking that sends Galicia slightly delirious every year, is that it only happens *once* a year. I've already had chorizos in Vila de Cruce's Carnival opener, followed by Laza's pig head bacchanal. But in fact I crammed in a third Carnival event this year, in a place called Lalín, which schedules its annual *cocido* month (yes, you read it right) to coincide with the pre-Lenten festive period.

The town of Lalín calls itself the 'Kilometre Zero of Galicia'. At its dead geographical centre point, it is a quintessentially Galician sort of place, a farming town set amid old-fashioned, rolling, rain-sogged pastureland dotted with small holdings and roadside villages. The kind of town where ironmonger and public notary sit side by side on the same street. A perfectly formed place. And Lalín does Carnival in a big way. The papers said fifty thousand. That's a lot of people in a town of twenty thousand. It's supposed to start at ten. Being British, I get there at nine, to find myself alone. Galicians just don't do 'beating the crowds'.

In many parts of the world, from the Canary Isles to the Caribbean, from the Alps to the Andes, people celebrate Carnival. Its origins, though, are hard to pin down. It falls immediately before Lent, the forty-day period running up to Easter when Christians symbolically recall Christ's forty days in the wilderness, when he was tempted by the Devil. During Lent some form of privation has traditionally been expected of believers. Giving up meat was common, although in the Middle Ages, Lenten food prohibitions could run to bans on meat, dairy, and eggs, or even to eating anything at all during daylight hours. Lent was clearly not a time for partying, so the days leading up to it were your opportunity to indulge.

Carnival also falls right at the end of winter, and coincides with the pre-Christian folk tradition of welcoming in the new spring, a time for letting one's hair down and splurging pagan-style. Indeed, Galician Carnival is called *Entroido*, literally 'the entrance,' and is thought to predate Christianity. It is perhaps this pagan element that not only gives Carnival everywhere its special edge, but also helps to explain why the Christian church has always been so resolutely opposed to it.

Whatever the history, Carnival is about pleasure and excess. In Germany and Poland, Fat Thursday is celebrated on the Thursday before Lent, and is simply a day for piling on the calories, for eating mountains of cakes and doughnuts, which are about to be banned for a long six weeks. The following Tuesday (Shrove Tuesday) is Mardi Gras (French for 'Fat Tuesday'), another such tradition, which in many cities around the world has burgeoned into a corpulent three days.

Lalín's annual *cocido* festival is one of the biggest of all Galicia's food festivals. Over the month of festivities, you can attend: a mass pig slaughter (fun for all the family), a televised gala, swimming and pistol-shooting tournaments, orchestral and pop concerts, motorbike trials, *divercocido* ('fun-cocido,' a stew-themed event for children), a running and cycling 'duathlon' . . . Lalín will also sponsor O Rally do Cocido, possibly the world's only professional automobile race in honour of pork stew. Meanwhile, in Nuremberg, Germany, there's an offshoot of the stew festivities, run by Lalínian émigrés who can't make it back home this time of year. No rally, though.

The centrepiece of the entire month's festivities, however, is Stew Day. All the town's restaurants are offering *cocido*, and although I have already sampled this particular dish on my pork tour of Galicia, the stew here is a bit special. Back in the *cantina* in January, I had a picnic of shoulder ham and assorted goodies. But that's also the problem with *cocido*: it's unpredictable. Will you get a snout? A slab of cheek meat? It's heads or tails, pure potluck. If you're going to eat the whole hog, you really need a plan. And this is where you'll find it.

The *cocido* in Lalín is, in many ways, 'the' *cocido*, the place where pork stew finds its greatest expression, standardised, regulated, perfected, and set on a pedestal. I am in the home of *cocido*.

The aroma of burning wood is already wafting through the streets, as cast-iron cooking ranges are plied with split logs, and big, bubbling pots fight for space on the hot plates. I'd like to say there's also a buzz in the air, but there isn't. It's drizzling and the streets are almost empty. Those few people who do appear are all carrying sports bags or shoulder bags, even plastic grocery bags . . .

At precisely ten minutes past ten a peal of fireworks signals sounds out. I look around, searching in vain for the source of the blasts as my eardrums collapse.

The horrendous noise reminds me of the Procession of Death Shrouds in the coastal village of A Pobra do Caramiñal. For the last five hundred years, survivors of near-fatal illnesses have gone to A Pobra for the yearly procession to give thanks to Jesus the Nazarene for their miraculous recoveries. Although I've never faced death myself, I went to A Pobra last year. A life-sized effigy of the Nazarene, dressed for the day in vivid purple and gold robes, is carried around the village, followed by eight or nine elaborately decorated coffins. A great many barefooted penitents walk behind the coffins, most wearing the purple robes of the Nazarene and bearing long candles. Some of them limp visibly. Others hold small wax reproductions of specific body parts, representing exactly where the healing took place (wax arms, heads, legs, etc., are for sale in a barn opposite the church). At last year's procession, several people carried wax effigies of newborn babies, while one young woman wore a full-face burns mask made of a thick, skin-coloured cloth pulled tight around her face, with holes for eyes, mouth, and nostrils.

Thousands lined the streets to watch. I have never, ever heard so many Galicians making so little noise. As if to compensate for such an excess of peace and quiet, an unholy barrage of fireworks was unleashed. They were being launched from about one hundred yards behind me, which, in terms of industrial-strength pyrotechnics, is just too close. In the sky there was nothing but a series of little twists of smoke (white on white; the day was cloudy and wet). In Galician they are called *bombas* (bombs), which is about right. Each wicked blast was followed by another, just a tiny fraction louder, just a fraction closer to the last, in a *crescendo-accelerando* that seemed to announce the coming Armageddon. My ears began to hum, then to throb. People nearby were laughing, gazing up into the sky with delight as they enjoyed the annual simulacrum of the 1990 aerial bombardment of Baghdad.

All of Spain loves very loud explosions. Galicia, so often the exception, is no exception when it comes to *bombas*.

With my ears still numb after Lalín's morning pyrotechnics, I head down to Loriga Park, which

188

overlooks Lalín Town Hall at the bottom of town. The park is named after Joaquín Loriga, Lalín's first (and, I am guessing, only) pioneering aviator, who flew solo to the Philippines in 1926. I try to imagine living in deepest rural Galicia in 1926. I don't think flying to the Philippines would have been on my mind. Joaquín must have been a rare dreamer.

A bus pulls up and out hops a man in a grey tweed jacket, a white cravat, and a large red carnation in his lapel. About thirty others now descend from the bus, the men all tweeded and cravated, the women in full-length crimson dresses with white trim. Everyone bears a carnation and a smile. A few wear floppy purple velvet caps, like medieval burghers' hats, squashed down and worn at jaunty angles.

Others carry baskets of flowers. A man with a shiny face and sporting a cloth flat cap lights a cigarette extravagantly, and another twirls a walking stick in little Chaplinesque loops, prodding at things in the gardens as he shuffles along. They all make their way across to the back of the park and disappear.

Puzzled by the carnation wearers, I wander the short distance back up into the main shopping area of town, where a *charanga* band in jazzy waistcoats has just struck up: trumpets, saxophones, a tuba, and someone playing a side drum, cymbal, and cowbell combo. Despite the drizzle, a couple of pensioners decide to dance, carrying their own umbrella above their heads as they smooch. Around them, people applaud.

189

A little way off a pig stands on the pavement, nearly four feet high and beautifully cast in bronze. I stop to look, and am joined by a man who tries a number of conversational gambits on me, then, when I sidle away, follows me. He's on his own, and he's lonely; I attract solitary types. I try shaking him off with an act of journalistic auto-determination, scribbling this very note into my Moleskine notebook with exaggerated concentration, as if to *write* him out of the narrative. Finally he goes. I should have told him I was a writer. No one knows what to say when you tell them you're a writer. It's like shaking someone's hand and farting at the same time.

A stage has been erected where the two main shopping streets cross. It is empty, but the loud-speakers now begin to belt out Galician bagpipe rock. The native pipes here are smaller than their Scottish equivalents, although they make almost as ferocious a noise. They are a powerful symbol of Galician identity, and their gastric drone is a fitting expression of Galicia's historical and cultural pull away from all those stereotypical notions of Spanishness. Piping features prominently in all manner of Galician celebrations. We had some at our own wedding a few years ago; it was intense and wildly uplifting, although my ninety-year-old granddad had to plug his ears with his fingers.

The pipes are associated with Galicia's Celtic origins. The Celts arrived here between the eighth and fifth centuries B.C. The remains of their hill fort settlements (called *castros*), composed of small roundhouses, can still be seen. The word *castro* also became a common surname here, later exported to the Caribbean.

It is sometimes claimed that the Galicians are in fact Celts. But why the Celts in particular are credited with providing Galicia with its unique character is not immediately obvious, because almost everyone else invaded here as well, coming from every imaginable direction:

AN ITEMISED HISTORY OF GALICIA AND THOSE WHO INVADED IT

1. Megalithic, dolmen-building culture develops (c. 3000 B.C.).
2. Celtic migration into Galicia from central Europe (c. eighth through fifth centuries B.C.), introducing hill fort settlements, prospecting for gold, and flatbread.
3. Romans next (third century B.C.). They extend their empire right up to Galicia's Coast of Death. They thought this was the end of the world, naming it Finnisterrae.
4. The Germanic Suebi tribes succeed the Romans in calling Galicia their own (fifth century A.D.). Over the course of a relatively uneventful 175-year reign, they go from paganism to Christianity.

5. The Suebi kingdom is annexed by the Visigoths, who are all over the peninsula at the time, like a bad German rash (sixth century).

6. The Moors come (eighth century), set up a garrison, but don't really like it here. In any case, they are driven out by the King of Asturias. They do, however, leave almonds, which become the basis for almost all Galician cakes, not least Santiago cake, which bears an image of the Moor-slayer's sword in the frosting. How's that for sweet irony!

7. Galicia is conquered by the neighbouring Asturians (late eighth century) and subsumed into their kingdom.

8. Vikings and Normans mount raids on the Galician coast (ninth century), keeping it up for two centuries. Meanwhile, Galicia's aristocrats exist in a fluctuating state of semi-obedience to a variety of nearby rulers.

9. The Kingdom of Galicia and Portugal formed (1065), with Garcia (a Castilian prince) as monarch. It lasts seven years, in which time Garcia is defeated in battle by his brother Sancho ('the strong'), who grabs Galicia for himself, before being assassinated. Galicia is then taken by Garcia's other brother, Alfonso ('the noble'). Garcia is now

imprisoned, which gives him time to think up a decent nickname.

10. Galicia is then given as part of a wedding present to Alfonso's daughter, Urraca (late eleventh century). Things get complicated for a few hundred years. Galicia continues in a state of semi-obedience to different kingdoms, little more than a makeweight in aristocratic bartering and territorial aggrandisement.

11. The 'Catholic Monarchs,' Ferdinand and Isabella, annex Galicia (fifteenth century), as they lay the foundations for the modern Spanish state.

12. Galicia has remained part of Spain ever since.

13. They're Celts, you know.

You won't find many Galicians boasting about their Visigoth heritage, just the Celtic one. The true extent of the Celts' formative influence here is widely debated; no spoken Celtic language survives in Galicia, as it does in those cultures with which Galicians sometimes claim kinship, the so-called Celtic Belt of Western Europe (Scotland, Ireland, Wales, Cornwall, Isle of Man, Brittany). Nevertheless, this mystical Celtic history is certainly an attractive one, as if Galicia is somehow culturally and geographically ambiguous. Terra Meiga, they call it, 'Land of Witches,' and also of bagpipes, dark, thick forests, cold, persistent rain . . . The whole place should be towed up into the Irish Sea and grafted onto the bottom of County Cork, or plonked down in the heart of rural Wales.

Back in Lalín two festival buffoons appear: a young man dressed as an ancient crone (black skirt, thick grey stockings, dustpan, and brush), and a young woman dressed as a sort of red leprechaun with a large green diaper on. People gather around as the buffoons skip and dance and do buffoonish things. These characters also have the perfect right to humiliate and accost members of the crowd, drawing the willing public into demonstrations of carefree madness. In this regard I am unwilling.

I find myself edging back into a doorway, heart rate already triple digiting, only to see that to my immediate right some members of the crowd are being lampooned by a man in a medieval pilgrim outfit and a comedy staff. I freeze and avoid eye contact until they have all gone away.

Today's pork stew celebrations are part of a festival that dates back to 1968, during the dictatorship of General Franco (the Galician they all want to forget). It is planned to coincide with Carnival, although back in 1968, I suspect things were rather different. As we already know, Franco hated Carnival so much that he banned it. But why?

Among the oldest traditions of Carnival are parodying those in power, role reversal, crossdressing, the concealment of one's identity, and a

194

general abandonment of the traditional constraints of good behaviour. Such practices were common in the Saturnalia festival of ancient Rome (thought to have influenced modern Italian Carnival), and as far back as the Dionysian festival of ancient Greece, the practice of mocking those in positions of power was permitted. Laza's *peliqueiros* are a good example of this, local citizens dressing up like lords and wielding a symbolic, satirical form of authority.

Carnival acts as a kind of social safety valve, a time for throwing off the normal routines of life, of thumbing your nose at those in power, of masks and disguises and dancing in the streets. Of laughing at authority, subversion, losing your head and your inhibitions . . . not the kind of thing an uptight military-Catholic dictatorship would countenance.

Franco did permit affluent, well-connected citizens to attend society balls at Carnival time. The 1951 directive from Franco's Office of General Security is worth reading in full:

> During the week prior to Lent, the following prohibitions will remain in force: all manifestations of street carnival, although private society balls held in private will be tolerated, given that period formal dress (not disguises) be worn, and that faces remain uncovered at all times; the spontaneous appearance of these suitably dressed people

195

in the street is also prohibited, since this might give rise to the pretext for others to appear in public disguised in shabby clothes, others indulging in the unoriginal and objectionable extravagance of dressing in the clothes of the opposite sex, faces blackened and making an exhibition of themselves in gaudy groups and exhibiting a noisy euphoria which is seldom far from the ingestion of alcohol (which helps them overcome the shame of their ridiculous situation); in order to avoid these excesses, then, the existing prohibitions are reiterated, and it is to be made public that agents of the authorities will detain these obstinate individuals of such bad taste, who will be severely sanctioned.

Passage quoted in Federico Cocho,
O Carnaval en Galicia.
Edicións Xerais de Galicia, 2008
(first edition 1990), pp.252–53.

It's not difficult to perceive, below the trumped-up provincial snobbery of the directive, the high-handedness of absolute power wielded arbitrarily. Also, if Carnival had been permitted, it's not hard to guess who would have been mocked. If you really want to know what a genuinely disagreeable person Franco was, ask his biographer Professor Paul Preston. On finishing *Franco*, his monumental, thousand-page biography of the dictator,

Preston commented that he had wanted to be able to say at least one positive thing about his subject in the book, just for balance, but couldn't come up with anything.

After Franco died in 1975 and democracy was established, many of the old Carnival traditions had been lost, especially in Galicia, where the years of the dictatorship had witnessed a prolonged wave of emigration, stripping many villages of their younger generations. It was feared that Carnival was as good as dead, and some went so far as to place death notices of Carnival in newspapers. But they were wrong. The fun returned, and the 'good taste' of society balls gave way to the thoroughly bad taste of street parties, cheeky disguises, and eating till you burst.

I slip into one of Lalín's bakeries and get myself a couple of *cañas* (cream horns). I don't know whether they short-horn me deliberately, due to my foreign accent, but one of the horns is very small. Back outside, a kazoo and drum band marches past in formation: twenty-five men and women dressed as cavemen and – women (cavepeople?), all playing something loud and jazzy on kazoos, the kind that look like trumpets and saxophones.

Farther down the street I see that busload of carnation-bearing folk approach. They sing and dance as they move along in a slow promenade, the ladies carrying big baskets of flowers. The group is a *ruada*, which I guess translates as 'a good-humoured, lively group of people,' a troupe of jesters and singers and mirth makers whose role is simply to bring good cheer wherever they go. And today, in the light but persistent drizzle, they're doing a great job; the whole street seems to heave a small sigh of happiness as they arrive.

Meanwhile, I see two young men stop for a cigarette on the corner. They are dressed in sequinned purple frock coats with silver epaulettes, voluminous silver trousers with purple chevron motifs at the ankle, and glittery boots. They are both carrying bags.

It is almost half past twelve, but still nothing seems to have happened. I go back to Loriga Park. Despite the drizzle, a bagpipe and drum band is playing on the forecourt of the town hall just below. They are in traditional Galician costume: fawn, white, and black troubadour outfits for the men, white blouses and great big heavy full-length skirts for the ladies. The ceremonial procession will (eventually) set off from the town hall, and make its way up to the stage in the centre of town. At the head of the procession will be Karlos.

One of Spain's most famous chefs, Karlos Arguiñano is today being inducted into A Encomenda do Cocido ('The Order of the Pork Stew'), a group of illustrious pork lovers whose aim is to promote Lalín *cocido* and the *cocido* fair in general. The *encomenda* is a closed order, like the Masons. You can't just join, or I'd be straight

198

in there. Can you just *imagine* the Christmas dinner? No, it's a shadowy organisation, the influence of which may extend farther than we know. Certainly, there are the telltale signs of conspiracy: ceremonial vestments (double-layered brown capes, reminiscent of the habits of Franciscan monks) and a suspicious paucity of females among the order's number. There may be secret handshakes, or mutual squeals of identification sotto voce between members. I don't detect anything as I watch the men of the order gather below, but that just goes to show how far and how proficiently the conspiracy has been extended.

Mercs and Audis now appear in front of the town hall, arriving thick and fast, as if a bottleneck of luxury cars has just been cleared some way up the road. Brown-caped dignitaries climb out, shaking the creases from their vestments and looking up at the unpromising sky. Finally, a limo with police outriders sweeps down to the town hall, and out steps Karlos.

Karlos Arguiñano is from the Basque Country. He is one of my heroes. His lunchtime cookery program was the first thing I ever watched on Spanish TV He used to do simple recipes, the kind of stuff you could actually cook yourself. *Con fundamento!* he would cry as he chopped and fried – With the fundamentals! – imploring us to use good, fresh ingredients and to cook properly. Watching TV chefs is a great way to learn a language. For a start, you can see the things they are referring to, and they keep repeating everything. You quickly get familiar with 'chop' and 'fry' and 'simmer'.

Arguiñano was a great teacher. Fluent and relaxed in the kitchen, he would tell jokes, sing, and occasionally dance as he worked. He's still on TV, all these years later, having become a Spanish institution, sort of a Martha Stewart without the soft furnishings and false accounting. Apart from the media stardom, he's also a highly respected chef, a populist version of the Spanish *superchef*, and responsible, alongside the likes of Pedro Subijana, Juan Mari Arzak, and Ferran Adrià (three Michelin stars apiece), of elevating and popularising Basque and Spanish cuisine, a process that has transformed Spain into one of the hot spots in world cuisine.

He steps out of the municipal Mercedes, brown cape buffeted by the damp wind. A celebrity frisson courses through the air. He and nine others have just been inducted into the order (previous inductees include Julio Iglesias). God only knows what the initiation rites were. Karlos is also going to act as the festival's *pregoeiro*, a town crier figure who will head up the proceedings and make a public speech in which, ideally, he should come out fairly strongly in favour of pork stew.

On seeing the great chef emerge from the car, a man to my right bellows out: *Con fundamento,*

Karlos! Con fundamento! Arguiñano glances up and grins painfully, an expression which suggests, I think, that some awful bloke bawls *con fundamento* at him every few hours of his life.

An entourage slowly forms, and they begin their slow walk up the road. When they reach the top of the park Arguiñano is introduced to the vice president of Galicia, who has been loitering there.

Some background: Lalín is a conservative stronghold. Many of the important men here today are conservatives. But also here is Anxo Quintana, our vice president. Quintana is a socialist, and leader of the left-wing BNG, the Galician Nationalist Party. Preferring not to join the caped dignitaries down at the town hall, he is hovering at the park's top edge, like the time Sinn Féin's Gerry Adams hung about in a Dublin doorway so that President Clinton could give him the officially unofficial handshake during a walkabout of the city.

After the two men have shaken hands, the massed members of the Order of the Pork Stew make their slow, processional way up toward the crossroads and the covered stage, a journey of some hundred yards. The press corps has run ahead to take up positions, and I realise that I am now the only person walking directly behind the procession.

Thousands of people are crowded into the streets up by the stage. Civil Guards have cordoned off a clear path through for the caped dignitaries. It occurs to me that the only way for

201

me to get anywhere near the stage now is to keep walking ceremoniously on. Suddenly I am beating *all* the crowd, fifty thousand of them.

When we reach the crossroads a pack of bossy un-Civil Guards ushers us into the cordoned-off space that runs down the centre of the street. I find myself inside the barriers with Karlos et al. Flashbulbs burst and flicker around us as the entourage shuffles to a halt. Then, one of the Guards, not long out of school and wearing unreasonably large boots, senses that I am not a dignitary. (How does he know this?) *Get out!* he tells me, pointing to the barrier.

The crowds on the other side of the barriers are very dense. And, having taken up their frontline spots, no one looks disposed to let me through. Big Boots repeats his order. So I make my solitary way along the street, still inside the barriers. As I go, there's a slight dip in the crowd noise, the onlookers perhaps thinking that I am a stray dignitary, or a one-man *ruada* who's run out of good cheer.

Right at the top of the street all the marching and strolling groups, including the pipers, the prehistoric kazoo band, and the *ruada* are waiting. There are also pastiche military bands, a float carrying a festive Louis XIV and Marie Antoinette on thrones, dancing girls with sequinned costumes and nine-foot sprays of brightly coloured, spangly feathers coming out of their behinds, like the rumps of psychedelic monster peacocks.

This explains the bags: this morning the town was full of people carrying their outfits, hundreds of them, all trying to find their group, or just waiting to get changed.

Fancy dress is common during Galicia's Carnival. Personally, I haven't done it for about ten years, after I turned myself into a rather attractive young woman, makeup and all, only to discover that our friends had all decided against dressing up that evening. Susana was also in plain clothes, but in a fit of pique I refused to back down, and drove to the restaurant in miniskirt and eyeliner.

Lalín this morning has definitely decided to dress up, and seems to have turned itself into Rio de Janeiro. But this is not Rio. This is Galicia. The rain, which has been a constant but unobtrusive companion all morning, suddenly turns into a foul-mouthed drunk, pissing on our parade before it even begins. In the frenzy of umbrella-unfurling I seize my chance and push through the crowds on one side, shoulder-barging a man who just will not move other than by force.

I make my way up around the top of town. From here I listen to Karlos as he finally makes his pro-pork speech, in which he suggests naming a street after *cocido*. Belly Pork Alley? The idea garners polite applause.

Pork stew, though, is why I am here. Lalín is *cocido* capital of the world. In 2006 an enclave of Galician chefs was convened here, their task to decide on the perfect recipe for the stew. When white smoke finally rose from the stove, the following was declared official:

Lalín Cocido
recipe for ten people

Ingredients (all pork unless stated)

½ head
2 lb. cured foreleg (shoulder) ham
3 lb. backbone
2 tails
1½ lb. streaky bacon
1 side of ribs
3 snouts
5 ears
5 trotters (feet)
10 chorizos from Lalín
5 onion chorizos
4 tongues
1 free-range hen
2 lb. veal (hock or skirt)
½ lb. pork lard
2 lb. chickpeas
1 lb. dried broad beans
12 lb. *grelos*
3 lb. potatoes

All that lot, with the exception of the veal and hen, would be salt cured. And all of it, by the way, is readily available in Galicia, especially around Carnival time. Lots of people make *cocido* at home, in which case you just use whatever you fancy. Susana once did a *cocido* using vegetarian sausages and tofu. Just the once. When it comes to cooking the official Lalín version, you'll probably need to take a trip to the hardware store first, because this is a very pot-heavy process:

Preparation

Four days before: Soak the shoulder ham in cold water to desalinate. Change the water every day.
Two days before: Thoroughly wash all remaining pieces from the pig. Soak in cold water. Change water after 24 hours.
One day before: Put the broad beans and chickpeas to soak. Day of cooking: Put a large pot of cold water to heat (preferably on a wood-burning stove) and add a little lard. Add the shoulder ham and simmer for $2-2\frac{1}{2}$ hours, skimming throughout. Toward the end of this period, add the head and other bits and bobs of pork. Continue cooking until they are all done.
Put another pot of cold water to heat, then add a little pork fat, plus the hen and veal, leaving to cook for about an hour. Add salt.

In a third pot, simmer the chickpeas and beans for about an hour. As they cook, add the chorizos, skimming throughout.

In a fourth pot, boil the *grelos* (to death, preferably), using some of the stock (strained) from the first meat pot.

In a fifth pot boil the potatoes, using the remaining meat stock.

Serve: on one platter the potatoes and *grelos*; on a second, the chorizos, chickpeas, and beans; on a third platter all the meats.

Eat until your stomach lining tears.

The Carnival procession is still going strong. On a street below the main event I find the parade disgorging. Young women huddle around the open doors of cars in various degrees of undress, struggling to peel off their Carnival costumes and simultaneously slither into their regular clothes. Meanwhile, clowns continue to clown and unicyclists are letting people try out the cycles. It's a whole different scene, a reverse parade, deconstructed and experimental, with plenty of people watching. It strikes me as pleasingly postmodern. It also strikes me that I'm hungry. The fiesta's been going for four hours, and all I've eaten is a couple of short cream horns.

The only restaurant I can see looks like a pretty good one. It's now half past two. What are the chances of getting a table for one at peak time on the day of the *cocido* fair in a good restaurant in a town of twenty thousand that has fifty thousand people in it when the whole point is to come and have *cocido* in a restaurant at lunchtime? Answer: no problem at all! Lalín is old school. They don't beat the crowds here, and they don't book. Reservations are for wimps. I guess they've never tried to get a table in one of those cantinas.

Just fifteen minutes after I sit down, the restaurant is a solid mass of bodies, all in need of a table, all without a reservation. More people are arriving all the time. They squeeze together in little huddles of hopefulness between tables and over by the bar, getting in the way of the waiters, who with difficulty transport great platters of steaming pork in and out of the human traffic jam.

For the record, it is the best *cocido* I have ever tasted. And over the years I have eaten enough to keep a minke whale going through a pretty severe arctic winter. There's a half ear, slit down the middle in perfect symmetry, but not tempting me any. I've already tasted ear, but now, just to fulfil my own pledge, I cut myself an eighth of a lobe. As I expected, it has a greasy, almost plastic taste. My wedge of pig's tongue, however, is sweet, dark, and scrumptious, with a tickle of nuttiness to it. Then there are two wobbling slabs of snout, which I am very eager to sample. Fergus Henderson, the British chef famous for cooking the less fashionable parts of animals, has this to say: 'The snout is neither fat nor meat: do not be discouraged, it is delicious in your brawn' (Fergus Henderson, *The Whole Beast: Nose to Tail Eating*, Ecco, 2004, p. 39). Brawn (headcheese, if you're asking) must be the secret, then. I take a big forkful of snout, but it presents me with some swallowing issues, and I resort to chomping it up quickly and sluicing it down with wine in a flurry of rapid jaw movements. I really wanted to like the snout, but I just don't. It is loose and fatty in texture, but tastes how I imagine the stuff that periodically clogs the dishwasher would taste, and is thoroughly unpork-like. The confusion makes me think that there's some sort of deception going on in my mouth, like sucking a lollipop that tastes of chicken curry.

The rest of the meal, though, is so good that I take pictures of it as I go, and commend myself on a job well done. Having sampled snout, ear, and tongue, plus the cheek in Laza, I've now made a decent tour of the head. There's the small matter of brains, but that can wait.

I sit back and congratulate myself with a big slug of chilled Ribeiro white. To my right a family of five are served a platter that is bigger than the wheel hub of a Volvo truck. They stare down at it momentarily before diving in, elbows raised, knives and forks brandished with boisterous enthusiasm. Elsewhere people are in animated conversation, hoisting big clumps of dripping *grelos* onto their plates and struggling to get a flap of ear or snout into their yattering mouths. In the past they would have been stuffing themselves in preparation for the miserable privations of a meatless Lent, although *that* tradition has now been well and truly banished. Thank God.

A FOOT IN THE JOAN AGE

Back in the mountains of Os Ancares, looking for trotters. And this time I've brought the family. As we drive along high, winding roads, we start to see giant toadstools, each one as big as a house. Most of the isolated hamlets we pass seem to have a couple of them, and you really wouldn't want to meet the leprechauns that sit on these things.

Nico is missing all this, asleep in the back of the car. He's precisely one year old, and unaware that he is about to spend the first day of the second year of his life looking for pig feet up a mountain spotted with gigantic fungi. I hope one day he'll appreciate the start in life we're giving him.

The mushrooms that we keep seeing are *pallozas*, circular or oval stone-built dwellings with enormous conical thatched roofs. They are reminiscent of the houses found in Celtic hill fort settlements that began to emerge in northwestern Spain sometime around the eighth century B.C., surviving until at least the time of the Roman invasions. It was in fact the Romans who gave these settlements the name *castros* (from the Latin *castra*, 'walled settlement'), a word that also took root over in England, thanks to the Romans, to live on in place-names such as Lan*caster*, Glou*cester*, Man*chester*, etc. Back in Galicia, as we know, *castro* also became a surname.

No one is sure exactly how the Iron Age, Celtic culture of the *castros* fed into the rural architecture of Os Ancares, although the *palloza* design is sometimes said to date back to pre-Roman times. Incredibly, these strange thatched dwellings that dot the sweeping sierra of Os Ancares were inhabited until about twenty years ago, the ancient, self-sufficient form of life that they made possible going on much as it had done for innumerable centuries. The normal way of experiencing the past might be through excavations and museum reconstructions, but *pallozas* are a living link to an Iron Age existence, perhaps the last link. And the very last bit of the last link is in Piornedo. His name is Pepe.

Don Pepe might be fifty-five or eighty. It's hard to tell. He has a full head of grey hair and walks in a pensive, self-contained way. He's slight of build, but not frail; later in the afternoon we see him working in a nearby field.

Casa Casao ('House of the Casoas') is one of two *pallozas* in the village of Piornedo that have been preserved in their traditional state, and which you can visit for the ridiculous sum of one euro. It's all very relaxed, but there's also a certain oddness in knowing that this building represents a rural culture that in some circuitous, un-fathomable (i.e., Galician) way stretches unbroken back to pre-Christian times.

Pepe hangs around inside, pointing things out if you wish, leaving you alone if you don't. It's very black inside. There's no chimney up in that towering thatch, and the place looks as if it has hosted the European finals of Pipe Smoker of the Year ever since Christopher Columbus won the inaugural event.

Pepe was born here, and lived most of his life under the soot-stained straw, just as his forebears had done for countless centuries. No phone, no electricity, no running water, and no significant contact with the world beyond the mountainside. In the 1980s the last human beings to have lived this Iron Age existence finally moved into more modern accommodations. In the case of Pepe that was the house next door, and he keeps the *palloza* just as it was, including all its other occupants . . .

Casa Casao is thirty feet high and oval in shape, perhaps forty feet at its longest, with thick, low stone walls, and above them the huge lump of weather-browned thatch. There are a couple of low-wattage lightbulbs, installed several years ago for the tourists. Before the arrival of electricity, thin holly branches were used as candle sub-stitutes. At first glance it's a barn, the kind that P. T. Barnum might have designed in a playfully spooky mood.

Running from one end to the other is a wide passageway – the *ástrago* – which serves as the general living area. All the farming and domestic paraphernalia that an extended family of anything up to about thirty people would need to survive is here: hay forks, butter churns, hunting traps, water pots, dog skins (for keeping the cattle warm). Off the main thoroughfare are small low-ceilinged workrooms, one for spinning, another with a loom. At one end is a kitchen, and at the other a bedroom. Above all this are massive haylofts on each side, dark and ethereal, like planetariums without the planets. This is where you and your many kith and kin would sleep, right on the hay, or on one of the various beds up there.

The centrepiece of the interior design, roughly in the middle of the *palloza* on the ground floor, is the stone oven, with enough room inside to bake a month's supply of bread for the whole clan, usually a coarse sort of corn-flour bread, but before the arrival of corn from South America in the late fifteenth century it was probably millet. If anyone wants to open a pizzeria in Os Ancares, a *palloza* would be perfect. Even the fumes from the oven's fire play their part in a *palloza*'s design; with no vents in the thatch, the rising smoke keeps the straw dry and rot-free, as well as discouraging the insects and rodents that would otherwise nibble it to bits. Smoke, in addition, is a disinfectant and a deodorant, minimising animal fumes

213

and the germs they might carry. If you want virtue out of necessity, come to Piornedo.

On the other side of the central aisle, beneath the hayloft, are low-slung stables, the dark wooden doors lacquered to a deep waxiness with several centuries of hand grease. From behind one door comes the shuffle of hoofs, and a disc of glistening pink snout snaffles at our heels from the gap beneath another. What with Porky, the cows, and a bunch of chickens flapping free around our heads, Casa Casao has its own distinctive fragrance. The menagerie is no recent innovation, either. Families and livestock lived together in these structures, not least to provide warmth for the human residents, and also because there was nowhere else for the animals to go through the long, killing winters up here.

Don Pepe does his best to explain the significance of all that lies within this cold, somewhat mysterious place. Yet there's a gulf of understanding between us. I try to imagine the rhythms and exigencies of the life he describes. The sum total of his existence rests within this single structure, where every member of his family would have been born, lived, and died. One can almost hear the echoes of former happiness, and of grief, of adored children and the promise of more, of work-worn adults, the laughter and sleep and shivering, the lingering diseases, the deaths . . . A history stretching back beyond the scope of memory. It's always a little uncomfortable to walk into someone else's home, to see their daily lives laid out bare. When it's hundreds of years of living, condensed and confined inside such a space, it really is bewildering.

Most of today's visitors spend less than five minutes inside Pepe's *palloza*. Their vacant coming and going suggests that the place is a sort of comedy grotto that everyone should sneak a quick look at. Some are amused at what they find, while others look mildly disgusted. It's a pattern the world over, I guess; once people with their roots in the land get all urbanised and modern, they start to feel patronising toward the quaintness of village life. This is happening in Galicia, where the countryside is rapidly becoming a playground for weekend excursions, for bargain purchases of locally produced honey and cheese and *orujo*, the local firewater that tastes every bit as raw and hangover-inducing as grappa, aquavit, or whatever your local moonshine happens to be.

The only future for rapidly depopulating places like Os Ancares appears to be tourism. 'Sun, sand and sangria' holidays are one of Spain's biggest sources of income. There's neither sand nor sangria up here in high-altitude Galicia, though, and I wouldn't make a definite date with the sun either. On the other hand, you can go barrel-to-snout with a wild boar if you dare, there's plenty of trout (less scary, but they do have snappy little teeth, you know), and if you're after an adrenaline rush, just take your big, luxurious never-off-roader and drive in an upward direction more or less anywhere.

The flight from countryside to urban centres in Galicia occurred on a large scale only in the past four decades or so. Susana always bemoans the fact that when they were young she and her sister were often the only children in the barrio at the weekend, since many children would go with their parents to visit 'the village' and see grandparents. She still feels quietly jealous of people who have a village. A lot of city-living Galicians, then, still have fairly recent links to the countryside, and this proximity to the chicken shit makes the more snobby urbanites desperate to distance themselves from the smell. 'Modern Galician identity,' says Galician essayist Antón Baamonde, 'is founded to a great extent on a censure of origin.' You can say that again.

I recall Baamonde's words as a fat bloke in a white shirt way too small for him waddles in. The resemblance to Peter Griffin from *Family Guy* is undeniable. He casts negligent glances at the smoke-blackened planetarium above, and at the haylofts chockablock with domestic implements of every imaginable kind.

'You've done this up like a museum, have you?' he says in a voice that I consider to be too loud, waving his pudgy hand at some mysterious, withered leather straps that hang nearby on the wall, so entangled that they might be clumps of tagliatelle left there to gather dust.

For him, Don Pepe is a wily peasant turning a quick buck on his old cowshed, and Piornedo is a stop-off to stretch his legs before he hauls his guts back into the Audi A6 and rolls down the hill in search of a big plate of *cocido*. I want to throw the slob in with the pigs, bolt the door, and see if they really do eat everything. Don Pepe tells him that, no, the *palloza* is just as it was left when they finally moved out. The whole exchange is conducted in a matter-of-fact way.

With Mr Griffin now tagging along, Pepe shows us the tiny downstairs bedroom. By tradition the oldest members of the family would sleep here. But the youngest would also get a berth, snug between Grandma and Grandpa, so as not to die from the cold. As Pepe explains this, he appears to be apologising, not for the fact that infants could easily freeze to death, but because they slept in the adults' beds. Susana mentions that it's not such a bad thing for a baby to sleep in bed with adults; they do in many cultures. Pepe nods. Perhaps, he says, although here it was out of necessity.

'*¡Que no! No, no* . . .' says Mr Griffin. 'Not so! They should have their own beds. It's better for 'em.' He strides up and peeks in through the bedroom door. 'How old are you talking about, anyway?'

At this moment we are in the company of one of the last remaining Galicians who followed an ancient, brutally self-sufficient life of hunting and subsistence agriculture, right here in the very roundhouse where he lived, looking into the bedroom where he was born, where he slept as an infant, and where each generation of his family would have died. And fatboy is picking an argument with my wife about child rearing.

Galicians, who relish just about everything else a pig has to offer, don't make a big deal about the feet. Unlike the head (especially the ears) and even the tail, pig feet are not a widely appreciated delicacy. So Piornedo, recommended as a trotter destination by Doña Marisol, was my big chance.

After my first, petrifying trip up the mountains here we found a map of the area in a cupboard at home, one of those small, 3-D maps pressed from a sheet of plastic that shows the contours of the land in colours, brown for peaks, graduating to green for valleys. We traced my previous journey, and I'd been pretty much in the brown up there.

Piornedo is right on the eastern border of Galicia. On the bump map it is quite brown. We got a reservation at the Piornedo Hotel. A twenty-three-room hotel in a village of about thirty-five inhabitants? It seemed a little excessive. Piornedo, though, is Palloza City. PRE-ROMAN VILLAGE, says the sign that greets you as you make it up the last bit of road leading here. Between the normal stone cottages some dozen straw-topped *pallozas* sprout, the whole place surrounded by painfully green slant-pasture through which crystalline brooks gurgle, and winding country tracks taper off into the misty distance. If you are a hopeless photographer, just go to Piornedo, hold your camera in the air, and push the button. It's that pretty.

After checking in, I had asked Carmen where I could get a plate of trotters. She and her husband, Manolo, opened the Piornedo Hotel in 1990, coincidentally at the very moment the last *pallozas* were vacated. Her face never slipped, although she seemed perhaps just a touch surprised: we were in one of the most majestic parts of Northern Spain, the hunting, hiking, and fishing all superb, views that make your heart explode . . . and I was looking for a pig's foot, the lowest point on the quotidian, the cloven hoof of mud-caked mundaneity. No, she told me, the season is over. By which she meant the cold months, when you eat *cocido*. Of course! They don't eat the feet as a *delicacy* in Piornedo. It's not a speciality, they just toss the feet into the pot along with everything else. Somehow I had nurtured the idea that I was going to find pigs' feet slow-braised in a little Marsala Superiore with rosemary and garlic.

We wandered up from the hotel to the village, passing an old *paisano* returning from the fields, a long-handled fork on his shoulder and a black beret on his head. We bid him good day. City dwellers bid everyone good day when they're in the countryside. Greet-the-Yokel is second only to the practice of filling one's lungs with country air twice as often and twice as deeply as necessary every time you stop to take in the views.

219

The old man plodded on. A dark blue Saab approached. It slowed, the occupants staring through tinted windows. The world froze for an instant, an instant photo perhaps, a snapshot of premodernity. What is it like, I wonder, to be a *typical feature*, something so delightfully original that people cannot but cast you a stare of satisfaction, of gratitude almost, when they lay eyes on you. The old peasants who still work the land in these rural tourist spots are providing a service, fulfilling our expectations and making it all so real. And what is the Observer Effect here? Does he glance in the mirror before stepping outside of a morning, just a tiny bit self-conscious, cocking his beret at a jaunty angle? Do those gaudily coloured Gore-Tex waterproofs that his granddaughter bought him hang unused in the closet? Does he care?

I am aware that such questions presuppose all manner of ridiculously arrogant assumptions on my part. The metropolitan conception of the simple country life as somehow 'authentic' is hardly a new one. Yet what is striking in Galicia is the relationship between the (Galician) tourist and this 'real' environment. Urbanisation happened here so quickly, and so recently, that people who now live in cities and towns (well over half the population) appear to be conflicted about the countryside and their relationship to it. On the one hand, they are keen to pay homage, knowing that the rural landscape is a formative element in their own history. Yet they are also aware that it was from this very rural environment that they, their parents, or their grandparents flew in search of modern houses, modern jobs, and everything else that the poor, limiting countryside denied them. Not so much 'censure of origin', as Baamonde argues, but rather uncertainty as to what to do with those origins.

After our visit to Casa Casao we loop around the lanes that twist between the village's thatched ovals. These lanes are steep, laid with stones so weather-worn they're like fossilised loaves of bread. And on the loaves is much evidence of cows. Nico hangs on to the side of his stroller as if he's on a foul-smelling roller coaster.

Amid the houses and the *pallozas* there are a number of thatched *horreos* (corn stores) on stilts, many of them looking rather snazzy. Indeed, the whole place is well scrubbed. This gets me suspicious. Just how self-conscious has the village become? Is it already at the tipping point of self-exhibitionism, turning itself by slow degrees into a sanitised re-creation of a bygone Piornedo? (Think Ye Olde Shakespearean Tea Shoppe, think Big Chief Smoking Wigwam Gift Centre.)

Then we round a corner and find our way blocked by a six-foot pile of manure-soaked straw. It has just been shovelled out of another *palloza*, one which is in use as a cowshed, and is now seeping a dark green liquid that runs down between the stone loaves toward us. Three men set about forking it up onto the back of a tractor. I rest easy.

Having negotiated our way around the shit heap we see Bar Piornedo, which boasts a fluorescent strip light and a football table, and looks like the kind of place where tough Piornedans hang out. Table football, by the way, was invented by the Galician poet Alejandro Campos Ramírez; you probably do not need to know this. Bar Piornedo is on the ground floor of a large brick building that has been given over, at the back, to hay storage. The entire back wall is missing, and the rooms are on full view, like a dolls' house with the panel removed. Each room is filled to the ceiling with bales of hay, even the rooms up on the second floor. I don't know how they're going to get the stuff down again, because directly adjacent to the wall-less end of the building is a ten-foot foundation pit for a house that was never built. Come to think of it, I don't know how they got it up there to begin with. I could go into the bar and ask one of the toughs. But I decide not to.

After staggering with the stroller up more fossilised bread lanes we make it to Casa do Sesto ('House of the Sestos'), the other visitable *palloza* in the village. It is run by Fuco Peréz, an intense-looking guy with an intellectual's beard and a thick pullover. And he speaks Galician rather than Spanish. There's no way that you can discern a person's political views by looking at him, but beards, jerseys, and speaking Galician are all pretty typical of Galician nationalists, and many nationalists support the Bloque Nacionalista Galego, the left-leaning party that seeks greater independence for Galicia and which actually has a clause prohibiting neckties in its statutes.

Dress is very conveniently codified for politics here, at least for men. Flannel trousers and a blazer are for conservatives and churchgoers (who are often conservatives); smart-casual to off-the-peg suits mean the socialist (social democratic) party. In Galicia these two groups are more likely to speak Spanish than Galician, although the more casually attired 'socialists' might do a line or two of the latter at the weekend. The beardy-jersey brigade, on the other hand, will speak Galician, very occasionally in the face of over-whelming evidence that the listener doesn't understand a word.

This is not the case with Fuco. He asks whether I understand Galician, and when I say that I do (in Spanish) he continues in Galician and I continue in Spanish. This is a common feature of conversation these days, a relaxed sort of bilin-gualism. And it says a lot about the tolerant nature of Galicians; in Catalonia, by contrast, I have occa-sionally been obliged to resort to English, however poorly the other person speaks it, because some Catalan nationalists would rather have their tongue removed with a rusty penknife than speak the Spanish language.

Fuco is just a handful of years older than me, and one of the last people to have been born in a *palloza*. His family moved out in 1970, although the animals stayed on, as was the common practice. Nothing was changed or taken away from Casa do Sesto. Years later, when the tourists began to arrive, Fuco had a museum on his hands.

At this point Peter Griffin shows up again, poking a chubby finger at a wall on which wood planes and other carpentry tools are hung. There is a plethora of other implements, but Peter hasn't noticed. He does recognise a saw, however.

'Carpenters, then, were they?'

Fuco seems only mildly irritated as he explains that they were entirely self-sufficient – carpenters, blacksmiths, weavers, hunters, farmers, butchers . . .

Griffin wanders off, and Fuco shows us around. It really is a *palloza* deluxe. The stables, for example, are walled off behind the main living area. There are no heavy beasts in residence these days, although the original cow cart remains, along with a *coroza*, a cape made entirely of long flat bundles of straw laid on top of each other, and covering you from head to foot. The *coroza*, which turns the wearer into a walking haystack, was the traditional rainwear in these parts until extreme modernisation pushed those flappy, arm-restricting mackintoshes on the population.

Back in the main area, the *ástrago* is exciting, and that's not something you say every day about someone's front room. Wherever you look there's another relic of Fuco's family, of the cheek-by-jowl life they calmly turned away from thirty-odd years ago: clog-making tools, an iron cauldron straight out of Harry Potter, scythes, thatchers' prodders, axes, wicker snowshoes, a worryingly short boar spear (they had to get *that* close?).

Where Don Pepe was wistful, Fuco is proud. Between visitors he sits in a chair reading a book, and one can see that he still feels at home here. And if Pepe's *palloza*, with its animals and old farming equipment, gave a sense of the practical hardships of life spent in these amazing dwellings, Casa do Sesto also manages to convey the domestic reality of life, with egg baskets, wool combs, washboards and irons, as well as those details that somehow let you a little too far into the private precinct of a family's ancestral past: a tambourine, a rough-hewn baby's seat.

The open hearth is enclosed on three sides by benches where the family would sit to keep warm, to read, sew, and to talk and tell stories in the evenings. (Where do you sit around to talk and tell stories in your house?) The whole place is, if not perfect, then *perfected*, the solution to a cramped, communal form of family living.

As you stand in Casa do Sesto and contemplate all this, the distribution of its space, with great haylofts above you on either side, the little workshop-like rooms and stables below, you start to wonder what it would all look like with a little backlighting up in the cavernous dome, a skylight or two, grey slate floors . . . because a *palloza* is really a double mezzanine loft. (Take note, Tribeca; the Galicians did it first.) The cow stables could be turned into an amazing wine cellar, and there's so much room for your turntables and retro vinyl collection upstairs it's crazy. You have a place to sit around and talk, if you still know how to do that, and provided you install central heating your babies should be okay. Why, if you're the hippie type, they could snuggle down with you.

I poke my head out the back door. Three pigs are rummaging around in a sty built onto the side of the *palloza*. They look unperturbed by my presence, their snouts twitching just a touch as they notice me there. Pigs are sociable animals (unlike the thoroughly unsociable wild boar). Perhaps this characteristic made them such an obvious candidate for domestication all those millennia ago, the instinct they have for cohabitation, for getting along with one another and those around them. Pablo Valledor told me that the Celtics in the woods near Fonsagrada sleep in large groups, all huddled up together under a tree, taking turns at the warm centre. It's almost touching, such a natural instinct for sharing and mutual protection. I think the notion that pigs are a dirty version of ourselves is wrong; if anything, we are the imperfect version of the pig, the gentlest and most unassuming of animals, as well as the tastiest.

I consult Fuco about the pigs. This might mean that he has pork, pig feet, even. He rubs his intellectual bristles. Too late, he tells me. Anything else I could try, any other unusual pork dish? I ask in desperation. More chin rubbing. I glance at the Harry Potter iron cauldron over by the fireplace and wonder how many trotters that pot has seen over the centuries.

I've blown it, at least until the winter.

The next day, and we are gunning along the mountainside in a brazen third gear. The invigoration of taking Wild Nature head-on is tempered only by the warbling-shrieking cries of anguish from my wife, as she goes through the experience that I had on my first trip up these high, narrow roads.

In Doiras, Doña Marisol's eyes are as kind and mischievous as ever. She tells me that the chiropidist was here, asking about me. It seems that I am going from nuisance to minor pork celebrity. Basking in my newfound fame I leave Nico with his somewhat becalmed mother in Doña Marisol's bar, along with an old man with a walking stick who doesn't appear to be in a hurry to go anywhere. I stride out toward the castle, where I have some unfinished business with the author of *Don Quixote*: I intend to be the first ever visitor on the Cervantes culture trail.

The sun is getting a bit naughty, and those square battlements seem a long way up. The track is steep, but what's more disconcerting is that my path is barred by an iron gate, which is padlocked. The road to the almost-certainly-related-to-Cervantes castle is a hard one, and it looks as if the owners (private) are not interested in turning a profit on the great man's name. I struggle to push myself under the gate, where a puddle-filled space just big enough for my body awaits.

Ten gasping minutes later I am on a high dome of a hill with a deserted medieval castle on it, technically a *fortaleza inexpugnable*, an 'unassailable fortress'. There's no messing about with decorative touches and faux features here; the walls are five feet thick and twenty-six feet tall.

I sit down on the grass, take off my T-shirt, and drape it over a gorse bush to drip-dry. The only sound is the distant clunking of cowbells. Way across on the next hillside I see them, orange-brown beasts idling away the morning on a postage stamp of shocking green pasture. I wonder who's going to bring them in tonight, and whether he was born in a mezzanine loft apartment.

The castle is abandoned, and its cloister is bare and rather spooky. Up at rampart level in one corner is an enclosed living space, although the windowpanes are gone. By the look of it, someone was living here not that many years ago. Location, location, location, they say. The castle is a bijou residence, no doubt. But in comparison to a *palloza* it lacks something, a certain intelligence in the use of space, in the distribution. A castle isn't cozy, and quite frankly I don't know where you'd put all your vinyls. Another thing: it's medieval. I prefer something a little older, Iron Age if possible.

I look down at Doiras way below, just a handful of buildings on a fork in the road. The trout stream sends out flickering sparks of sunlight as it runs past the village, then on through untouched meadowland to the next. Green meadow. Greenfield. That's where the car park would go. And a riverside picnic area. People love picnics. Then, a cow cart up to the Cervantes Castle Experience, driver in a straw overcoat, tour guides armed with old hay forks.

There'd be pig feet for everyone.

ATILANO'S VIRGIN HAM

The bare wooden floorboards are caked hard with mud and chicken shit. Atilano, a fit-looking eighty-year-old in bright blue overalls, leads me down the passageway. There are doors to my right and left. Through one of them I see a black hen loitering by an olive green bidet. More birds frequent the passageway itself, strutting in and out of rooms at will. Above our heads hang two partially depleted racks of ribs and a side of bacon. Their musty hog aromas add a welcome note of sweetness to the air. The pork is a good sign. It is the best sign.

Last door on the left is the kitchen. We enter. And I, like one of those interior designers on daytime TV, immediately *get* the place. The room just *speaks* to me: 'They have no cleaner,' it says loudly.

The walls are dark brown, flaking to black. It may be the other way around; between the brown and the black it is impossible to tell which is paint-related and which is growth.

In the middle of the room is an iron cooking range, set within a stone-topped surround perhaps

230

ten feet by three, with wooden benches around it, the standard country kitchen arrangement. The surface is littered with exhibits from a peep show of domestic horrors. A prodigious glass jar, like the ones Victorian freak museums used to keep pickled babies in, contains a dozen chorizos that lurk in a sump of cloudy oil. Next to the jar is a plate of old cheese rinds, like huge reptile nail clippings, and they too sit in suspicious oil. A second specimen jar is brimfull of honey. Then there are pots, a rusty ladle, scatterings of orphaned cutlery, at least three iron frying pans bearing the pox of unchecked corrosion and soot, a hen, a plastic jug ringed with brown stains that lend it the muted Ulster of Etruscan earthenware, a small bowl that seems to be made of mahogany, in it the darkened smear of something organic around which a colony of ant pupae ripples with life.

Atilano pulls one of the benches out for me and brushes the stone worktop clear so I have somewhere to rest my elbows. The hen, who has been patrolling the middle part of the range-cum-table, pecking at a wide selection of available foodstuffs there, now stalks in my direction and does some concerted pecking in front of me, making it perfectly clear who has crumb rights in this kitchen.

I laugh nervously. The bird takes offence, extending its wings in a territorial flap-squawk. Atilano, who is over by the sink looking for a clean wine tumbler, turns around, shouts, seizes a broom, and sweeps the hen off the range and out the door.

I am in Atilano's kitchen quite by accident. About twenty minutes earlier I had been, as usual, lost up Déjà Vu Mountain, when I discovered that the narrow (and wrong) track I had taken was about to turn from degraded asphalt to loose stone, right at the point where there was a great deal of mountainside off to my right. I could not turn around, and stopping was not a useful option, although I tried it for a while. On I went, and eventually spotted a house halfway down the valley, some way in the distance.

Drawing cautiously up to the place, I saw that there was nothing else roundabouts. The track itself stopped, and there was not a single other building in sight. I felt almost proud: this was getting lost on the grand scale. I could not, physically, have got any loster.

Out came Atilano, marshalling two pony-sized hounds. Through the car window I asked if I was in Monteseiro, a remote mountain area close to Galicia's eastern border, not far from where Pablo Valledor has his Celtic pig forests. I had come to Monteseiro for two reasons. First, it is said to be almost untouched by modernity. Second, this high-lying area is one of the best places in Galicia for dry-curing hams. The combination looked good: if anyone was rearing and curing traditional country hams, it was going to be here in the altitudes that time forgot.

'Monteseiro?' he said, weighing up what seemed like a number of cockeyed answers. I sensed that we were about to enter the *retranca* zone. He repeated my original question, which is a Galician trope if ever there was one. Finally he pointed at my car keys and instructed me to turn off the motor. Apparently, it was just not that simple. We would need something to drink before the issue could be resolved.

The Etruscan plastic jug now disappears with Atilano, and returns full of white wine. Then he's off again, to reappear with a big lump of goat cheese. Then a large, round loaf. He sets everything down on a cloth between us, finds a knife, and implores me to cut myself some bread, which is heavy and moist and delicious, especially with the cheese.

After a lot of fussing, he sits down himself, and together we have a mid-morning snifter of crisp, floral white wine. Don't be shy, he says, nodding at the cheese, which I am already eating without the least shyness. I am, frankly, starving. Getting lost today was a long process, and my breakfast had been a Toblerone. Spanish breakfast, in case you didn't know, is coffee and cigarettes. In a café there might be a dry, bready croissant or an industrial bun in a cellophane packet. Spain is just not a morning sort of country.

'Where did you say you were going?' he asked.

Atilano is somewhat deaf. To complicate the issue, I am trying to explain to him, in my loud, foreign-accented voice, that I am on a quest to eat all the various bits of a pig, a notion that, once it gets through, meets with some suspicion. Do you have pigs? I ask. There is, apparently, no straightforward answer to this.

I proceed with my inquiries, more questions, more derailments on the mainline to Factuality Central. Atilano seems perfectly happy to sit and mull things over here in his kitchen, which looks like a pack of feral bachelors are in residence, and no one drew up a rota for the chores.

The house is only fifty years old, built by Atilano himself upon the cellar and foundations of a previous house. And just wait till you see the cellar! he says. I get all this in snippets, between the wine and the cheese and more wine. I nudge toward pork several more times. Yet despite the damning evidence that hangs in the passageway, no confirmation is forthcoming.

Enter Candido, son of the father, who has been out tending grapevines. Candido is perhaps in his late thirties, slight of frame, and intensely timid. He speaks not in Spanish, like his father, but in Galician, using words with extreme economy, staring down at the floor in front of him as if disowning each phrase as soon as it leaves his mouth.

He shuffles onto one of the benches around the

range and lights a Ducados. I explain my presence by telling him that I'm a visitor who got lost. This information strikes Candido as only marginally more interesting than the cigarette between his lips.

Atilano and I continue talking, hindered by deafness, foreign accents, conceptual non sequiturs, and hints about pigs that are continually unanswered. Then Candido is told to wash the mahogany bowl. It leaks, he says, as he washes it in the sink, the kitchen's next ant generation quickly smudged under his thumb.

'Let's have a look at the cellar,' Atilano says.

The cellar and the animal stables together occupy the foundation floor, and are built right into the slate mountainside. The back wall is solid rock, hacked out by hand untold centuries ago, and the basis for an unknown number of dwellings going no one knows how long. Atilano has old land deeds which cite the fifteenth century, but that's just modern stuff.

Inside there is hardly any light, and the air is cool and musty. The wine press, also said to be from the fifteenth century, is essentially a squared-off tree trunk, almost two feet thick, pivoted at one end and supported at the other on a carved wooden corkscrew the girth of my thigh. Several stone counterweights sit within the superstructure, which is composed of improbably large chunks of wood, all of which have names, and each of which I am taught; there is some intergenerational disagreement as to what exactly a *frog* is (it is the stumpy vertical support of the output tray of the press, not the top piece of the support). The press is so perfectly crafted that the corkscrew turns easily with a pole slotted through it, inching the trunk up or down fractionally with a loud creaking sound. It's one big bastard of a thing, however old it is.

Opposite the press stand four wine barrels, chest-high, Jacuzzi-sized ones, the kind of oddly massive containers that naturally make you wonder if you could have sex inside them, and if so how you'd go on in terms of leverage, knee scrape, etc. Atilano and Candido make somewhere in excess of five hundred gallons of wine each year from the white, acidic grapes of their own vines, the equivalent of about 2,500 bottles, all for domestic consumption. Some members of the extended family are involved in this consumption, I understand, although I am doing my bit this morning to help out.

The mahogany ant bowl now reappears, and is filled with wine from a smaller barrel by the door and offered to me. Hospitality cuts both ways, and I really do not have any options at this point. We pass the leaking bowl around and take long draughts. Do ants have spores? I think as I take a sip. No, that's mushrooms. Ants have eggs. But how small are these eggs? And how resistant are they to things like gastric juices? I imagine how my innards are going to look in a couple of days'

236

time: armies of fat-thoraxed ants marching through my gibbering liver, already crisscrossed with glistening ant walkways and tunnels . . .

After a good bit more wine and chitchat, Candido gives me a tour of the mountainside, thickly wooded right down to the stream at the bottom of the valley: oak, birch, chestnut, pine, plus a good selection of apple and cherry trees. We pay a visit to the old shrine, a tiny slate-built place of garden shed proportions with a confessional, the modesty grill just a wood plank with irregular holes drilled in it. This whole valley side was once populated, a house every mile or two, and a priest from Fonsagrada (about ten hard miles away) would somehow make it all the way down here to hold mass.

'Fifteen days!' Candido says. (Fifteen days is a fortnight in metric, FYI). 'Fifteen days!' as he looks up at the holes in the roof. 'That's all this'll last.'

He pulls bits of the deteriorating mud-plasterwork from the wall. The place is about a hundred years old, but might well be on the site of earlier makeshift chapels. Fifteen days!

As we make our way through the trees Candido changes dramatically. For well over an hour he hardly shuts up, liberated perhaps by the release of being outside, of wandering free through the woods that are, these days, his own private domain. There's almost no tree that doesn't have a story to tell; no twist in the overgrown tracks that wind along the steeply inclined land, no spring or dried-out cattle pool that doesn't prompt him to a new snippet of information, a story, a memory.

I learn things that are probably never going to be of much use to me. When you collect chestnuts, for example, four bucketfuls in your sack is enough; you think you can carry more, but . . . ; wild boars are mad for grapes (who knew!); cherrywood burns like buggery.

We eventually reach the nearest neighbour's house. They moved out a few years ago, drawn to the bright lights of Fonsagrada (population two thousand). But the abandoned house still has all the necessaries – stables, cellars, vines, apple and fig trees, a spring. On the whitewashed walls of the main house the year of my birth is daubed roughly in blue paint. It sends me momentarily loose-kneed, the result of too many *Hammer House of Horror* films in my youth.

That's one of ours, he says, indicating a cherry tree as we begin our return journey. He does this repeatedly, indicating pines and cherries and half a dozen other kinds of tree, all of which belong to someone in particular, the land on which they grow held in common. We talk in a seemingly natural mishmash of Galician and Spanish and smoke his Ducados. Where am I from? he asks. Did I come on an airplane? The car, is it mine? Have I got a place here in Galicia? Is it rented or bought? Did I buy it furnished?

The questions start to get a little bit confusing. When I go back home do I take my furniture

238

with me? After a while I realise what the problem is. I explain to Candido that I live here, for the moment. Here is my home. In Spain, in Galicia. Your place over there is boarded up, then? he asks. I have no place in England, I tell him.

That's the problem. And whereas it is the lack of a *place* – a house, a permanent residence in my native land – that puzzles him, he also seems to be expressing something about *a place in the world*. It strikes me that Candido's place in the world is of a different order to my own. The mountainside here resonates with the arduous, unfaltering life of a millennium, perhaps longer. And to all this Candido adds his own sweat, his own work, his intense, unhurried sense of belonging. I, by contrast, come on an airplane and buy my furniture in flat packs.

Back up at the house we have more wine. I plug away at the question of the day, of the year. It turns out they buy them at a few months old at a nearby livestock fair, then fatten them up here for the slaughter. This is increasingly how country folk are doing it in Galicia. Why go through all the trouble of keeping a sow and getting her serviced? Who knows, what with the depopulation of these remote parts, where the nearest available breeding boar might be? Then there's the birthing in the middle of the night, the vet's bills, the dead runts to bury . . . I'm sure once you've stopped breeding pigs at home, you don't miss it.

239

And everywhere it's the same story. The traditional *house pig*, the all-year-round domestic waste disposal unit and bacon supplier, is disappearing so fast you can hear its grunts trailing off into the distance.

Atilano, though, does at least have ham. Candido is sent off to fetch it, while I cover up my body jerk of elation by asking permission to photograph the sides of bacon hanging in the passageway. The ham is duly brought and presented for inspection. It looks good, very good, pristine. Not too big, not too small, a little lean of fat on the outside, but oh so beautiful. It is hung up alongside the bacon for better photos. Then we return to the kitchen and avail ourselves of more wine. The ham is left swinging in the passageway. When you live this far out, I guess you've got to husband your stocks well. My year-long quest for all the pork will have to wait, and I can't really grumble.

We wander through into the living room. A brochure is retrieved from a high shelf. A cloud of dust follows it down. No offence to the feminists, but that dust simply would not be there if a woman lived in the house. Or one of those queer-eye guys from the TV. In the brochure is a picture of Atilano's daughter, who was the queen of a local country fair in 1980. There are several more children, and on the wall are perhaps ten framed swimming certificates, all the same size apart from one, which is smaller.

'That's mine,' says Candido.

Another glass of wine, and then comes the cigar box with family photos: a handful of sunny afternoons sometime in the 1960s and '70s, the colours faded, the yellowed faces smiling and fresh, sons and daughters, a woman sitting astride a donkey, and then tending to some meat on an improvised barbecue.

'*E miña paisana!*' Atilano says. *It's my wife!* literally 'my country girl' or 'my peasant girl'. He is talking in Galician now, spluttering a bit into a handkerchief, laughing with joy, his eyes glazed a little with tears.

It's time to go.

Driving back along the mountain track doesn't seem that bad. I've been lost most of the day up a mountain, having resigned myself sometime around midmorning not to finding Monteseiro. In fact that is exactly where I have been, the last house in Monteseiro. It's just that when I arrived, Atilano wasn't too sure. The whole day has been a bit like the kind of answer a Galician might give you to a straightforward question; what it lacks in definition and clarity it more than makes up for in unexpected digressions. It's not the arriving, they say, it's the journey you take that matters. Today I got both.

Homeward I go, porkless but happy, all the way back to Coruña. It might not be my place in the world forever, and the furniture might be from Ikea, but my peasant girl's there.

TO MARKET, TO MARKET . . .

In Coruña, the city in northwest Galicia where we live, there is a glorious indoor food market, best known for its great, bustling expanse of fresh fish and seafood stalls that takes up an entire floor. The market has recently been rebuilt, and the meat section these days is rather muted and neat. But in the past it was like walking into a bloodstained grotto of death, with animals swinging from frighteningly large hooks as they were hacked at by cleaver-wielding men with solemn faces and sadistic moustaches, their gruesome stalls festooned with strings of deep red chorizo bunting. Rabbits and hares lay together in bunches, their dead, blooded eyes staring pathetically out at you. All manner of flesh was on display, from pig heads cleft in two, to skinned calf tails, sides of ribs, piles of gleaming liver and kidneys, swathes of deep red fillet, furry grey ox tongues . . .

That is what a five-year-old girl saw every time she accompanied her mum to market. There was the stench of cold blood, and the grisly thump of those cleavers as they scythed through meat and bone, hitting the butcher's block like guillotines. Then, one day, that little girl made a connection between what she saw during those scary trips to market and the fluffy bunnies, bleating lambs, and grunting piglets of her picture books at home. Always a sensitive child, Susana's horror was so intense that she refused to go inside the market again, and had to be left with Angelita, a curly-haired fruiterer on a different floor of the market, while her mum did the meat shopping alone. From that day on, the taste of meat made little Susana retch. Without knowing it, she had declared herself a vegetarian, a state reinforced by all those visits to the fruit and veg section, where she was petted over and given cherries and apricots, as well as fresh country cheese from a stall right next to Angelita's.

The doctor was eventually called, to see if he could cure her of this strange illness. He suggested that wafer-thin slices of cured *ibérico* ham might serve as a good source of protein if fresh meat was off the menu. It was a good suggestion, because *ibérico* ham isn't really meat, it's something higher, better, something way above mere animal flesh. Reluctantly, she managed to force a bit down.

As a result of all this trauma in early life, the separation between meat and nonmeat in our kitchen these days is almost kosher-like in its strict observance. But it's not a religious thing, just that she cannot tolerate the merest speck of it anywhere near her plate. Nevertheless, from time to time I am allowed to purchase whole legs of acorn-fed *ibérico* ham, the most expensive pork product on the planet, because the doctor prescribed it in 1974.

Today I am in the food market, shopping for sausages. I get a *morcilla*, blood sausage. It is black, as thick as a child's arm, and almost two feet long. Hanging there, doubled over a high steel bar in an inverted U shape, it looks like the yoke for a Shetland pony. In Galicia, *morcillas* are only found in the provinces of Coruña and Pontevedra. In the provinces of Lugo and Ourense, there is no blood sausage.

'In Lugo they don't know what it is!' the woman serving tells me, one of those frightening females in aprons who stand behind their market stalls and look as if at any moment they might bound up to the counter and challenge you to an arm wrestle.

I nod.

'They've never heard of them, eh?' she continues. 'They've never heard of *morcillas* at all. They just don't –'

All *right*, lady.

I also intend to get a *longaniza*, a sort of bargain-basement chorizo that I have read can also contain finely chopped lungs, heart, and any other oddments at hand. But the lady shrugs, says it's just like chorizo but longer. She lets me taste a slice. It's not very interesting, and I plump instead for three gloriously orange chorizos made from

Galician Celtic pork that are actually blowing me kisses from behind the counter. I also get an entire *salchichón*, made of very finely chopped pork meat (the greasy stuff) with pepper prominent in the spicing, the equivalent of a thin salami. That's enough, I reckon. It's only for a starter. I've already got the meat for the main course: pig hearts.

Then, as I'm wandering down the aisle on my way out, I get suckered by another of those arm-wrestling women. She catches me glancing up at a dark brown object suspended with string from the eaves of her stall. It's lumpy and irregular, clearly made from part of the large intestine, and looks like an old leather football that's been kicked to absolute shit.

'Is that –'

'*Muy bueno, buen'simo . . .*' – 'Good, really good' – she says, quickly pulling the thing down. You see, I have paused midstep. I have shown weakness. Like a nervous gazelle fawn, frozen in its tracks at the sight of the leopard sprinting toward it, I am now easy prey. *Muy bueno . . .* A big sheet of wrapping paper is torn from the roll and the knobbly football dropped enthusiastically onto it. *Buen'simo.* My dithering indecision is pathetic. *Muy, muuuy rico . . .* The horrid ball of broken bones is wrapped and handed to me. It weighs three pounds. It is, of course, a *botelo*.

Back home I don't bother to unload my sausages. In the fridge, right down at the back of the salad drawer, hidden beneath the remains of last week's wilting leeks, are two pig hearts, plus pig kidneys, in a tightly bound carrier bag. I got them fresh yesterday from a pork butcher in Santiago, who didn't even bother charging me for them. That's how much value is placed on the pig heart these days.

Having sneaked the hearts into the house, I am now going to sneak them out again. There's no point cooking them here. To a vegetarian, it doesn't get much more offensive than pig hearts, and using one of our baking tins for this recipe might lead to divorce. Remember: if my marriage crumbles then so too will my excuse for buying £350 hams.

My hearts and I go across the road. You might not think that having your in-laws live twenty-five paces away is such a great idea, but when you need a place to cook and a few appreciative carnivores, it's quite a boon.

Mercedes hovers at the door of her kitchen. She looks unsure, unsure as to whether this was a good idea (the idea of consenting to the marriage of her daughter to me). A variety of large sausages are lying around, two deep red pig hearts sit on a plate, and I am about to drop what looks like a ball of hardened elephant dung into an eight-quart pot of boiling water.

After just a few seconds, the rank smell of festering *botelo* rises up on the steam and makes me shudder. At some point I also throw the

246

chorizos into the pot. Antonio has by now appeared at the doorway alongside Mercedes. Neither of them has ever had *botelo*, and they are curious, but not in a good way.

With the nasty bag filling my lungs with its foul stink, I chop the onion finely and sweat it down, then add some white wine and reduce. In a separate pan I fry a little pig kidney, then chop it finely. When the onion is off the heat and somewhat cooled, in goes the kidney, followed by a plateful of bread crumbs that I made yesterday, grating the end of my middle finger in the process. Salt to taste.

A pig heart is the size of a man's fist. Mine have been slit down one side, I don't know why, but one ventricle is laid wide open. Luckily I have some thread and a needle, and I sew them back up. There are two ventricles, which are the large chambers, and two atria, the smaller ones. All four get stuffed, after which I drape streaky bacon over the top, sit them up in a little baking pan, and bathe them in ham stock, which I bought earlier. Fact: you can tell the precise moment someone becomes a foodie-cum-kitchen ponce: They acquire a stockpot. I don't have a stockpot.

I join Antonio in the living room. In the past we might have played chess before lunch, but as the years went by he started beating me in more outrageous and humiliating ways; I'm on safer ground with a newspaper. As far as the approaching meal is concerned, I'm glad we're going to give *botelo*

247

a try. Earlier on my pork tour I dissed the *botelo* pretty thoroughly, only to discover later that it is a cherished dish in Eastern Galicia and also in the Bierzo area of neighbouring León, where they call it by its Spanish name: *botillo*. My sister-in-law says *botillo* is delicious, rather like *zorza* (spiced pork). I am intrigued.

The hearts take two hours to cook.

Our appetisers are not such a success. The *salchichón* is like a bland salami. Antonio refuses it, saying it brings back bad memories of the Civil War and its austere aftermath, when *salchichónes* were often of the very worst quality. Food is a massive memory trigger, and it strikes me that sausages are pretty bad offenders. Just ask anyone who lived through the Second World War in Britain about sawdust bangers; on the other hand, don't we all have at least one great hot dog moment in our lives? Meanwhile, I have removed the skin from a section of the fat, limp *morcilla* and shaped the black contents into thin little patties. In other parts of northern Spain *morcillas* contain rice and sultanas mixed in with the blood, but in the parts of Galicia where *morcillas* are made (not Lugo, obviously) it's blood, sultanas, and pine nuts.

A pig slaughter in Galicia would normally involve collecting the animal's blood, beating eggs and sugar in it, and making pancakes. Today I'm making myself the next best thing, sweet blood patties. I pan-fry them for a minute on each side in a little olive oil, and they are magnificent, crazily sweet, but a sprinkling of salt brings out the savoury taste of the blood as well. I eat them alone, my parents-in-law watching with quizzical amusement. Mercedes says they remind her of the horrendous process of making blood sausages when she was a child (another sausage trigger). The blood, apparently, has to be boiled before it is coaxed into the skins, and it makes for a messy, stomach-curdling afternoon's work. Good thing Susana never witnessed that as a five-year-old.

Then comes the *botelo*, steaming on the platter, the intestine bag straining, bones poking through here and there. I cut into it, which is not that easy, since inside is a three-dimensional crisscross of bones. It looks like a month-old car crash that no one bothered to clean up. We each get a stubby bit of bone onto which dark meat clings. The bones have been steeped in so much paprika and garlic that they sting your mouth. It is just awful. Mercedes brings her piece to her mouth, and fifty milliseconds later it is back on the plate, her face suddenly like that of a bulldog that's swallowed a wasp. Antonio picks the meat from two small pieces of bone, but I think it's just to make a point; he's fairly serious about his eating, and I've rarely outdone him over the years.

So, I am very sorry to all lovers of Galician *botelo*. I have it on good authority that the *botillo* from the Bierzo is better. It certainly could not be worse.

'Heart' is such a complex word. It's impossible to ignore its many connotations as you take your first tentative bite. And the notion of eating another being's heart, the very centre of its physical existence, the tight little muscle that has been its sine qua non since before it was born, is somewhat disconcerting. Of course, we've all had heart before, minced up and processed, in sausages and pies and goodness knows what else. But the entire lump of it, stuffed and roasted in stock, is a challenge. The stretched, oven-darkened muscle tissue reminds me of something from an anatomy diagram. And in terms of my journey from nose to tail, you really can't get deeper into the animal than by devouring its heart.

'Devour' is the word too. My in-laws love it. I had expected them to refuse it, period. Because this is a pretty classy household when it comes to food. Mealtime here is a big deal. Across the very table where we are now tucking into the hearts, I have witnessed long, earnest discussions about the relative merits of bull crab and spider crab, and I have been present at meals of many courses during which the only topic of conversation has been food, often the food we were eating: Antonio's slightly spicy octopus stew, Mercedes's lamb braised in wine (*estofado*) with saffron potatoes, pile after pile of langoustine and prawns and all that crowd . . . Galicia is not just about pork. The food here is tremendously varied. I've had more monkfish at this table than you could get on the back of a pickup truck, plus turbot, haddock, grouper, hake, mussels, clams big, clams baby, clams razor . . . But of all the many things on offer in this part of the world, pig is the only one that really satisfies me 100 per cent. It squeals *meat* when you chew it, the fat is sweet and unashamed and authentic. There's no mistaking it, no disguising it, nothing *tastes-a-bit-like-chicken* about it. The real deal, the king of meats. Choose life! Choose pork!

Dark red-grey, the hearts have a tight, almost springy texture, like a hard ox tongue. I have overdone them. But apart from that, they are a delight. The taste is of pure muscle. Fat is like a court jester, the funny turn that lends meat its all-round appeal and jolliness. A heart, by contrast, is meat gone all serious, fatless, scowling meat, if you will. There is a slight fustiness, plus a liverish taste of blood, almost bovine in some ways. It's a serious taste, somehow, and I love it. We all do. So let's remove all pretence of modesty: my hearts are stratospheric.

The only slight quibble with this particular part of the pig was the recurring thought that the very heart I was eating might just as easily have been my own. Of all the pig's organs, none is more compatible with the human equivalent. So, if you really want to get to the heart of things, this probably tastes quite a bit like you do. And make no mistake: you taste damn good with a bit of kidney stuffing. *Oink oink.*

FOUR STOPS IN NEGUEIRA

1. *Last Mule East*

A wooden-railed walkway goes right around two sides of the old, weathered house. From it you can look out across a gaping valley and beyond, to the green-grey mountains of Asturias, the neighbouring region to the north-east of Galicia. An overhanging roof protects the walkway, each of its slates dark and rounded, like the chocolate button roof on Hansel and Gretel's house. Such is the slope of the valley that the front of the building is propped up on two six-foot stone piles, the back moored to the earth with built-in stables and a mini-courtyard. Until 1987 there was neither electricity nor running water.

I am in the extreme east of Galicia, and this is the very last dwelling before Asturias begins. I knock.

'What was it like before 1987?' is my dumb question to the elderly lady who has lived here all her life, after I finally coax her out from the dark interior of her quietly clucking home.

'It was a pain,' she says.

'But at least you have these magnificent views,' I add, dumber still.

'You just got here,' she says with a derisory shrug. 'Try living here all year long, back and forth to the well, buckets of water on your head. It was nothing special.'

She casts glances over her shoulder at the hens inside, and shuffles from one foot to the other. She does not want to talk about her waterless, unelectrified life here. You can hardly blame her.

I mention my quest for pigs. Meeting the very last pig in Galicia would be quite a feat. At least I think so. But she no longer keeps pigs, saying that she's too old. There's a mule, though. I go and find the last mule in Galicia. It doesn't look very pleased to see me. When I return to the house, the lady is gone.

Negueira de Muñiz is beyond the last mountain ridge, one of the most easterly points in Galicia, and with just over two hundred inhabitants spread around its nearly thirty square miles, the most sparsely populated part of the region. In 2006 not a single newborn baby was registered in the municipality.

Sticking out into Asturias, it's a little knuckle of secluded, high-lying land that nestles in the mountains on Galicia's northeastern flank. There's a beguiling sense of peace here, a touch of utopia, of a sleepy Lost Paradise. It is also, by some considerable margin, the most beautiful place I have been on my Galician travels.

There used to be a river gorge in Negueira, but the river was dammed back in the 1950s to service a hydroelectric power station farther downstream. Nowadays a long, wide reservoir curls north-south through the area, banked on both sides by steep, wooded mountains. On the map it looks like a python that found itself in the small-mammals enclosure at the zoo and is now regretting that last muskrat.

Returning from my meeting with the remote mule, I spot the village of Entralgo. Viewed from the mountainside road, far above, it looks confusing. Literally *between something*, Entralgo lies on a finger of land that pokes into the snake's belly. There is just enough room for three or four houses and some small vegetable plots before the road descends into the water. I decide to go down and take a look.

At the centre of the sliver of land, like a chunky diamond on a dowager's frail finger, is a large house, square, ancestral, perhaps a couple of centuries old, perhaps more. It is built of thin layers of gneiss, a local stone with red, brown, and dark grey tones, rather like slate. Through the top half of the stable-style door, which hangs open, I can see that the interior has its original stone floors and old, time-darkened woodwork, the real deal. There is even a thin line of smoke coming from the chimney. Jackpot.

I sling my camera over my shoulder and, like a stout version of Clint Eastwood in *The Bridges of Madison County*, stride out. An old lady is tending vegetables nearby. I ask her if I can take a picture of the house. She looks at me with *that* expression. Someone on his first trip into rural Galicia might mistake it for ironising disdain, or hardly disguised contempt. It is not. It is blanket disinterest. After some *uhming* and *ah*ing, the effort of which seems to make her physically uncomfortable, she tells me to go ask inside the house. I do. I knock on the double door. A younger woman appears. I ask about the picture. No, she says, you can't.

The only other person I can see is a lady in purple trousers tending plants in the adjacent plot, the last one before the road dives into the silent reservoir and Entralgo meets its watery end. Can I photograph *her* house? She says I can take whatever photos I want, and immediately turns her back and continues to work, ignoring me as I mooch disconsolately around her property taking consolation snaps.

Asking permission to take a picture is a means of breaking the ice. Photos are all very well, but what I'm really after is to get someone talking, preferably about pigs and how to eat them. But Between Somewhere has spurned me. Smiling, foreign-accented Me! Good-mannered, Nike-whooshed, motherable Me! Women of a certain age never turn me away. They take me in and give me food. Feedability is my most endearing feature. Plus, and I say this without undue vanity, I must, by default, be the most interesting visitor they've had here all week.

Are they not just a little bit intrigued? No?

No.

Off I go.

A little farther along the valley is a sign to Sanformar. There is just one house in Sanformar. I drive down a bumpy track, overgrown with long, stiff grass that spanks the undercarriage of my car mercilessly as I rumble cautiously on. I come to a gate, chained shut, and wired to the gateposts at several points on both sides for extra shut-ness. I can take a hint.

Pablo Valledor told me about the area of Negueira de Muñiz. He used to visit one or two farms here when he was starting out as a vet, and described it as an isolated, almost untouched place, a step into the past. He also mentioned that there were a few Celtic pigs here. I didn't think much more about it, until a few weeks later, when the Galician local elections were held, with Negueira notching up some pretty notable results: the four conservative party candidates amassed a combined total of zero votes, not even voting for themselves; the Cannabis Party, meanwhile, beat the lot of them with a single vote. I decided to go.

Negueira village itself, the municipal centre (population twenty-eight to thirty-two, depending who you ask), has two bars. I have a room above the older of these, having decided to stay the night. After an unpromising start to my trip, I call at the local council offices and ask the two girls there if any old farmers are still working the land in the area, or if anybody is still living in traditional, unmodernised houses. Although I had a couple of vague leads from Pablo, now that I was here I wanted to see everything. Negueira de Muñiz is, somehow, a tiny bit magical; it draws you in, you don't know why.

The girls look at each other. There's Joselín, one of them says, up at Tres Montes ('Three Mountains'). She tells me that he lives alone in an old house miles from anywhere with no electricity or water. And when someone from Negueira says miles from anywhere, this is no figure of speech. But immediately they turn to each other and shake their heads. The eighty-year-old sole resident of Three Mountains is not going to talk to me. He might hide, they say, or run away. No, forget Joselín.

Across the street, the proprietor of Negueira's newer bar is also sceptical. He warns me not to bother going up to Three Mountains, although he does explain how to get there.

I go. But I go the wrong way, parking the car and hiking into the wrong forest altogether. The sun is now on full beam, and even in the shade of the trees it is hot and humid. On I struggle, over the mouldering remains of dead trunks and through an undergrowth that seems to be a fifty-fifty bramble-fern weave. Eventually, with still no buildings in sight, I can go no farther. A hart springs out in front of me, and we both shit ourselves. It takes me half an hour to fight my way back out, by which time a swarm of flies is taking good advantage of my exposed bits, now hot and juicy. To shake the flies off I have to go several paces away from the car, turn, and take a run at it, jumping in through the door and slamming it shut behind me. A change of shirt and several minutes of AC-wallowing follow.

Finally I manage to find Three Mountains, an eerie, abandoned hamlet of four houses up an otherwise untouched mountainside. I knock on the door of the last house, which is supposed to be Joselín's. No one answers. I walk around, calling out *buenos dias* and *hola*. I knock on other doors, just in case I got it wrong. No one is here, and I'm so freaked and hot and exhausted now that the situation sends me a little light-headed. I watch some lizards scamper along stone walls, and remember that I once had a very nice job teaching English in a university.

A friendly short-toed eagle follows my car part of the way back to Negueira village. I call in at the council building again. The hippies! I say, lead me to the hippies! I'd heard that there was a hippie commune somewhere around here. I was saving it for tomorrow. But today has not been a screaming success. I get hippie directions.

A longish drive around and across the reservoir leads me to Cancio village, mentioned by the girls. There are no hippies here. There are no humans here. I drive a little farther, as instructed, but the road turns to a dirt track, and my breakfast was a small industrial bun in a cellophane wrapper. I'm not intrepid. I'm hungry. I turn around.

2. The Land That Bridges Forgot

Aurora complains about the sun, which is high in the sky. She has just come up from the fields, greeting me with a smile as she dabs her brow with a handkerchief. And after the morning I've had, her smile is like a draught of the warm south.

I had been on my way back from the deserted village of Cancio when I spotted Santalla, a cluster of substantial old houses on a sweeping valley side of powerful, almost blinding green. Someone must still live there, I thought, and pulled over.

Santalla is the kind of hamlet where people would always have been self-sufficient. Aurora and her husband, José, still are. Until last year they had eight head of cattle, some sheep and chickens, plus the pigs, which I can already hear grunting. They've sold most of the cows now, but the rest of the livestock remains, as the couple move slowly toward what looks like it will be a sublimely contented retirement.

José appears. He doesn't seem ready to retire. He looks fit and alert, the kind of person that management consultancies should sign up to teach burned-out executives about the all-important mind-body balance. Perhaps the local conditions keep José and Aurora young. Negueira has a warm microclimate, ridiculously fertile soil, and a shimmering, unrestrained beauty. Almost anything will grow here, including some pretty good red grapes, and – apparently – even better marijuana, although I haven't found the hippies yet.

I chat to José, who is quiet and has the air of a college professor on sabbatical. Meanwhile, Aurora, who has the air of a professor's wife (the ones who are charming, great cooks, and known by everyone on the faculty to be smarter than their husbands), herds four goodly porkers out from the dark, ground-floor vestibule of the farmhouse for their midday stroll. This shared entrance leads to the family's living quarters, above, and the stables and sties below. She tosses dark, floppy cabbage leaves onto the ground and herds the animals toward them with a casual flick of the foot.

The farmhouse, stolid, spacious, and unmodernised, is a perfect example of how things used to be. The whole hamlet has an unchanged atmosphere to it. And there's a reason for this, which José now explains.

Santalla sits about halfway up the mountainous eastern side of the reservoir valley; imagine a scale model of Switzerland dunked partway in a tub of water. When the river was dammed, in 1952, this and other villages on the eastern side found themselves looking out over a slice of water-filled Swiss Galicia with no bridges across it. And the bridgelessness was a bit of a killer, because in the other direction, right behind them, was a range of treacherous Asturian mountains with no way through. A whole strip of Negueira found itself suddenly cut off from the world.

About a dozen hamlets disappeared below the water, as well as half of Entralgo. There wasn't much consultation with the inhabitants, and the compensation they finally received was a lot less than had been promised. But this was during Spain's dictatorship, and organised protest was not really an option. Many of the displaced residents moved to the neighbouring area of Terra Chá, where they formed 'colonies' of ex-Negueirans in two villages there.

José was a boy at the time, and he recalls all this with perfect clarity. He looks down his sloping farmland, all the way to the water far below, and tells me that when the dam suddenly rose, overnight, villagers in places like Santalla made a startling discovery: no one had a boat. The hills were alive, I imagine, with the sound of *Oh shit*.

They managed to acquire a few rowboats. Everything had to be brought over the water, then hauled home up the steep banks. When they wanted to take a cow to market, same thing, people and beast huddled together, bobbing precariously in a launch just about big enough for

261

the purpose. Farming machinery, nope; tractors, sorry. There was a suspension footbridge some miles upriver that sheep and goats could, at a pinch, be driven across one at a time. No electricity or running water either, by the way.

The isolation lasted until 1982, when a mountain track was laid eastward through to Asturias; in November of that year an automobile appeared for the first time ever in Santalla. A little later they got a bridge across the reservoir back into Galicia. But for three decades a string of villages up this side of the reservoir were stranded.

An invitation to a cool beer leads us into the kitchen, where Aurora tells me about the birth of her son Félix, back in the days of isolation. When contractions began she and José had to trek down the mountainside to the water's edge, get across the water in a rowboat, struggle up the opposite bank, find someone with a car and beg a lift to Negueira, then phone for a taxi to take her over another mountain to the hospital at Fonsagrada. The pains, she recalls, began at midnight. Would you like to stay for something to eat?

Were words ever so sweet?

I nip outside with José to take some pictures of the valley while the table is laid. Félix now arrives with his girlfriend, Monica. They work in Gijón, a three-hour drive east in Asturias, but they come back here as often as they can. Félix looks none the worse for his adventurous start in life, and rowing across a reservoir every day to go to school no doubt toughened him up plenty. Monica, who is just about to take the exams to join the hallowed ranks of Spain's *funcionarios*, is back visiting her own parents, who live not far away.

We sit down to eat. There is a big pot in the middle of the table. Aurora removes the lid.

'Do you like pig feet?'

I don't know. They float in a stew of potatoes and chickpeas, the surface freckled with tiny droplets of orange, paprikainfused oil. I have failed to eat trotters twice so far on this year's quest, and I had more or less given up hope. I can't believe my luck.

I am invited to serve myself. Pig feet are never going to win prizes for beauty. Even a pig lover will admit that they are hunched up and inelegant, as if the animal has spent its life in a tutu trying to master ballet pointe. These feet have been cut in half, the bony, skinwrapped ankles separated from the hoof. There's not much evidence of meat on either part. *Leave them if you don't like them!* they all keep telling me, as they serve themselves and tuck in, holding their pieces of foot with their fingertips and nibbling expertly.

I start with the stew, which is the golden orange hue that a *refrito* has lent it. The potatoes are earthy and almost sweet to the taste. They come from the hillside just beyond the kitchen window. The chickpeas, meanwhile, are soft, oozing a fatty flavour that is not obviously meaty but has an

263

alluring kind of meat reminder to it, somewhat like *callos* (stewed tripe with chickpeas). The gravy is thick and very slightly sticky, and could easily be eaten with bread as a meal in itself.

For a while that's what I do, skipping between the feet, mopping up the unctuous paprika-flecked gravy with lumps of heavy bread that I hack inexpertly from a large, round loaf. For extra rustic élan I try to cut myself a slice while holding the loaf in the air, like my grandmother used to do. I fumble and drop it.

Finally, it's time to start pedalling. I pick one up and hold it up to my eyes. I take a . . . what? A bite? Not really. A whole new technique is required, part bite, part chew, part suck. I watch the others, who strip their feet of skin and meat in a matter of seconds. It reminds me of the way the Spanish have of popping a sunflower seed pod between their teeth, cracking it, extracting the seed with their tongue, then removing the husk from puckered lips with finger and thumb, all in about half a second. My own foot technique is slow and fumbling, more a matter of exploration. Each mouthful involves a snap-crunch of cartilage, a twang of chewy outer skin, then the slurp of sticky-sweet fat beneath as it disintegrates on your tongue. Somewhere in all this, down in the nether regions of backtastes and aftertastes, is something deeply porklike, which I find, curiously, the least appealing part of the experience.

Leave them if you don't like them! they continue to

tell me as they eat their *manos de cerdo* – literally 'pigs' hands'. I don't leave them, but I don't love them either. Not really. There's a savoury squashiness as I chew, and flaps of thick skin that look like soggy bandage on the way in turn to pure glutinosity as I bring my teeth cautiously together. I'm not quite relishing the experience, but it is certainly fascinating.

If nothing else, there's a lot of novel things going on in my mouth, a quick-fire vaudeville show of every act you can muster from a pig foot. The star must surely be the hoof itself. Divested of the hard outer nail, it's like a little bishop's mitre, covered in a fine dark brown coat that looks like deer velvet and tastes fusty and faintly bloody as you suck-nibble it away from the bone. And it's a curiously pleasurable experience, knowing that you've got a pig's big toe in your mouth.

My next helping includes fewer feet and more of the chickpea stew, which is fabulously satisfying, a perfect combination of flavours and textures. This is how to make it:

Trotter Stew, Doña Aurora

1 lb. fresh pig feet, cut into pieces
chickpeas
potatoes
refrito (paprika, finely chopped garlic and onion, softened in olive oil)
salt

Soak the chickpeas, then cook in a large pot with water. Add the feet, and a little later the potatoes, cut into medium-sized pieces. Cover and simmer for 30–45 minutes. Add the *refrito* and mix through. Salt to taste.

'There's nothing to it,' Aurora says. 'I get the feet fresh, though,' she adds.

So is that the secret? The trotters are fresh, not salt-cured. Perhaps a dried, salted foot would have given a sharper, hoggier taste, its fat and skin reduced and condensed, adding the slight bitterness that dried skin sometimes carries. Apart from this, the recipe really is simplicity itself.

'They take about forty-five minutes,' she explains, 'but try them after half an hour. It depends on your pot. Your wife'll know.'

She bloody won't.

The kitchen windows are open, and a breeze from the valley enters, carrying with it the chirping of a little blue songbird in a tree by the window. We drink José's cool, slightly sweet rosé, which confirms the quality of his vines, and we get through a lot of pigs' hands. I ask Félix and Monica whether they would consider coming back here to live. Never has a no been expressed with so much yes in it. They have thought about it. But they won't. Félix grew up in this house and he knows what's involved. There's no lie-ins when you're milking, he says, no holidays, no sick days. No one comes back, not to farm.

The conversation around the table is friendly and generous. I am given the lowdown on the hippies, who seem to be regarded with fondness, although with a degree of incomprehension. There are snippets of other local information. Aurora knows Atilano over in Monteseiro, and they all know the reticent lady in Entralgo, who turns out to be the mayor's mum. Félix tells me a good place to find the otherwise reclusive Joselín on a Friday night: the older of the two bars in Negueira village, which is lucky, because that's where I'm staying.

I have more of José's wine, and reflect on the fact that the life he and Aurora live is as good as over. They are the last in Santalla to work the land; indeed, they are almost the last in Santalla. After that there's no way back. Villages such as these simply wither and die. I've seen it up and down the valley – sinking roofs, crumbling walls, then nothing. Nobody even bothers to pull the houses down.

Coffee and a cigarette. Then José has work to do, and Félix is off trout fishing. It's been a normal lunchtime in Santalla. And if you didn't know better, in such wonderful company, in such a place, you might have thought that this life could go on forever, like it always has.

3. Trouble in Paradise

A couple of villages past yesterday's stop for pig feet on the wrong side of the reservoir, and I am driving down a narrow dirt track that leads off a slightly wider dirt track. It is midmorning, and I have high hopes for today's visit.

Foxo, a tiny hamlet of perhaps a dozen old stone houses, sits on a slope close to the water. Set amid fairly dense woodland, its darkness is lifted here and there by traces of purple, turquoise, red, and yellow on doors and walls, the fading rainbow fingerprints of a hippie commune.

Some of the houses are falling down, their roofs sagging, patched with tarps, others already collapsed, and the old, multicoloured daubings lend the place a melancholy aspect. Black hosepipes wind through the village like darkened veins, bringing water from a spring somewhere up above, although I don't know how many residents are still here to drink it. Three or four houses, I have been told, are inhabited, but no one's about when I arrive. There are cattle down in the pastureland near the water's edge; one or two more beasts amble within the settlement itself.

Yes? Hello? The voice comes from the biggest house. And it's not a greeting, it's a question. At an upstairs window is an attractive young woman in a white T-shirt that does her justice. I tell her I'm a journalist, and ask her if I can take some pictures. Not of this house, you can't, she says, and quickly demands to know which newspaper I work for, in a way that seems intended to wrong-foot me. It does. I stutter, inventing a magazine called FSG (the initials of this book's publisher), and in a spontaneous attempt to impress her I mention that it is American. If she is impressed she manages to hide it well, and sends me away with a flea in my ear.

I wander around for a while. But I am feeling uncomfortable. Music comes from another house, but now I hardly dare knock. Even the cows have a smouldering, don't mess with me look in their eyes, and I find myself making a detour between two silent, tumble-down cottages to avoid a loitering bovine that guards the route back to my car.

A young woman and a bare-assed toddler appear. They crouch down and peep into a chicken coop, trying to spy a rabbit that's got in with the birds. I introduce myself. She tells me I can take whatever pictures I want, then ignores me rather pointedly.

Well, brotherly love, go screw yourself. These hippies are sourpusses. To me the word 'hippie' means Ken Kesey and the Merry Pranksters. It means a bighearted grab for peace and happiness, the kind of people I have always admired, if only for having the courage to be openly, colourfully idealistic. This is the first time I have been in a hippie commune. I've really been looking forward to coming. But quite frankly, in this particular paradise, they have no manners.

Dejected, I make my way back to the car, past a new, shining Citroën (suspicious), a rusted-up hunk of former Ford (better, more fitting), an old airport luggage wagon or some such bit of beat-up industrial detritus (commune material par excellence). I sit and ponder my options.

The Negueira commune was established by Nilo Seira, Galicia's answer to Kesey. He ditched his high-paying job in Barcelona and founded an alternative community here on the banks of the reservoir in the seventies, during the prebridge days of isolation. For the next three decades people came here to live, not only from Spain, but from Holland, Italy, Norway, Finland, Argentina, and the United States, moving into five of the most remote villages up the valley, where most of the old stone houses were already abandoned. From a high point of well over a hundred, there are now about forty individuals left, including a pack of children who were born here.

Foxo is one of those five villages. But Foxo has not shown me much of a welcome. All the doors have remained closed, and I feel like an intruder in a village called Fuck Off Intruder. Just getting here has involved driving down several sides of the reservoir (the reservoir has tendrils; it's complicated) on narrow country roads and a dirt track, and I'm not likely to be in another hippie commune anytime soon. I decide to give it another shot.

Back at the house with the chicken coop I hear rock music playing. Not the Grateful Dead, but something reassuringly similar.

I knock.

Out pokes a head. A gaunt, bright-eyed,

messianic face draped with long, straggly hair and a wild beard. Hi, he says, bounding down the steps in aged boots. I apologise for the intrusion. You're not intruding, he says with a smile; beatific may be going too far, but it's a damn good smile.

His name is Speed. He's as skinny as a rake, and has been in the commune for over twenty years. He's only visiting Foxo today and is nursing a hangover after some unspecified shenanigans the previous night. He perches himself down on the stoop of the house's entrance and I tell him I'm interested in pigs. The eyes get brighter.

Three young children emerge, dressed in tie-dyed orange and flower-power purple, three of the most delightful children I have ever seen.

'Get Porki!' Speed tells them.

Porki is duly brought, a black and white sow who immediately starts digging up the soil next to the house, then lies in it.

'She's a Celtic!' I say, recognising the big ears and long back.

'Yep,' says Speed. 'And there's more where I live.'

Before I can ask where that is, Isabel emerges from the house, the woman from the chicken coop, and the mother of the three kaleidoscopic angels. She spends a long time berating everyone else for the loss of her lighter, an unlit cigarette dangling from her lips. We don't like journalists, she tells me, as her lighter is finally found. Then she disappears inside again.

One of the kids is now riding Porki up and down

in front of us like a pony. Isabel reemerges from the house with a book of press cuttings, articles about the commune from local newspapers. I guess that for a place like Negueira, the real ass-end of Galicia's rural hinterland, a hippie commune must have been quite an unexpected development. The journalists come smiling, she says, then they print whatever they like.

I scan the articles in the folder. The main point of contention, I surmise, is the issue of drugs, although I have to say that no one offers me any. I promise her that on no account will I print whatever I like. I explain that I am interested in pigs, not communes. This pacifies her somewhat, and as if to demonstrate the fact she gets a long stick, orders her daughter to dismount, and starts scratching Porki on the back, which the animal clearly finds mighty pleasurable, rolling right over onto its side and throwing its head back in guttural throes of ecstasy.

Before you get all sentimental about the scene I am painting, it is worth bearing in mind that Isabel's partner, who is not at home this morning, used to be a butcher in Madrid. The hog will become Porki chops soon enough.

'If you're interested in pigs,' says Speed, 'my Celtics are up in Vilar.'

An incredible stroke of luck. The porkers in Vilar village were already on my radar. The people back in the council buildings yesterday had mentioned them; in Santalla too, although Monica had added that Vilar is a little tricky to get to. You see, in Negueira everyone knows everyone and every-thing. Meeting people here is like clicking on a series of real-life hyperlinks, one leading right on to the next. Everyone I have spoken to knows the story of the commune, including the narrative of its partial unfolding; Speed knows Aurora and José over in Santalla; absolutely everyone has a story or two about old Joselín up at Three Mountains . . . On it goes. *Click click.* As for the girl in the fetching white T-shirt, she's not from the commune at all, I now learn, but the granddaughter of one of the village's prior residents, back to look over the old family house. She's *police*.

So, I walk into a hippie commune in a remote rural paradise and the first person I meet is a police officer in a tight-fitting T-shirt who inter-rogates me from an upstairs window. What are the chances of that?

Speed and I now set out for Vilar in my car. We emerge from the steep track out of Foxo, and he immediately points to a track in front of us that stretches upward at what seems like a ludicrous angle. It is still under construction, merely a strip of loose rock, like the ribbon on a gift-wrapped mountain.

We ascend. It is far too steep. Cars should not point up at the sky like this; it's not natural. I don't want to wimp out, though, and I keep going, never once getting out of first gear. Partway up, the track is storm damaged, with deep channels where the rock has been washed away. The wheels spin and whiz, and my poor automobile is thrown violently about, as if the mountain is actually sodomising it. We are humped rudely across a bed of loose boulders until we slip toward the edge. A sinister smell comes from the tires or the brakes or the gearbox or somewhere, as the vehicle begins to exude a gaseous musk of anxiety. I lose my nerve.

It's a long walk.

'We didn't want the track anyway,' Speed tells me as we hike upward, pointing across to the ancient footpath that snakes up the roughly gorsed mountainside way off to our left. The sun is painfully intense. I have started to perspire and to gasp. 'We're all thin up here,' he says, 'it's the hiking everywhere that keeps you fit.'

I get the message.

'By the way,' I say, changing the subject, 'who voted for the Cannabis Party?'

'Nobody knows!' he shrieks, guffawing with laughter.

Rounding a bend we see Vilar, a hamlet of (you guessed?) several stone cottages clustered together. *Vilar* simply means 'village' in Galician, and there are lots and lots of Vilars, although none, I would imagine, is as hard to get to as this one. In the past Galicians tended to give a name to every hamlet. As you drive through the countryside it is not uncommon to see a name sign, two houses, and an old tractor, then nothing more. Taking Spain as a whole, thirty thousand places are listed in the atlas, from cities and towns to the smallest recognised villages and hamlets; half of all these are in Galicia, which occupies a mere 6 per cent of the Spanish landmass and a similar percentage of its population.

Panting, and dabbing my neck with a handkerchief so heavy with perspiration that it's debatable whether I'm taking the stuff off or simply moving it about, I tell Speed that yesterday I had assumed Santalla was pretty much the end of the road. He laughs, because it turns out that Santalla is the Big Apple in comparison with Vilar village, which is in a perversely isolated spot, secluded to an extent that seems almost contrived to be so. Why? Why on earth build a village here? Then the reservoir came, which just made things worse. *Why-village*, it should be renamed, *the place they stranded twice*.

You really need a very good reason to come to Vilar. And my specific line of thought goes something like this: commune, communal, common ownership, sharing, sharers. Sharers of Celtic pigs. Which I am going to consume.

We arrive. I look as if I've just done the hundred-metre butterfly in my jeans and T-shirt. Fortunately, it's cool and shady in Neka's kitchen, where he slouches in a battered old armchair, a log fire sizzling and clicking in the open hearth at his feet. The room is as close as I have come to untouched antiquity: lumpen, irregular stone walls limed white a million times, dark wooden beams overhead (not far over), a cockeyed imprecision to everything, like a Hobbit's kitchen. Neka gets up, pottering about in a pair of stripy pyjama bottoms and a jumper that's seen better decades. He puts some coffee on and rolls himself a cigarette.

Vilar has not changed much since the real Big Apple was called New Amsterdam, other than in population. The houses here were abandoned progressively during the waves of emigration that have slowly eaten away at Galicia's rural population since the second half of the nineteenth century. The commune had no problem requisitioning them, because there was nobody here to argue.

Neka has long, fine hair and moves slowly, deliberately, hardly making a sound. He didn't say a word when Speed came through the door (sign on it: DO NOT LOCK) with a gasping, sweat-dripping stranger dressed in black and looking neither turned on nor tuned in, and dropping only in the sense of onto a wooden bench in exhaustion.

We sit at the rough-hewn table and chew the fat. Speed has stories to recount of last night's mischief, and takes a little wine to knock the edge off his hangover. There's gossip, complaints about money, stories of who said what to whom, all of which passes me by and allows me to absorb the atmosphere, which is quiet, so quiet that it is noisily quiet, a violent rush of not-noise pinning you back and forcing you to relax.

The population of Vilar numbers five adults, two young boys (incalculably adorable), six pigs, a herd of sheep, chickens aplenty, various dogs (there are always various dogs), and a venerable old cedar tree at the centre of things that is a sort of slow-beating spiritual heart to the place. I mention the pigs. We go take a look at Speed's specimens, which live in a barn nearby. My thoughts are already turning to a ham lunch. His animals are young, frisky, long-backed Celtics. Unfortunately, they are his first stab at pig rearing.

There is, then, no Celtic ham in Vilar. The news, the dreadful news, hardly has time to sink in when a big 4x4 pickup rumbles along the unfinished track, laden with firefighting equipment. The main source of work for those still living in the commune villages these days is Negueira's local council, and today's crew has been on municipal forest fire patrol.

Four people get out. One of the women looks like Nico's paediatrician, which unnerves me for a second or two as I try to remember if his stools have been soft this week. Then there's Guillermiña, with long, flowing auburn hair and an endlessly kind face, half Amazonian warrior, half Pre-Raphaelite beauty. She's lived in another of the five commune villages for over a quarter of a century, surrendering to electricity and running water only when she had children; when she first lived here she used to get around on a horse. Meanwhile, the two guys wear regulation bushy beards and long, tied-back hair, and don't look afraid of a bit of work. In fact, they all seem to be tough and hardened, not floppy and saggy-limbed like hippies are supposed to be. Life up here, I gather, is a mixture of physical toil and overwhelming peace, precisely the two things lacking from many people's lives, certainly from my own. Who knows, toil and peace may be good for you. I've never had much of either.

Things in the multivillage commune are not quite as communal as they once were. People have drifted away. Nilo Seira, the patriarch, has moved on, although he comes back for visits now and then. Others have set up home together, becoming more conjugal than communal. What is left is not a commune but a loose network of friends. Yet something special remains, you can sense it up here in Neka's kitchen, with Speed and the part-time firefighters, although I don't know exactly what it is. A sort of resilient gentleness. Perhaps they've found true peace, or happiness. Or both. I don't know. They look happy enough, but then again, the boozed-up tramp that begs for money at the end of our street in Coruña laughs and jokes as if he's just won the lotto. Happiness, it's a difficult one to gauge, although when one of the two incalculably adorable boys from the hamlet joins us, taking Guillermiña and me to see his pet sheep, there is little doubt that he is blissfully happy up here in Vilar.

We return to Neka's place just in time. Everyone else is now crowded onto the small, creaky porch, and from there we watch the first bolt of lightning. It splits the sky right out in front of us, at eye level. This is one drawback to paradise; the humid microclimate, the altitude, the between-mountain-ness . . . it's a recipe for thunderstorms. In two days I found myself in the middle of three, and on each occasion the lightning came far too near, as if someone up there had spotted a new face and was trying to see how high he'd jump. Except for Speed (fingers in ears) and me (fingers in ears and expression of Mother-where-art-thou horror) everyone toughs it out. But the storm is so loud and so bladder-strickeningly close that I immediately understand why villages up these mountains never grew to more than a few houses; any sane person would be sheltering down in the valley bottom. The hailstones are huge, like frozen lychees, hitting the ground so hard that they seem to have been catapulted out of the sky.

There we remain, smoking (everyone in a commune must smoke cigarettes, it's a rule), and an improvised lunch of chorizo and potato stew is orchestrated. I am thinking, first, that the torrents of rain now coursing down the disintegrating mountain track might at any moment send my car over the edge where we abandoned it, and, second, what happens if this rain doesn't stop? The third scenario, in which both of the above transpire, somehow never occurs to me, which is just as well. Because I'm not going anywhere till we've had lunch.

279

4. Joselin

It's my second evening in Negueira de Muñiz. The rain in Vilar finally stopped, and now I'm back in Negueira village. I decide to give Joselín another go. Why? Ask Edmund Hillary and Sherpa Tenzing why they risked life and limb to scale Everest. Joselín is my Himalayan peak, and I don't know when I'll get another chance at scaling him. I book in for another night at the *hostal*, then phone home. Susana's patience is holding up well, although it probably shouldn't be.

Back in Three Mountains, my luck has changed. As I make my way into the spooky ghost-hamlet for a second time, there he is, lean and alert, his movements slow but deliberate. He wears a blue pullover, and carries a plastic bucket brim-full of water from the communal spring in the hamlet.

Buenas tardes! I shout as I emerge from between two of the abandoned cottages, finding myself on the familiar path that runs through the tiny settlement, skirts a swathe of sloping pastureland just beyond, then disappears over a bush-covered ridge. We are fifty or sixty yards apart at this point, and I press on with the 'good evening's and the 'hello's as I mince along the muddy, rock-strewn path.

He stops, turns his head a little, and waves an arm out behind him in the air, as if swatting me away. Then he continues on his way with the bucket.

I am undeterred. He may be ignoring me, but I have a theory about recluses: they are just big show-offs who have taken things to extremes. Underneath all that Greta Garbo braggadocio lies an exhibitionist desperate for a bit of attention. And besides, I've been in this very spot before, shouting 'excuse me's and 'hello's at abandoned buildings. At least I have an audience this time.

So I continue after him in resolute but very well-mannered pursuit. Eventually he stops, puts down the bucket, and turns. He screws up his eyes, puts his hands on his hips, and watches as a stoutish man in jeans and T-shirt comes stumbling along the path, shouting apologies in a foreign accent and looking like the kind of person you don't really expect to see late on a Saturday afternoon up at Three Mountains.

Thus do I finally meet Joselín. He accepts my hand warily, shaking it as if it's puzzling but not *that* puzzling. I tell him that I have come to photograph old houses in the region. Without much fuss he says I can come and take pictures of his house. He has an angular, weatherworn face and short-cropped silver hair, and is gently spoken and seems to be a calm, thoughtful man. Not the unpredictable ogre I had been expecting. Something doesn't square with everything I've been told about Joselín, and the only conclusion I can draw is that an aura builds up around recluses, one which conceals the truth.

I follow him as he makes his way up the single-file track that winds over the ridge, then through thick heather and gorse bushes for quite a way. It turns out that he doesn't live in Three Mountains at all, but farther on, over the horizon, deeper still into the woods. He is talking in Galician, and as I walk behind, trying to listen, I realise that he is precisely what linguists call a NORM (nonmobile, old, rural male). It used to be thought that old, rural men were the most representative speakers of a dialect, perhaps because they were the most conservative, unadventurous speakers. Much fieldwork in the study of dialectology involved just what I am doing now, finding old, nonmobile men to talk to. Since the 1960s it has slowly been ceded in dialectological circles that younger people also speak in dialects, even women.

As Joselín talks, explaining the kind of hunting he gets up here (boars, if you know what you're doing, even harts), and the plants that grow (anything at all, it sounds like), I realise that he is the most extreme NORM I have ever met. Plus, he is up ahead of me, and I can't see his face, nor read his expressions. If you really want to test your language skills, try listening to the back of a NORM's head as he leads you up over a deserted mountain with a bucket of water at dusk.

We eventually come to his house, which is large, two stories, six big bedrooms I would say, although some of them are now gone, part of the roof having given way, like a collapsed pie crust, and been left that way. Built from the local gneiss stone, yellowish grey and dry-layered in thin slabs all the way up to its elegantly finished eaves, this is a substantial building in anyone's book, but especially so when you consider its location. Who built it here? And why? Were they sick of the bustling four-cottage metropolis over at Three Mountains? Was the deafening gurgle of the spring too much to bear? And what has gone on within these walls over the years, so isolated and untouched by human commerce?

There is no running water and no electricity. A single gas light provides illumination, plus there are some candles *if you need them*, he explains. Usually, when you visit an 'unchanged' house, the slow creep of modernity is somewhere evident: a furtive TV aerial, or a solitary lightbulb hanging from the ceiling. But this is the real deal. Apart from the scandalous innovation of the gaslight, this is exactly as it would have been a couple of hundred years ago, although its current single male occupant probably worries less about putting things away than a proud nineteenth-century Galician housewife would have.

The thick wooden floorboards are so irregular that they might be the knobbly skin of a house-sized reptile. The ground-level open hearth that takes up one corner of the room is surrounded on three sides by wooden benches, just like in the *pallozas* in Piornedo. Everything is blackened with soot and age, although the absence of light makes it difficult to see much at all, other than the mammoth clutter of pots and jars and mysterious sacks of stuff that stretches off into the penumbra of Joselín's ancient front room. He offers me a drink of homemade wine from a wine sack. It is strong and characterful, and I make great show of just how well I can handle a wine bag, though it turns out that a black T-shirt was an opportune choice.

There are two small windows, mostly the wooden framing and holes, just two handkerchief-sized panes of cracked glass. I take a picture of the hearth, then show him the little screen of my camera. I don't know why. He nods noncommittally, as if he doesn't know why either. And thus we stand, in the darkness, as I try to decide what one might say in such a situation. What I want to say is, *Jesus wept, you actually live in a place like this!* Not out of disgust or shock, but wonder, sheer amazement.

Joselín has been on the mountain thirty years, and in that time he has seen the residents of the nearby hamlet leave one by one, until only he remained. The mayor of Negueira has been trying to persuade him to move to the village centre for years, but Joselín doesn't seem to be the kind of person who responds much to persuasion.

Back outside, he dithers by the house as I take more pictures. I even manage to get him to pose for a shot. He seems to accept all this happily enough, and tolerates my questions with patience. His words are softly uttered, and they tail off as if he thinks perhaps I don't really want to hear them. Yet I do, and also how he came to be here, and why he stays. These, though, are not questions you can easily ask. I've intruded far enough into his life just by being here.

The house itself sits just about plumb on the Galician border. At the back is a small apple orchard, after which a dense forest spreads out as the mountain slopes off into Asturias. It really is an incredible place. Although, as I wander down between the apple trees at the back to take photos, little crackles and snaps from the adjoining forest do worrying things to my heart, which feels as if someone is injecting it with amphetamines. To live here alone, in terrifyingly silent seclusion, would not be many people's idea of paradise. And when a wild boar comes a-prowling on a cold, windswept night, or a wolf, or an Asturian bear, most people would want more than a gaslight and candles.

I wander back up from the orchard. He is pottering around, waiting for me at the front of the house, the bucket of water outside the door where he left it when we arrived. He gives me a handful of *pexegos*, a Galician fruit somewhere between an apple and a peach, just picked from a tree right outside his front door. He doesn't really want me there any longer, though. I guess you don't go and live up beyond Three Mountains on your own if you relish the company of unknown visitors.

I offer to send him copies of the photos I have taken.

'Should I just address them to Señor Joselín, Three Mountains?' I ask.

'Yes,' he says. 'Everybody knows me around here.'

That evening, my last in the area, I walk down toward the water's edge. Over the last couple of days I've finally managed to sample pig feet, and that alone earns this trip a prime spot on my pork-chasing itinerary. But there's something else, and it's not just the hippies, or Joselín, or the folks in Santalla, something that has left a profound impression on me. Whether it's the majesty of the landscape, or the atmosphere of its silent hamlets, there's a calming and vaguely dreamlike feeling to Negueira de Muñiz. It raises your spirits, yet smoothes them as well. The kind of place where as soon as you arrive you know you'll be back.

The banks of the reservoir lie just below Negueira village, separated by a strip of ground perhaps a quarter of a mile wide. Small plantations of apple and cherry trees dot its gently sloping surface. At the far edge, flanked on two sides by a crowding of mature Spanish firs, and with the water right behind, is the village church, entirely isolated, the sole building on this strange band of land.

Fat, heavy raindrops begin to fall, rolling lazily out of the sky and spattering around me. I take cover beneath a cherry tree, its laden branches offering me refuge against the rain, and eat small pink cherries. They have a fragrant, almost perfumed taste.

I look at the deserted church, and listen to the *tick-tock* of the falling rain, which is the only sound to be heard tonight in Negueira.

THE TAIL IN THE EAR

Spain is a hot country. In Seville and Granada temperatures tickle the seventies all winter long, and are lodged firmly in the hundreds through the infernal summers. But the Iberian Peninsula, especially its interior, is full of extremes. Castile's searing summer months give way to freezing winters: *nine months of winter, three months of hell*, as they say in Madrid.

Up here in Galicia the estuary-laced coastline serves to regulate temperatures, perhaps explaining why over half of the region's three million inhabitants live on or near the coast. Away from the sea, though, the place is a bewildering patchwork of contrasting weather conditions. The climate here is like an irritating old friend you never liked much, with bits of food between his teeth and social skills that make you wince, but who you've somehow grown to need, if only so you can complain about him to everyone else.

Today I'm in Ourense, administrative centre of Galicia's southeastern province (also called Ourense), a city with an excellently variable microclimate: wet, cold, ferociously hot, dry, humid.

Not in that order, necessarily. I'm glad to be back, because on a previous trip here I missed something pretty special. And it was staring me right in the face.

Manolo stirs the simmering pot. There are forty-five pig ears in it, a light brown colour, each one slightly bigger and chunkier than you would imagine. Pig ears really are a funny sort of size: too big to fit snugly into the palm of your hand, but too small to hit someone with. A second, equally large pot contains 130 off-white tails that quiver in frothy, bubbling water.

I tell him that I have tasted the tail here before, during that incredibly hot July we had a while back (see below). We're in the galley kitchen of A Orella ('The Ear'), and it's almost as hot now, what with the heat that those ears are throwing off. Manolo, tall and energetic, with a clean-shaved head and a thick black beard that makes him look like Rasputin's good-natured younger brother, is showing me how to prepare ears and tails the traditional way.

'The secret is there's no secret,' he says. 'Just good-quality products, and getting the cooking time right.'

The Ear was opened in 1952 by Manolo's dad, and Manolo himself, who is about my age, has been cooking all parts of a pig here in the bar for most of his adult life.

'Same with the *cachucha*,' he adds, pulling open the door of a cold storage unit and dragging out a large plastic bucket in which two halves of a pig's head are soaking in slightly scummy water.

These heads are the reason for my visit. Throughout my Galicia-wide quest for all the pork, I've carried with me a Moleskine notebook. Onto one of its pages is pasted a diagram of a pig, conveniently divided up along butcherly lines. Each time I sample a new part of the animal, I shade in the corresponding area. So far, blackened areas include: shoulder ham, loin, neck and shoulder meat, ribs and bone marrow, vertebrae, ear, snout, tongue, belly pork, bacon, trotters, heart, kidneys. For several months now I have also been boasting about the *cachucha* (head) I ate in Laza. But the truth is, in Laza I ate only a square of fat and meat from the cheek. And although I swallowed ear, snout, and tongue in Lalín, it was as if I'd been avoiding the issue, nibbling rather than diving headfirst into one of Galicia's true classics: *cachucha prensada*, pressed whole head of pig.

Last week I got an unexpected opportunity to redeem myself. I had given Manolo a ring to ask about cooking times for ears. But when he started telling me about the pressed pig head he makes, describing it with an infectious, almost boyish enthusiasm – part gourmet chef, part mad scientist – I thought I'd better get down here and try some.

But first, that scorching July . . .

It was a couple of years ago, and although we did not know it, we were about to climb aboard the

290

high-speed, rudderless toboggan ride down the sleepless vale of tears known as parenthood. But even then, still blissfully unaware that we would soon be three, coming to Ourense in July sounded daunting. People up in Coruña-by-the-sea shook their heads in pity and made just about as many references to sweat glands as was decent. Paco once forfeited a tennis match here rather than die of heat exhaustion. More frighteningly still, a troupe of ceremonial drummers from Burundi I met at a music festival last summer told me that when they visited the city they simply couldn't sleep at night, such was the heat. These were fit young men who in sub-Saharan Africa could dance and sing while balancing seventy-pound drums made from hollowed-out tree trunks on their heads.

Ourense is a massive, over-urbanised crater in the earth. The drop from valley top to city centre is about four miles of spiralling divided highway. I guess if you lived in Ourense when travelling was still a quadrupedal affair, then you either had a very committed donkey or you didn't get out of town much.

The Romans came here and left a bridge (still in use) and thermal baths (ditto). They also gave the place its original name, Auria – 'place of gold'. The golden city then got a Spanish name, Orense. More recently still it was changed to the Galician spelling, Ourense. All place-names were changed from Spanish to Galician in the 1980s, all except

291

La Coruña, which sometimes changed and some-times didn't. Confused? You will be.

Anyway: we head downward into the golden crater, still carefree and childless. The car's ther-mometer, which has been loitering at about eighty degrees for most of our journey, begins to creep up. The weather has been a feature of every radio bulletin this morning, as Spain slips into its first truly hot spell of the summer. Hospitals are seeing the first victims of the heat, and ridiculously obvious advice on how to combat the intense temperatures is everywhere (stay out of the sun, drink plenty of water, dance a lively tarantella at high noon). I detest the heat, but I think even a draught-fearing Galician would quail now, as the worst possible news comes across the airwaves: Hell today will be Ourense.

With the knowledge that we are in the hottest place in Spain, we enter the city. Driving here is a motorised version of doing the Rubik's Cube. You retrace your steps time and time again, trying desperately to remember the street sequence. The journey from the city limits to our hotel, being a distance that one could express in yards rather than miles, takes us close to half an hour, which I consider more than reasonable.

Hotel Parque has been here since before anyone can remember, and has that look of gentle postwar malaise, the kind of place that has been left behind by progress and doesn't give a shit about it. The lobby, when we finally make it, is full of old-age pensioners. It is stiflingly hot, and they sit motionless on plastic sofas that line the walls. Galicians, as we know, like it stuffy. Draughts are the devil's bad breath, and sitting by an open window is actually against the law. The pensioners in the lobby keep dead still as they talk, looking straight ahead. They might be stuck to the plastic. I don't know. Every one of them is in a heavy-duty cardigan buttoned right up to the neck. *Se queres criarte gordo e san, a roupa do inverno pouna no verán . . .* 'Wear your winter clothes in summer if you want to be fat and healthy . . .'

The reception desk is cramped, and behind it on the wall are pigeonholes for residents' mail. The man on duty manages to exude both intolerance and indifference, and gives the definite impression that he is busying himself with other things just to keep us waiting.

When he decides to grant us an audience, there is a complication with our booking, some trivial piece of information is missing, our blood groups, or the name of our childhood pets. There is always a little problem in Galicia, some small issue that crops up whenever paperwork or any remotely official-looking operation has to be gone through. Susana was born to it. I edge out of the conversation's range, having never acquired even a smattering of patience in such situations. And I've been to Mexico.

Upstairs, our sheets are nylon and the timeworn pillows are like bags of leftover oatmeal mush.

I throw open the sash window. The warm air from outside is marginally cooler, as if I've jumped from a scalding sauna into a fractionally less scalding hot tub. In our bathroom there's a midget bath, measuring three feet (length, not width); if you actually wanted to sit there, you'd have to soap yourself just to get in.

Back downstairs, the difficulties continue. We inform Mr Passive-Aggressive that there is no toilet paper in the room. Later on we see that he's left us a roll in our pigeonhole. Next, the car. Hotel Parque has underground parking space in an adjacent building. You borrow the garage key from the reception, then, on exiting the car park, you leave your vehicle on the sidewalk (blocking it entirely) and return the key to the hotel. If you are alone in the car, this is particularly annoying. Guests with cars cannot keep their garage keys for the duration of their stay, it is explained, because there are not enough keys. For a moment I consider making a suggestion. But I let it pass. In any case, there are no suggestion boxes in Galicia. Your opinion is not welcome.

Across the road is Saint Lazarus Park, about as big as a football pitch, and full of elderly people shuffling along the winding paths in their slippers. Our hotel doubles as a permanent residence for old folks, an arrangement that used to be more common in Spain a few decades ago, before retirement homes became common. We take a drink on a terrace just above the park, and watch people come and go.

The women in Ourense look good, really good. Not as got-up as Coruña's starched-out señoras, but with loads more flair. A great deal of money has been lavished on their shoulders, my better-informed wife tells me, noting that Ourense is pretty well served by fashion designers: Carolina Herrera has a shop here, as do Adolfo Domínguez, Purificación García, and Roberto Verino (all Galicians, by the way); then there's an array of small, bijou boutiques for all your Chanel, Prada, and D &G needs.

This degree of fashion surprises me, because Ourense is at the heart of farming country. The province itself has a history of grinding rural poverty that forced countless thousands to emigrate in search of a better life, some as recently as the 1970s. Many emigrants from Ourense went to South America and prospered there. A few of them prospered spectacularly well, and émigré families have been known to pop across the Atlantic for the day in private jets. Ourense is also known for its itinerant knife sharpeners, who travel from town to town playing ocarinas to advertise their services. I wasn't expecting Wellies in the city, but Ourense is surprisingly elegant. Even the young have made an effort, some of them with an understated designer-post-grunge look, and others seeming to be stylish without trying at all, which of course is the most difficult and expensive.

I consider myself: black nylon shorts and a blue Adidas top. Not scruffy so much as sadly, hopelessly foreign.

Susana now leaves. She is the reason for our visit. She has work this afternoon, a term which in Spain corresponds to 4 to 8.30 p.m. She is a *funcionaria*, and has been called to sit on a public tribunal that will decide who else will be allowed to join the hallowed ranks of civil servants. If you want to be a tenured school or university teacher in Spain, you have to undergo this horribly stressful form of public humiliation, known as an opposition (*oposición*). Same goes for many other careers in the public sector. The system is designed to be scrupulously open and fair, and also so your competitors can sit in the gallery and watch you squirm before the judges. These trials benefit the economy too; literally tons of sedatives and tranquilizers are prescribed each time a new round of *oposiciones* take place.

Finding myself alone, I wander down to the bottom of the park, where a clock thermometer tells us that the temperature has reached 114 degrees. People glance up as they walk past, people in suits and ties, people going about their business as if it were a fresh spring morning. A young couple stops, and the guy takes a photo of his girlfriend as she points proudly at the sign. They should have waited, because not long after they leave it clicks up to 115.

A Orella has two grinning pigs printed on its

296

paper serviettes. Personally, if I'm going to be tucking into some very identifiable bits of an animal, I don't really want to see the animal casting me a cheeky smile. Galicians are less squeamish. In Coruña I once saw a display of wild game in the window of a delicatessen. The display's centrepiece was a dead rabbit dressed up like a hunter, complete with miniature deer-stalker hat and rifle.

Pig's ear is a traditional delicacy in Galicia. And there's not much in the way of fancy preparation. As Gertrude Stein might have said, in Galicia a pig's ear is a pig's ear is a pig's ear, although she would probably have made it scan better. Manolo simply gets fresh ears, salted and with a touch of smoking, and simmers them for half an hour, then lets them stand in the water the same length of time. That's it. No secrets. You eat them in big wobbly strips, normally as a tapa.

What I really fancied in The Ear, on that first trip in a blistering July, was the tail. I saw the word *rabo* on the menu board, and it conjured up in my mind the delights of oxtail, *rabo de buey*. I will walk a long way to eat oxtail, to tease those deep, dark brown strands of beefy caramel meat away from the bone, globules of sticky, amber-hued fat adding silky succulence. The word *rabo* must have provoked some kind of synaptic misfiring in that part of my brain that stores infor-mation pertaining to tail and tail-related things. In a dither of confused greed, then, I plump not for a modest *tapa*, but for the more substantial *media ración* (half a portion).

The culinary arts, I guess, often involve *artifice*. Things are cooked so as to disguise their ugly origins. An oxtail, for example, doesn't really look like an ox's tail; it looks brown and glazed and beautiful, like a slow-roasted half-brogue. When my *media ración* arrives it looks as if Gertude Stein has prepared it, simply boiled then cut into single-vertebra pieces. The pieces are a sullen grey on the outside, and the skin is wrinkly. Underneath is a layer of blubber, which together with the skin can, I imagine, be pulled away from the meaty bone inside. I try to do this, but the fatty skin disintegrates as it comes away, gooking up my fingers like boogers that I can't get rid of no matter where I wipe. It takes about a dozen grinning serviettes to get the worst of it off, and by now my hands are tar-and-feathered in tail slime and tissue paper.

What I am left with, on the plate, is a curious little nub of bone with some pink meat on it. It smells distantly familiar, but I cannot say why. With my determination quickly draining away, I make a grab for the paprika dispenser and shake until the vertebra looks as if it's been swabbed in iron oxide. In it goes. I run it around my mouth, sucking the soft meat from the bone. The taste is instantly recognisable: economy pork sausages, those bright pink fellas bursting with our old friend 'mechanically recovered meat' (known informally in the British meat trade as 'eyeholes, earholes, and arseholes'), absolutely the last bits of a pig that can be pried away from the bones and pummelled into an edible form. MRM is used to make the kind of commercial, mass-produced sausages that I have loved since childhood. Today, I am simply extracting the meat with my tongue. Susana asks what it tastes of. Cheap, I say. It tastes of cheap.

Armed with a couple of toothpicks, I start to deskin a second piece. It's relatively large, from the thick end of the tail, and I ignore the few short black bristles that protrude. After teasing away the skin, I send great clouds of deep red paprika downward, then place it into my reluctant mouth. The plate, smeared with paprika-stained skin and fat, looks like a flesh-and-blood Barbie has been butchered to death there.

With manly determination I eat as much as I can, about half the tail, turning the vertebra around in my mouth, drinking lots of beer, lots, lots. Susana stares, as if she is watching an act of desperate self-harm that she can do nothing about. She rings María. 'Can you believe John's eating pig tail?' Even the cell phone shudders.

That's it. I give up. I might love low-grade sausages, but now, after sampling the kind of stuff that goes into them in its neat and unblended form, I come to understand the truth: it's ketchup that I love, not thirty-six-for-a-dollar pork bangers. The remaining pieces lie on the plate amid the carnage. It would have been less embarrassing to send the half serving back than to eat *half* of it.

As I contemplate my failure, a young woman perched on a stool behind us catches my attention. She is wearing a pristine lime green trouser suit straight out of one of the city's upscale boutiques, plus quite a bit of jewellery, and she is busy pronging piece after piece of her own *rabo* and popping them into her mouth whole, bristly skin and all. She is also talking nonstop, yet within minutes nothing remains on her plate but a small pile of vertebrae, each one sucked to a pearly white. That's my problem. I'm just not dressed for the occasion.

After the *rabo*, our evening turns into a tapa endurance test. We leave the ear bar and wander around the narrow streets of the Old Town. At one place I have a mini-steak in pepper sauce, and at another the best hot pork and wild mushroom sandwich that ever existed in time and space. Susana, meanwhile, has skewers of langoustine and monkfish. We eat tons of thick, juicy potato tortillas, and runny white cheese spiked with freshly milled black pepper then drizzled with extra virgin olive oil . . . and everything comes with a large chunk of bread. This is no ordinary bread, either. In Cea, just north of the city, bread making has been going on in the same communal stone ovens since at least the thirteenth century. It seems unlikely that bread could in itself excite strong culinary passions, but Cea's loaves come pretty close. They are made with unbleached wheat and baked over wood, and the bread has a spongy but robust texture that seems to resent the indignity of being torn into pieces and eaten. It is the only bread in the world to carry its own denomination-of-origin label of authenticity, and is sold in rounded loaves of biblical dimensions. Each loaf carries its own unique identification number. Naturally, there is an annual bread festival.

Later in the evening I return to the pork and wild mushroom place for seconds, and in an overemotional moment I almost French-kiss my sandwich. It's now well past midnight, the temperature is down to a chilling ninety degrees, and the streets are heaving with people eating and drinking. This is another seemingly incomprehensible quirk of Spain, that people stay up – and invariably that means staying *out* – until ridiculously late, go home at dawn, sleep for eleven minutes, get up again, and go off to work.

When we get back to our fanless room in Hotel Parque I lean out the window, willing the light breeze to insinuate its way inside my foreigner's Adidas top. I look down at the road outside the hotel, a single-lane, one-way street. In the space where a second lane might go is a taxi rank that extends all the way up. From time to time people walk to the top of the street, stop at the first taxi, pause as someone on the other side of the street shouts something to them, then they walk all the way down the street again and take the *last* taxi in the line. When this taxi files off with its passengers, the rest of the drivers, who are in the habit of sitting on benches across the road for a chat, return to their vehicles, reverse downward a space en masse, then make their way back over to the benches. Meanwhile, new taxis join the reversing line at the top of the street and wait to shuffle backward toward the back-to-front line. There are so many reasons why this just *cannot* be a good system, I surmise that there must be an over-ridingly brilliant reason why it is.

Against all good advice and reason we leave the window open almost six inches, which I consider a coup on a grand scale. We do not die of draught. The bass rumble of traffic continues late into the night, accompanied by the constant shriek of seagulls, although we're inland and they can't be seagulls. Whatever they are, they shriek. The taxi rank is now in full backward swing, and it has a telephone, mounted at the bottom of the street (twenty yards from us), which rings constantly, an old, clangy bell that no one answers because they're all on the benches opposite having a chin wag. In the park a young man has decided that tonight is bongo night. And the telephone. And the landlocked gulls. And no fan. Somehow, in the Hotel Parque, we sleep. I dream of oxtails.

Pressed head of pig doesn't sound that tempting. All I can say is give Manolo a call, he might persuade you otherwise. After the *cachucha* is

302

simmered until soft, the bones are removed. The two half-head pieces are then crammed into a steel press about half the size of a shoe box, and pressure is applied until all the squeal's gone out of it.

Back in the bar, two years after my first visit, he cuts me some pressed pig head using a bacon slicer. The block of head that happens to be on the machine is no bigger than a pack of cigarettes, and the wafer-thin slices he cuts give the impression that this is something to prize, a select delicacy, in contrast to the great greasy slabs of ear and the nodules of cheap tail that people all around me are tucking into.

Each small, rectangular slice of head is like a fragment of embroidered lace, like a tiny abstract painting, with daubs of pink and grey-brown, glistening flecks of jelly, and threads of white snaking across the canvas.

'There's twenty-four different tastes in a head,' he tells me as I pop the first jiggling wafer into my mouth.

I don't count them, but there's a real cacophony of flavours, from the familiar sweetness of boiled ham to the earthy notes of the skin. All the different bacon you've ever eaten comes back to say hello, from the musty, the salty, to the downright hoary. It's like a chorus of chattering pork voices in your mouth. Like an amazing pig cocktail. A guessing game. Plus, there's a delicate crunch from tiny strings of cartilage, just to give it an edge.

I order some more. And as I eat, I remember that drunken evening in Laza during Carnival, standing on broken glass as I tore bits of meat from a slab of hot, greasy jowl. Then, as I savour all twenty-four of those excellent tastes, I take out my notebook and with a delicious sense of achievement I scratch out the entire head of the pig.

ENCOUNTERS WITH EMINENT GALICIANS II: ANTÓN OF ESPASANTE

I drive north of Coruña, up past the city of Ferrol, birthplace of General Franco. Ferrol del Caudillo ('Ferrol of the Boss'), they used to call it, and to celebrate the fact, in 1967 an eight-ton, twenty-foot bronze statue of the Boss on a horse was erected. The Caudillo himself refused to inaugurate the monument because it was so ugly.

After Franco's death the statue survived a number of attempts to blow it up. Then, to mark the twenty-fifth anniversary of the end of the dictatorship, a group of radical Galician nationalists painted both dictator and horse a striking Chanel pink. The thing was finally removed to make way for a car park, and these days General Francisco Paulino Hermenegildo Teódulo Franco Bahamonde (El Caudillo for short) resides in Ferrol's naval museum.

Farther up the coastal road is Ortigueira, which must surely have the most lyrical place-name in the world (ORR-ti-*GAYYYYYYYY*ra). It is here that the annual Celtic Music Festival is held, further cementing Galicia's position as a proud member of Europe's Celtic fringe. Just past Ortigueira is Espasante, where I see signs for Antón Beach and San Antonio's church. The prevalence of Anthonys, whatever the spelling, is propitious, because I've come to see one.

I park and walk along the seafront of the Tony-rich village of Espasante. We are now entering Galician autumn (less sun, just as much rain), although today threatens to be sunny and warm. A wooden shack that houses the village's public toilets has been spray-painted with the words ONLY LOCALS, in English. What could possibly have prompted such feelings in Espasante's home-grown graffitists? I imagine hoards of Australian backpackers messily missing the urinal, and tight-lipped Japanese gentlemen quietly swiping the toilet rolls on their way out.

I shun all thoughts of conveniences and call in at a corner shop, one of those old-fashioned places that sells everything from cabbages to boot polish, axe heads to balls of string (the sign of a good corner shop is if it sells string). I ask about the whereabouts of Antón. Two ladies suspend their chat to give me directions, unsurprised that I am enquiring about him, perhaps seeing the camera hanging from my shoulder.

Following their instructions, I walk back up the road that led me into the village, but I cannot see Antón. Cutting down a lane between two small patches of scrubland haphazardly planted with corn and *grelos* I find myself in the narrow, close-knit streets of Espasante's small urban nucleus. I ask in a bar, only to be sent back up past the scrub.

Crossing the road, I walk a little way out of town, where I find an old couple at work in their dilapidated but picturesque small holding. It appears to have been constructed from scraps of wood and chicken wire by a trainee Cubist, the kind of dwelling that in about fifty years' time living museums will try to re-create. I ask them about Antón. The lady stops work and dries her hands on her blue pinafore. In Galician villages all ladies over a certain age wear blue pinafores. It's a statutory requirement. When they get too old to work they wear black. Again, mandatory.

The blue lady now points to a place just up ahead on the same side as we now are, the out-of-town side of the road. That's the thing: it had never occurred to me that Antón would live *across* the road from town. He's a pig, of course. Antón is the most famous pig in Galicia.

No one knows where the tradition comes from. *Older than memory* is the standard answer. Every June, Espasante acquires a young pig, names him Antón, and for the next six months he lives as guest of honour in the village. With a small bell around his neck, the animal – Toñito to his most intimate friends – is allowed to roam free, ambling up and down the crooked lanes of the old town, stopping here and there at the doors of houses, where people are in the habit of feeding him. He might wander onto the beach to take the sun, thence to cool his privileged trotters in the gentle surf, and by tradition he sleeps wherever the hell he fancies. This was all very well before the advent of motor vehicles, but these days it seems like madness. Antón, though, not only continues to enjoy his ancient freedoms, he even manages to cross the road on his own.

The noble tradition is coordinated by a committee that also oversees the village's *festas*, the celebrations in honour of the local patron saint, Anthony. The committee must comprise two married and two unmarried men; do not ask why, for this too is beyond memory. Most men in Espasante are fishermen, absent for much of the time, and so by a less noble tradition, a nonofficial committee of women has often done the bulk of the committee's work on the sly, while the men take the credit. This all came out into the open a few years ago when the de facto women's committee took control overtly, causing something of a stir. When it came to the swearing-in ceremony, however, none of the ladies would go on, for reasons that I could not ascertain. Whatever the problem, the result was that no pig was bought and named Antón that year. Thus do timeless traditions die.

And what a tradition! People used to walk into

their living rooms and find Antón curled up there asleep. They used to pet him and stroke him and allow him free reign of their gardens. They'd hose him down in the heat and rub sunblock onto his big, sensitive ears. He would steal towels and bags from sunbathers on the beach and snaffle anything he came across. His antics were tolerated. He was well cared for. He was, in effect, a great big spoilt patron saint of a pig.

On another occasion, at the height of summer, Antón got so merry trotting around town that he overheated and dropped down dead. Another year he tumbled over the cliffs in a fit of euphoria, but was hoisted back up to safety by panic-stricken villagers. Despite all this, I heard no stories of the pig causing mayhem on the roads. Galician drivers cause enough mayhem them-selves; having a pig loose on the public highways probably serves to add a note of restraint to the traffic conditions.

These anecdotes, needless to say, refer to different Antóns, a new one each year. Yet the various Antóns are spoken of as if a single being, each year's beast assuming the sacred mantle and becoming *him*, a kind of linear reincarnation of the pig king. There's even a bronze version of the ur-Antón up near the beach, complete with a bell around its neck. As I photographed it, earlier this morning, a couple of young men in work overalls passed by, stopping to tinkle the bell and chuck the pig statue under the chin.

Now, after a hiatus of two years, the real-life Antón is back. And eventually, after quite a search, I find the evidence. These days Antón has bespoke lodgings for the night, an old, stone-built sty with a nice sloping slate roof, set in the corner of a patch of wasteland right by the road into town. The sty's door is open, and as I inch up close I see him slouched just inside, fast asleep. I get closer still and take a couple of pictures. Just momentarily he opens an eye, notices that he is being photographed, sighs as if the paparazzi thing is tiresome beyond words, and falls asleep again.

Once the potato crop is planted, Antón's wandering is curtailed somewhat, lest he munch his way through the lot. And by Christmas his days are numbered. On Twelfth Night the well-fattened animal has its own sort of Epiphany, as first prize in a raffle. After that, only the butcher's slab awaits. Live fast, die young, Tony.

Whenever I talk to someone about the raffle there's a very slight pursing of the lips, a stifled shudder. While the winners of Antón can in theory take his beloved carcass home with them, they almost always prefer to let the committee sell him discreetly on their behalf, receiving the proceeds of the sale in lieu of two hundred pounds of saintly pig meat; it's so much easier when your stewed shoulder ham does not bear a Christian name. I mean, could you eat the meat of an animal whose floppy ears you had dabbed with SPF-15?

I return to the sty several times during the morning, as the sun's rays intensify and lunch edges slowly into view. Antón does not move. I hesitate, wondering what to do. A man walks past, sees the camera, guesses what I'm up to, and asks me if he's still sleeping. I nod. *Poke him with a stick!* the man tells me. I laugh. But I've seen angry pigs, and I've seen their teeth.

This year has seen another incarnation of Antón. But with the village population in decline, and fewer people willing to take responsibility, how long will the tradition continue? Perhaps this is the last spoilt pig in Espasante.

I hang around, but the slob doesn't move. I decide to leave him in peace. The raffle's not that far off.

DRIVING SOUTH FOR *TETOTES*

My first car in Spain was a sporty little Citroën AX-GT, and was also the first vehicle I owned that did not have rust holes in the wheel arches that needed cramming with chicken wire then gumming up with underseal.

Some months after buying it (second-hand) I took it for its ITV test, Spain's official road-worthiness check. The car didn't make it as far as the ramp.

'Oh, no!' they said, tutting. 'No. *No!*' They waved me to one side of the inspection area as if they'd discovered a stack of Swedish porn on the back-seat. 'Look at those tires!' I looked. The tires were newish, plenty of tread. 'Look at your documents!' I looked. The tyres did not match the tyre size stipulated on the vehicle's documents. 'Can't pass this,' they said. 'Illegal tyres.'

'What do I do?' I asked.

They shrugged. 'You could ask Citroën to give you an official letter stating that these tyres are legal for this model.'

If you've lived in Spain any length of time you'll

know all about official letters and other pieces of official paper, all bearing official rubber stamps. The stamp can be from the president of the Mickey Mouse Club, it does not matter. But the great, flabbily inefficient state bureaucracy needs feeding continually with signed, stamped, official-looking papers from Mickey and Donald.

'Couldn't you just check about the tires?' I asked in the test centre. 'Isn't there a database?'

There isn't a database. There are just a lot of people going backward and forward to offices getting documents stamped in order to take them to other offices to satisfy the demands of low-ranking civil servants with bad teeth for whom the daily creation of these sub-Kafkaesque vortices of hopelessness is the only fun they get, now that the thrill of having a job for life has given way to the realisation that their world will never, ever change.

The man at the Citroën dealership tutted some more. Then, in an act of unprompted initiative – which immediately singled him out as *not* a state employee – he faxed the head office and told me he would be in touch when the answer came through. He rang that afternoon. The tires were horribly, impossibly illegal.

'So, what now?' I asked.

He knew what now. He knew exactly what. Yet he merely sighed, the sigh of a defence lawyer who knows that his client's best option is perjury, but cannot say so.

That evening I was explaining all this to Paco.

313

'My uncle'll sort it out,' he said.

If you want something done here, something that requires insider knowledge and just a touch of corner-cutting, you better have an uncle, or a friend with an uncle, or even an uncle with a friend who's an uncle. If you come from a long line of one-child families you're screwed.

Uncle, who owned a motor shop, switched the tyres, and I took another test. Then he switched them back again. I paid the equivalent of about six quid rent on the legal tyres, and as a little favour he took sixty thousand miles off the clock.

These days I have a sensible, well-shod vehicle, and this morning I have driven it south for breakfast in Vigo, Galicia's biggest city, and close to the border with Portugal. We lived here for a while in the 1990s, next door to a gay couple who spent much of the night having noisy sex to Barbra Streisand's *Broadway Album*. Sometimes they would also break into spontaneous bongo playing. I don't know whether this was during or after, but it strikes me now, as I write this, that I attract bongos.

Whenever I mention that I used to live in Vigo, people always ask if I took my car. This is because driving in Vigo is kind of exciting. At least, it is if your idea of excitement is being very scared.

Vigo's scary streets are often blamed on their proximity to Portugal, where driving is like an incomprehensible form of competitive circus entertainment. Fast-moving Portuguese clown cars cavort and race across the frontier and up to Vigo on weekends and bank holidays, to stock up on designer kitchen knives and the latest shower curtains at the El Corte Inglés department store in the centre of town. You can tell the Portuguese cars easily: they swerve continually between traffic lanes for no reason, and they travel at great speed, then immediately slow down to a crawl, again and again, fast-slow-fast, as if they're trying to leapfrog invisible obstacles on the road.

I arrive toward the end of morning rush hour, which in Vigo is like a vehicular running of the bulls. I stop to consult my city map. I am on Garcia Barbón, the very street where we used to listen to those sexed-up bongos. I am double-parked, but so are lots of other people, and the street is wide enough for no one to care.

A couple of cars up ahead of me a woman in a smart black trouser suit returns to her smart black Mercedes A Class, which is parked alongside the curb. She opens the door and throws her bags inside, then takes off her jacket and hangs it up, apparently heedless to the fact that a large, dusty Volvo has double-parked her and is blocking her in. She slips into her seat and sounds the horn, three long blasts. She makes a call on her cell phone, and sounds the horn again as she talks. In a beautifully subtle-surreal moment a traffic warden strolls slowly by, paying absolutely no attention to any of this, or to the line of double-parked cars that stretches right up the street, their hazard lights flashing in jolly unison.

Finally, after more blasts, a portly man idles – and I mean idles – back to his dusty Volvo, fumbling for his keys. He pulls his car forward just enough for the black Mercedes to leave. Neither driver looks at the other. She expresses no grievance, and he expresses no apology. When she's gone he reverses into the curbside space just vacated, locks up, and waddles off again. Within seconds the Volvo is blocked in by a white van.

Double-parking is a way of life in Spain. The double-parker simply keeps an ear peeled, and if an obstructed car wants to leave, its driver sounds the horn, using longish, repeated blasts. This system is universally understood. And once you have returned to your car to let the other driver leave, lo, there's a vacant space just waiting for you! It couldn't be better.

Unless you disappear from earshot. Or you forget all about your car, in which case the *toot-toot*ing can go on for a long time, each flurry of blasts just that bit longer and more irritable than the last. In busy areas there might be several drivers waiting to be liberated from the curbside at any one time, their horns echoing around the streets like the plaintive mating cries of stranded sea lions. Occasionally someone forgets to start their engine before tooting, and if they are too insistent or the toots too long (a very angry person might just hold the horn down continually) they flatten their battery, the dying tone taking on the sound of a slowly strangled Canada goose.

When it comes to parking, the rules are clear: Park anywhere. Park on street corners. Park on pedestrian crossings, at bus stops, park bumper to bumper, park where someone might reasonably want to cross the street. And block the sidewalk, *please* block the sidewalk.

This form of parking is the same throughout Spain. When it comes to driving, however, Galicia has some of its own idiosyncrasies. For one thing, Galicians are not as death-defyingly speedy as drivers in some parts of Spain. In Madrid, for example, you can actually find yourself being *impressed* by the sheer dangerousness of the traffic.

I've driven all over Galicia, and I have tried to look closely at road behaviour, to appreciate the complexities of the system, to ascertain whether there are deep cultural metaphors that explain the Galicians' approach to their cars. Is behaviour on the roads here underscored by sophisticated notions of private and public space? I think not. Like Mexicans can't make good wine, and the French can't be modest, the Galicians can't drive. Imagine a place populated entirely by giddy, egocentric children, each one of whom has been given a supercharged tractor for Christmas, without training or guidance. That's Galicia. Pedestrian crossings? Chance it if you want. Traffic lights? Merely suggestive. Indicate before you pull out? Fuck off.

Galicians often say that the worst drivers in Galicia are from the province of Lugo. Broadly speaking this is true, although it's a bit like Jack the Ripper calling Sweeney Todd a nasty piece of work. And if you want to know about driving in the rest of Spain, according to the European Union's statistics, of all the country's regions the safest roads are in Ceuta, a tiny Spanish enclave on the North African coast. The second safest are in Melilla, another African enclave. Spain's two safest places to drive are on another continent.

Finally I make my way through the traffic to the docks, where a cruise liner of gargantuan proportions has recently arrived, towering above the dockside buildings, making them seem like Monopoly hotels.

Down here beside the docks, basking in the morning sun, is Vigo's Old Town, a compact network of narrow streets and grand stone houses. There's a fresh food market right at the centre, and a steady bustle everywhere as deliveries are made and sun-stung tourists make their way over from the boat.

I head for Pescadería Street, a narrow pedestrian lane close to the market, where boxes of oysters are now being unloaded and stacked on the pavement. Venerable ladies in white aprons and coiffured hair are already at work with their stubby oyster knives. Two thousand years ago the Romans went mad for the oysters here, preserving them in *escabeche*, a vinegar-based sauce that is still used today for all manner of seafood. In Vigo, the tradition of eating oysters also continues.

I order a dozen from the only oyster lady who is smiling. She calls me *my little king* as she knifes them open. It's good to be a little king once more. I eat my breakfast at a terrace table, together with a benjamin of Cava from a nearby café. And after making my way through the city's traffic, it really is the least I deserve. Plus, after this I am off to investigate the dirty end of a pig.

Mari Carmen is talking so fast I am amazed I can follow what she is saying. Remember Karlos the TV chef? Well, Mari Carmen is also explaining how to cook something, and the pages of my Moleskine are filling up quickly. The phone here in her kitchen keeps ringing. Someone is pregnant. Someone else is ill. Her cell phone is buzzing as well, and at one point she has a phone to each ear, busily telling people to ring later, or that she'll ring back . . . Meanwhile, she keeps apologising for the interruptions, pouring me glasses of spring-water as the cookery class continues.

Cerdedo, in the hills about an hour's drive inland from Vigo, is desperately trying to hang on to its traditions and to halt the rapid depopulation that will see most of its outlying parishes abandoned within a generation. The mayor runs a wild boar festival to stimulate interest in the area. But the women's collective, of which Mari Carmen is the

319

go-ahead president, is stealing the local limelight by organising an annual bladder celebration.

'Isn't it *beautiful*,' she says, holding one up to the light.

It is dried to a yellow-brown and the size of a rutabaga. Naturally holding its spherical shape, it resembles a rough-hewn Chinese lantern, and absorbs the light in a curiously warm and delightful way. I did not expect to be bowled over by a pig's bladder, but yes, it is rather attractive.

I'm here in Cerdedo to collect a couple of the bladders and to get the low-down on how to make *vincha*, a sweet pudding that is cooked in the bladder itself. No one up in Coruña has ever heard of *vincha*, and even down here in Cerdedo it has never been commercialised. Apart from anything else, many families would have slaughtered just one pig each winter, and the single bladder would have been dried and kept until Carnival, when the *vincha* was made.

In *Galician Cooking*, Álvaro Cunqueiro includes the bladder recipe, although he calls it 'Buxo na Vixiga'; my best effort at a translation of that is 'boxwoods in bladder,' which perhaps suggests that these puddings are as solid and heavy as the wood of a boxwood tree. The festival is now in its eighth year, and last year they got through two hundred puddings. The ladies of Cerdedo and outlying parishes get together just before Carnival and cook up the *vinchas* in a mass pudding-making session. Just getting that many bladders and upward of fifty dozen free-range eggs is quite a task, Mari Carmen says, never mind the other ingredients, plus all the mixing. Well, this time around they're going to have an extra pair of hands to help out with the mixing: mine.

Having been invited to roll up my sleeves and pitch in with the forthcoming bladder pudding session, I thought I better get some practice, so I am here today to pick up my bladders and to make sure I understand the procedure in detail. I intend to have a couple of dummy runs at home before the big day. Susana doesn't know this yet.

Mari Carmen's mother is now called into the kitchen. We discuss various aspects of cooking the pudding. The two of them also try in vain to explain what exactly a *tetote* is, another local speciality that is cooked with the *cocido* at Carnival time. From everything they tell me, the two of them talking over each other, their descriptions wide-eyed and enthusiastic, the *tetote* is a dough-based python that lurks at the bottom of the stew pot, a sort of bottom feeder in the pork swamp. I might be wrong, though.

All of this, by the way, is conducted in Spanish. Mari Carmen, about my age, is equally fluent in Spanish and Galician. Her mother would normally speak Galician, which I tell her I understand fine. Yet she automatically switches to Spanish as she talks, and seems reticent to switch back. I don't know how anyone ever learns Galician; many of its speakers, especially the older ones, run away from their own language at the first sign of a foreigner.

Back at home my bladders were not welcome. I think Susana saw something ominous and vaguely threatening in them, as all vegetarians tend to when faced with unfamiliar dead things. They were put in a carrier bag, which was tied securely and stuffed down behind the washing machine. As far as I know, they're still there.

I went back to Cerdedo for the mass pudding-making session, which was to take place in the hills above Cerdedo. I had the phone number of Pura, the lady in charge. But my cell didn't work up in the hills, and when I finally asked my way to her house, she wasn't there. I spent a fruitless morning chasing from one hillside hamlet to another looking for her, before giving up and going to Mari Carmen's place.

But Mari Carmen wasn't there. Her mum, also called Mari Carmen, poked her head out and frowned in confusion.

'Can I come in and watch you make puddings, please?' I asked.

'Are you staying for lunch?' she said as I was ushered inside.

The bread, torn into pieces, is steeped overnight in a mixture of egg, sugar, a little milk, and a touch of cinnamon. There are also a few sultanas, but that's a modern innovation. In the past they were too poor for sultanas (or cinnamon), I am told. Meanwhile, the bladders are thoroughly washed in warm water, inside and out. You can also use vinegar if they smell. The bread mixture is poked carefully into a hole in one end, and the bladder sealed, traditionally with needle and thread. Today, however, a two-inch joiner's nail is pushed through the tightly gathered neck of the bladder, and twine is then used to bind it up. The twine is left long enough so that the puddings can be dangled from a stick that rests on the rim of an enormous pot of boiling water. Three such pots sit on the wood-burning range in the kitchen, each one steaming generously, and each one with five or six puddings bobbing and dancing inside.

Two or three hours later they're done: eggy cannonballs of sweet Galician pudding, eaten hot or cold in slices, no sauce. They taste great. Somehow, though, I don't think I'll be making them back in Coruña.

LUXURY RIBS

A woman dressed in a black trouser suit and a plain top of the same colour greets me. Black shoes too. She is friendly but not wordy, and there's a hint of jujitsu in the way she moves. The room is muted Zen, dark wood surfaces (brown not black), simple, minimalist furniture, a single camellia on each table. One wall, entirely glass, looks out across an intensely green valley; we seem to hang in midair, the atmosphere just a touch otherworldly. Then there's the rest of the calm-but-firm service staff, all black clad, all women. They make no noise and are reassuringly protective. I'm sure they would mother you (in a stern way) if it became necessary.

To the left another glass window, *Last Supper* dimensions, gives onto a shiny steel kitchen in which five silent chefs are at work. Amid the whites in the framed kitchen I spot my man, José (Pepe) González Solla, chef-owner of Casa Solla. His restaurant is getting something of a reputation.

Spain is currently living a kind of long and involved honeymoon with food. It started with Basque chefs like Juan Mari Arzak, who married the nouvelle-ish ideas of lightness and simple, pared-down preparation with the traditions of Spanish and Basque cooking. Ferran Adrià and the El Bulli phenomenon then emerged. And it just goes on and on, getting tastier.

Galicia, with its robust approach to food, has not led the way in this revolution. But things are changing double-fast. Galician cuisine is on a big, exciting upward surge. The new generation of chefs are doing broadly the same to Galician food as Arzak et al. have been doing since the eighties, taking what is best of traditional cooking, then modernising, refining, reaffirming. For a lover of the old, timeless tastes of Galician food, trying out modern interpretations is like discovering that there is a whole new brand of happiness that's just gone on sale. Right now, from a gastronomic perspective, there is absolutely no downside to being in Galicia; it's fun, fun, fun.

Above all else, Galicia has great raw ingredients. The proverbial million cows have a lot of lush, green grass to go at; apart from Friesians for milk and cheese, there's meat from those Galician Blondes that accosted me up a mountain in Os Ancares. Then there's our friend the wild boar and a variety of other game, small and large. The fish is tremendous, and the seafood is of special significance, much of it collected in the *rías* – wide, meandering fluvial estuaries that give form to the many-fingered coastline here, one of which you can see from the wall-sized window of Casa Solla.

Incidentally, Galicia's filigree coast made it a great place for smuggling, a noble tradition for centuries. Tobacco smuggling was particularly common. Big American brands have always been produced in Spain under license to the U. S. companies, and cigarettes smuggled from outside Spain were not only cheaper but said to be better quality. When I first lived here, many bars still kept special, smuggled packs of Winston under the counter that you had to ask for with a knowing wink. When the consumption of cocaine skyrocketed in Europe in the eighties, a smuggling network was already well established along the Galician coast; at one point half of all cocaine coming from South America to Europe passed through Galicia. Most of the drug barons responsible are now in jail, but you can still see smugglers' boats moored innocently in small fishing villages up and down the *rías*, modest fibreglass launches weighed down at the back by two, three, even four obscenely big outboard motors. When there's a chase on, the Civil Guard don't stand a chance.

Finally, there's the wine. Galicia's reds are a mixed bunch. Some are so lousy that they're drunk with lemonade. But at the other extreme, the more sophisticated ones are considered among the best hidden gems in the world of wine, two of them (El Pecado, from the Ribeira Sacra area, and A Trabe from the Monterrei area) recently achieving the hallowed 'extraordinary' rating from the influential U.S. wine critic Robert Parker. As for whites, Albariño is the best known, a light, crisp varietal wine. The grape is said to have arrived here in the twelfth century with monks from Cluny, and it produces wines with a slight acidity and delicate fruit. A very subtle accompaniment to seafood.

If a chef wanted to base his style on the purity of local ingredients, to abandon unnecessary culinary airs and get down to the essence of food, then Galicia is the ideal place. And they do not come much purer than Pepe Solla. He also happens to make the best ribs in the world. That's kind of official.

The man himself greets me, smiling, relaxed. Chefs are normally pasty and tired-eyed. They don't shave properly, and look like middle-aged medical students. Pepe Solla, by contrast, has an erect, commanding stature, lots of black hair, and there's an intelligence, an acuity in his expression. He looks like a poet who works on the stock exchange to support his art. Like a reformed Lord Byron. Like a man quietly in command of his genius.

He suggests I have the tasting menu, plus an Albariño. I nod like an altar boy on his first day. I've been in touch with Pepe about the ribs, which are not on the T-menu, but he's going to let me have them anyway, which is rather like Sinatra switching around his set to include your favourite song. He rejoins the characters in Michelangelo's last kitchen and I sit down. Out comes my Moleskine. Across glides a silent waiter in black with a jug of water. Off we go. Twelve courses.

Pepe inherited the restaurant from his father, also called Pepe. Close to the city of Pontevedra in the southwest of Galicia, Casa Solla had long been a reference point in Galician cooking, doing classic dishes with the kind of refinement that led to a Michelin star and a reputation to match. There have never been many Michelin stars handed out in Galicia, but Pepe Senior held on to his year after year. Recent developments at Casa Solla, then, are curious.

The Albariño is poured, and some snacks are brought: home roasted peanuts (not thoroughly roasted; their freshness remains), salt-encrusted roast corn, a little cheese and guacamole. So far so good, although to be honest, prestarters and edible aperitifs and handmade nibbles get on my nerves. I don't go somewhere to eat the stuff that arrives before the stuff I've gone to eat. I once ate at a (Michelin-starred) place where we ordered from armchairs in the lounge, to the accompaniment of a shot of chicken soup. Sod that. I'll have a gin to get appetised up, *merci*.

After a brief pause – a pause, not a wait – there's some liquid foreplay in the form of a hot, bright yellow pumpkin cream with a note of ham running after it, plus a small square of cockle *empanada*. We're rolling.

Young Pepe graduated in business studies. He did some front-of-housing for his dad, but never formally trained as a chef. When he finally crept into the kitchen, it was to experiment with some of his own ideas. One or two of his strange, avant-garde creations eventually found their way onto the menu. We're talking here about the menu of Pepe Solla, Senior, one of the most respected exponents of Galician gastronomy. Would you have let that happen? Personally, had I been Papá Pepe, I would have stood right next to the knife rack, Michelin star clasped to my breast, a tear in my eye, and a couple dozen faithful, traditionalist, high-end customers standing right behind me, and said: 'Son, I love you dearly, but hands off my fucking restaurant.' That's what I would have said.

An oyster arrives with a small crown of white foam on it. There's kind of a rule these days that to be taken seriously all Spanish menus must feature *espuma* (foam) at least once. Today's froth is made from *escabeche*, the vinegar-based preserving medium. It gives the oyster a cheeky kick. Yet it also manages to melt on the roof of the mouth as you are savouring the taste of the oyster below. The two separate tastes only really join hands for the big slurp-down that follows.

It's a good example of Solla's approach to food. Sourced from a nearby *ría*, the oyster is as local and as fresh as you can get. But the *escabeche* harks back two thousand years, to a time when the Romans collected oysters from the very same estuaries, preserving them and sending them far and wide across their dominions. He explains all this to me after the meal, and how his goal with this dish was to maintain the simple freshness of the local oyster and combine it with the historical reference. How to quote both, yet lose neither. The foam is added right at the last minute. They don't mingle. It's perfect.

By 2003 Pepe Senior was ready to hang up his whites and retire. The restaurant was gutted, its classic country-house elegance replaced by an assertive but not strident minimalism and a gleaming stainless steel kitchen. In pure business terms, bearing in mind the reputation that Casa Solla already had, plus the very conservative nature of Galicians when it comes to food, this was somewhere between walking the high wire across Niagara Falls and just throwing yourself straight into the water. It worked, though. José Carlos Capel, food critic of the newspaper *El País*, observed that seldom had a generational transition of this sort 'been accomplished with a grace so sensitive to the rhythm of two eras'. Young Pepe's intellectual, essentialist style lost some of the old customers along the way, he admits, but he did not lose his listing in the *Michelin Guide*, an achievement of which he is rightly proud. Since taking charge, he has become one of Spain's most exciting and individual chefs. The second star is said to be merely a matter of time.

A small section of lobster tail comes next, bobbing in a thin, clear broth composed principally of the lobster's own juices. It strikes me that I have never had lobster that didn't come blathered in something or other, my fault, I know, but given the option of butter/cream sauce/etc. – well, we all like melted butter (I think I am speaking for everyone here). At the bottom of the dish are some extra-thin noodles, which are intriguingly firm. The taste, the texture . . . I don't quite believe it, but they seem to taste of turnip. I deliver this brilliant observation after the meal when I talk to Pepe. Here's a tip: don't tell a Michelin-starred chef that his fine, Chinese wheat noodles cooked to a decided firmness in soy broth taste like turnips.

I look around as I eat the lobster, and wonder if everyone today is going through the same turnip/not turnip dilemma. The customers seem to be mainly businessmen, and at the largest table nine or ten of them are drinking a lot of champagne, which brings them right up in my estimation. Among their number, I am sure, is Sepp Blatter, president of FIFA. After some concerted rubbernecking it turns out not to be Blatter.

A calf's *molleja* then arrives. The *molleja* is part of the cheek, or so I think. Ignorance, bliss. It is crazy good, a soft cube of all the tastes in the world – salt, sweet, fat, meat, curry, floral – so wonderful that I almost lean back and tell the people at the next table; Casa Solla is just not the kind of place to eat alone. The *molleja* has been cooked with nothing but a little stock, oil, and the finest touch of powdered Szechuan pepper. (I am not, after the turnip/nonturnip-noodle debacle, going to pretend that I knew this at the time; I asked.) It tastes, though, as if every spice known to man – East and West, ancient and modern – has been injected into the fatty-soft flesh on my plate. It blasts you away with taste.

Back home, my *Collins Pocket Dictionary* is no help with *molleja*, and my medium-sized *Oxford* says sweetbread and gizzard. As far as I know, big lumbering bovines don't have gizzards, which goes to show that if you intend to take a dictionary to a fancy foreign restaurant, it's *Larousse* or nothing, although you'll need an extra place setting. *Larousse* says sweetbread. But sweetbreads are normally in the neck, and Pepe had subsequently made a point of explaining that these *mollejas* were not from the neck. I consult the *Oxford-Duden Pictorial* translator's dictionary to clarify matters. I am so glad I didn't know I was eating pancreas at the time; such a vile word, normally heard in its adjectival form ('there's no hope for him, it's p . . .'). Just to complicate matters, further correspondence has failed to clarify whether it really was the pancreas. I have not insisted. The memory of the probably-pancreas is perfect just as it is, whatever the truth.

Pepe wanders into the dining area to take someone's order. He stops to discuss the menu with another customer. Then he returns to the kitchen and starts preparing the order. It is all 100 per cent fuss-less. I watch the kitchen, and even when there is a sudden moment of dashing about, it looks scowl-free. A couple arrive with a toddler, who sits on her mother's knee, has some Michelin-starred milk, then wanders around the restaurant a bit while her parents eat. No one minds. This is how restaurants should be.

I have come for the pork. However, I have also come for an egg. There are no specialities at Casa Solla, but there is a signature dish: a poached egg on a piece of toast. I've read about this egg far and wide, it is a famous egg, and it is absolutely nothing more than a large egg yolk, poached at 64 degrees centigrade, served on a piece of deeply toasted bread with olive oil on it. The French might have three hundred, three thousand ways of cooking an egg, but they can go shove it; Pepe does the perfect egg. Dribbled around the egg are some tiny bits of black olive in oil. But they needn't be there, and in any case it's all but impossible to get them into your mouth because the egg on toast is to be eaten by hand (one of the black-clad ones whispers this as the plate, a square piece of black slate, is laid before you). More than the oyster, the egg sums up the essence of Pepe Solla's essentialist style. It is more egg than an egg. And this is not some El Bulli fantasy. It's a real egg, but one that has become, somehow, semantically richer, deeper, an extra line or two in the

333

dictionary. More *meaning*. Pepe Solla is, in fact, a lexicographer-chef. Egg? No, egg-plus. Egg-Solla.

Another man at the Champagne table stands. It seems to be César Lendoiro, president of Deportivo La Coruña (a big football club), but this too turns out to be false. Then, at the next table (the two tables are obviously full of local oligarchs; they all know each other, and they look like they do a lot of eating in these kinds of places), there's a man who bears a striking resemblance to Rupert Murdoch. Only then does it occur to me that after a certain age, and in good-quality worsteds – the kind that shine like satin – all rich/powerful/prominent men look more or less the same. Perhaps it's the potent mix of endorphins and testosterone that does it, all that alpha-male juice pumping through their bodies for years on end while they are being driven around in large German automobiles. No one is going to mistake me for a rich/powerful/prominent man in twenty years' time, no matter how expensive the suit. It kind of hurts to know that now, as I move toward middle age. But I guess it *is* better to know.

Fish next. I am not a huge fish lover. The grouper, though, is a wow-ratcheter. Cooked only until it is exactly *just done*, a step or two up from the texture of ceviche, its flesh retains that very slight chewiness which we home cooks avoid because it often leaves a taste of low tide on the fish. With a grouper that was still swimming in the sea twelve hours ago, it is heavenly. The fish comes with a watery-thin sauce of seaweed, plus tiny clams. The sauce looks banal, and there isn't even very much of it. Yet the degree of its seaness, with a hint of bitterness from the seaweed, sets up the different seaness of the fish itself. There are two distinct tastes of the sea in operation, and that's before you even get to the baby clams that loiter in the sauce.

The grouper, then, actually sums up Pepe Solla. There is, no doubt, a language somewhere in the world where 'simple' and 'essential' and 'beautiful' are subsumed into one single word (in Navajo, for example, there's a single word for both blue and green; yes, I too have Wikipedia). I am going to suggest 'sollaic' as an addition to the English lexicon. I know 'sollaic' sounds like a food intolerance, but *molleja* sounds like cancer, and that was delicious.

By now I'm scribbling in the Moleskine far too much. The black-clad ones try not to cast glances as they drift by. *They* don't know I'm a nobody who'll never look good in worsteds. I have a foreign accent, the boss came out to greet me and switched the menu around for my convenience. For all they know I might be important. And meanwhile, I sigh as I taste, grinning as much as I dare, nodding and shaking my head in disbelief. I just want to let someone know how much I am enjoying myself. The all-black brigade, though, studiously respect my privacy, which is frustrating, because this is the one time in my life that I actually want a member

335

of the wait staff to ask me, on removing my empty plate, whether I have enjoyed the dish. I don't need to know that she's called Debbie or that she's going to be my waitress today. But I would like to exchange a word or two.

Recently, Pepe Solla was in the United Nations building in New York cooking for the world's diplomats. Then in January he was cooking at Madrid Fusión, the big culinary jamboree attended by all of Spain's great chefs. He is undoubtedly a star. Yet he is understated, unpretentious, and his food is not flashy. He is not a celebrity chef. His ribs, on the other hand, are celebrities. They were on the menu at the Madrid Fusión gala dinner, which in most people's eyes is a greater honour than cooking for Nicaragua's deputy ambassador to the UN. José Carlos Capel, whom we have already met in his guise as food critic, is also the organiser of Madrid Fusión, and his verdict on the ribs was that they were the best pork dish he had ever tasted. For an *El País* writer, he gets to the point with refreshing brevity.

As an impromptu eighth course, then, I am served two half ribs sitting on five *petits pois* and half a potato. That's less than you get stuck between your teeth in Lalín. But the quantity, after so much fabulous stuff before, is just right. They are cooked *sous-vide* (more anon), and they make you cry when you eat them. They are about the best thing I have ever tasted. This is not making me sound like a very sophisticated food writer, I know, but what the hell do you want me to say? How big is the Grand Canyon? No idea, it's just very big, you know, it's really enormous. The *petits pois* are also, by the by, staggeringly tasteful, and I can guarantee you that I have never considered pea pods to be even remotely surprising, let alone staggering; another semantic shift on the plate, then.

While eating the ribs I come very close to making a fool of myself vis some teary-eyed behaviour, not just because I am emotional about food, but because it is such a shame that I have no one to share the experience with. My heart is ready to burst. But it's just me and Solla's food. I decide that these ribs, more than anything, sum up perfectly the chef's style. After the meal I get the recipe from the man himself.

Pepe Solla's Luxury Ribs

ibérico pork ribs
bay leaf
garlic
chicken stock
olive oil
pinch of Szechuan pepper
Cook *sous-vide* for 11 hours at exactly 70°C. Bone ribs, then pan-fry briefly to toast the skin.

Sous-vide is all the rage right now. Ingredients are vacuum-sealed in a plastic bag, and the bag is placed in water to cook, normally at low temperatures and for long periods. One of its advantages is control. You know just what's in the bag, nothing else gets in, nothing comes out – no leeching of flavours, no unintentional loss of juices or fat, no evaporation or reduction – and you can control times and temperatures rigorously. The boiling tank is specially designed and regulates the water's temperature exactly. It is perfect for Solla, whose cooking often involves very precise times and temperatures. The long, slow boil-in-the-bag process allows for a perfectly even distribution of heat, and leaves the ribs extraordinarily tender while maintaining their original shape.

The key to this dish, however, is *ibérico* pork. Good old white-breed pigs will do, or the newly resurrected Galician Celtic. But the world's best pork is *ibérico*. As the ribs sit in the gentle heat, that glorious, fat-infiltrated meat is slowly transformed into what was for me one of the most spellbinding dishes I have ever eaten. Solla talks about the choice of ribs with what I think is a touch of self-reproach. He is, above all else, a chef concerned with fresh, local produce, a regional chef, a Galician chef, yet his most famous creation uses pork only produced in the southwest of Spain.

Do I care? I do not care. As he reproaches himself, this is what I am thinking: the ribs in question are cooked *sous-vide*, a technique currently being embraced enthusiastically by some of Europe's best chefs (Paul Bocuse, Ferran Adrià, Joan Roca); Spain is arguably at the European culinary vanguard right now, and at Spain's premier gastronomic celebration, Madrid Fusión, the most celebrated pork dish was Pepe Solla's ribs. Hence, I consider that the ribs I have just eaten are the best *sous-vide* ribs in the world, and their creator is currently the world's master at cooking them. It's circuitous logic, perhaps, but in the world of food, a world of value judgements and competing opinions, how close can you come to saying, even with flimsy, rollicking logic, that you have tasted the best example of a particular dish on the planet? I think I have.

A black-clad one arrives bearing cheese. Four kinds. She extends an index finger and explains, thus: *cow, cow, goat, sheep*. Then she is gone. Sheep wins.

A deconstructed apple tartlet next: base of cream with apple slices on it, a tiny cinnamon biscuit on that, topped with a light, milky ice cream, whizzed up using the Pacojet, a whisk that makes ice cream that can be served at around eighteen degrees Fahrenheit, rather than the minus-four that ice cream normally demands. The result is a substance that changes form on the tongue, a soft melt that leaves your mouth ringing with taste and not shrieking with cold. Solla explains all this afterward with a glint of alchemy in his eye. You don't need to know about the Pacojet to enjoy the ice cream, though, which is basically less cold than normal ice cream, hence less annoying to eat. Normal ice cream is just too damn icy.

An assemblage of soft, freshly made chocolate creams follows. If I had less self-esteem I might call them orgasmic. Then petits fours. With coffee I have some Carlos I brandy. Then, as an added digestif, Pepe Solla emerges from the kitchen, which is already in its post-lunch phase, and talks to me until after six in the evening.

So what sums up Solla's cooking? There are no adornments. There is nothing added that could be left out. Come to think of it, I don't remember a single spice or herb speaking out on its own behalf (cinnamon in the apple tartlet the only exception). He uses words like 'empirical' and 'intellectual' to describe his work, and these do not sound out of place or high-falutin'. There is no gasp-factor in the presentation, no showiness, no chefiness. Humility, intimacy, precision, essence, simplicity – the same qualities, one suspects, that could describe Solla himself: a chef who has never worked or trained in another restaurant, and who has never seriously considered moving elsewhere. A chef who lives on the banks of the very *ría* where some of his freshest ingredients are harvested. Close to home.

APOCALYPSE THEN

Way back in 1992, as Pablo Valledor was rediscovering that Galician Celtic pigs wiggled like Jayne Mansfield, I was living in the flat in Santiago de Compostela with the five girls and an embargoed telephone. One evening we found a half-inch slip of paper in the mailbox. On it was a laser-printed note. *They have a laser printer*, I thought, *but they are economising on paper?*

The note came from the man who would for a short time be my boss, the head of English philology at the University of A Coruña, some fifty miles away. On the ticker-tape message was a number to call. But the phone in the flat (which I wasn't allowed to answer) also had a padlock on it: *nobody* was allowed to make outgoing calls, for reasons that I never fully understood. The issue of the phone was beginning to eat away at the edges of my soul. I went out and called from a bar. The head of English philology was brief. Did I want to teach English? Yes, I said. See you next term, he said.

This was just before Christmas, and the offer of

a proper job came as a relief. College friends of mine were by this time getting posted to New York and Hong Kong on corporate missions of one sort or another. Meanwhile, I was in Santiago teaching English conversation in bars for a fiver an hour.

After Christmas I awaited further instructions. None came. Then, on a Tuesday morning at 9:20 a.m., the padlocked phone rang. I was still in bed. Term, apparently, had started without me.

I arrived at the University of A Coruña an hour later. The cafeteria, nestling in the low-slung guts of a hideously ugly concrete toad, was full of students waiting for an English class. I was supposed to have known that term started today.

Professor Antonio de Toro treated me to a coffee. A short, stocky guy in his middle years with a big fat slug of a moustache, there was a shiftiness to him, as if he wanted to sell me some illegal pheasants he'd poached but didn't know how to raise the subject. Yet he also exuded paternal kindness, a batty sort of authority. Antonio, as I would soon learn, was an old-school insider, a campus wheeler-dealer, one of those university people you find on an awful lot of committees, but don't see in the library much. He tried to interest me in an apartment he'd got for rent in town. For all I knew this was normal practice in Spanish universities, but I rebuffed the offer; I did not want to get into any arguments about carpet stains with the man who paid my wages.

Antonio shifted the conversation from real estate to research. His own academic speciality was James Joyce. I listened to his English – which managed to be lumpen and squeaky at the same time – and thought, shit, Joyce. As we sipped our coffee he mentioned that he was president of Spain's Joyce Society. Of course he was. Probably the president of the Moustache Society as well. He also let slip the name of his brother, the novelist Suso de Toro. I'd heard of him? No, I answered, which was the wrong answer.

You'll be doing the phonetics classes, he told me, perhaps as a punishment for not knowing who his brother was. Phonetics, the study of pronunciation and how we produce speech sounds, is the nearest that students of languages get to real science while at university. And although I did not know this at the time, it's also the shitty stick of philology, the course that no one wants to teach. Go anywhere in the world, to any language department, and the youngest, most junior, most gullible member of faculty will be doing the phonetics course.

I began to explain to Antonio that I knew absolutely nothing about phonetics. He gave me a *don't bother me with that shit* flick of the eyes. Antonio de Toro was not one for the details. He was a man for the big picture. The 'de' of his surname stood for 'delegate'.

By now a lot of the students were staring at the rumpled, nervous, just-out-of-bed figure at the bar with the head of the department. And they were staring because I was about to replace Tim Quinn. Glamorous, blonde, brilliant Tim Quinn, the most popular phonetics teacher since Aristotle taught remedial Greek pronunciation to the Phoenicians. I had been called up to replace the Irreplaceable One, who had left suddenly in mysterious circumstances. That day's class was cancelled, and for the rest of the morning, as I was shown around, people looked me up and down with expressions of surprise, of disappointment, of pity. *You are no Tim*, their eyes said. Which was true.

That monstrous concrete amphibian of a faculty building became my Apocalypse Now, and Tim Quinn my jungle-bound Brando. I never did get to meet Tim, but his shadow cast a permanent darkness across my path. And at the heart of it all, in the office that I would share with María Jesús (a specialist in eighteenth-century literature who had studied in Oxford and had a mug from St Andrew's College, Oxford, to prove it) Tim-Kurtz had left an enormous footprint on the wall that I could not remove however hard I rubbed. Even in the cafeteria the shadow followed me. Davíd, the ebullient young barman, asked me what part of England I was from, then actually began to explain some of the regional variations in the English vowel system; Tim, you see, had been teaching him English pronunciation for his hotel studies exams. *Great bloke, Tim. Really great.*

Back in Santiago that evening I sat at the kitchen table as Susana delivered a crash course in English phonetics. Having studied the very same course at university a few years previously, she already had the textbooks. Thus did my Galician girlfriend begin to teach me how to speak English. The following morning at nine-fifteen I arrived in the lecture hall, shaking with nerves, pale-faced, and dehydrated after vomiting twice in the toilets. About sixty students stared at the new Tim – shorter, fatter, sweatier – who spent the next hour trying to remember what a diphthong was.

I stayed for two years, which is just about enough phonetics for anyone. During that time I relocated to a flat with a fully working phone in Coruña, which is our next stop.

THE CITY FORMERLY
KNOWN AS LA CORUÑA

D on Francisco Vázquez Vázquez, the mayor of Coruña, clears his throat. The council's ceremonial guards stand to attention behind him (maroon tunics, scarlet knickerbockers, hats festooned with sprays of white cockatoo plumage), as he breaks into a chorus of 'La-la-la', Spain's winning entry in the 1968 Eurovision Song Contest.

With thick pomaded hair scraped back over his scalp, and grinning from one rosy cheek to the other, Vázquez Vázquez looks like a naughty schoolboy, like a fat cat that got the cream. He has been the mayor of Coruña for almost a quarter of a century, and in Galician politics that's an awful lot of cream.

But now, quite unexpectedly, he has been named Spanish ambassador to the Vatican. At his official leave-taking ceremony, held in the sumptuous, neo-Christmas cake town hall, his impromptu rendition of 'La-la-la' makes everyone smile with pride. A moment to remember in the history of the city, for sure. But also the end of an era, the end of the *La* as we know it.

Let's get something straight. Coruña is my adoptive home. But it is Susana's unadopted, natural-born home, and also my son's. So here's a little snatch of history for Nico, because his hometown's past has a bit of an English flavour to it.

Built on a small peninsula that juts out into the Atlantic, Coruña is an old military and commercial port. In 1588, during the first Anglo-Spanish War (there were lots) Spain's *Invincible Armada*, on its way to invade England and restore Catholicism, stopped off here for supplies. It then headed up to the North Sea, where it sank invincibly. Sir Francis Drake, admiral of the English fleet, spent a long time laughing uncontrollably, before sailing down to Coruña to give the Spaniards a good hiding. Having breached the walls of the old city, he sent an ensign to hoist the English colours. The ensign, though, came face-to-face with a large, passionate woman called María Pita, who shot him dead. She then led a raggle-taggle citizen army that repelled the English with pitchforks and broom handles. Years later, toward the end of an eventful life in which the redoubtable Maria got through four husbands, she was granted a license to sell mules to Portugal. (Incidentally, Sir Francis Drake, the English naval hero, is known in Spain as a *pirata*, a pirate. Nico, you're going to be conflicted about that one. I only hope you finally make the right decision.)

More than two centuries later, Napoléon also failed to sack Coruña. Not many cities, I imagine, can boast of having repelled the dominant English navy of the sixteenth century and Napoléon's land forces of the early nineteenth. On this latter occasion, the English were the heroes. General Sir John Moore's English troops were in Spain, but were heading back to England, via the port of Coruña. Having drawn Napoléon's men northward after them, they had little choice but to defend the town, so as to make their own escape possible. During the fighting, Moore's shoulder was blown off, and he lost his life there in Coruña, a token of contrition, perhaps, for the unfortunate episode with Drake the hero-pirate all those years before.

The death of John Moore in Coruña was commemorated in a true tearjerker of a poem by Charles Wolfe:

THE BURIAL OF SIR JOHN MOORE AFTER CORUNNA

NOT a drum was heard, not a funeral note,
As his corse to the rampart we hurried;
Not a soldier discharged his farewell shot
O'er the grave where our hero we buried.

We buried him darkly at dead of night,
The sods with our bayonets turning,
By the struggling moonbeam's misty light
And the lanthorn dimly burning . . .

I'm walking down Calle Real ('Royal Street'), a marble-paved shopping lane at the heart of Coruña.

It seems to have changed little in a century, full of silversmiths, jewellers, fancy shoe shops, and slow-moving crowds of well-dressed Coruñans unhurriedly getting in one another's way in a serene mass promenade-cum-shuffle that ends just as it started, pointlessly. People here just love strolling.

As you move slowly along you might perhaps stop to browse the illegal CDs and DVDs laid out on large blankets by Senegalese street vendors. Then nip through to the tree-lined Méndez Núñez gardens nearby for an aperitif at the circular, glass-terraced Copa Cabana Bar ('the King of Fried Squid'), take in an exhibition at the beautiful art nouveau exhibition hall, or have an ice cream as you watch the locals (knickerbockered kids; bleached, Burberryed moms) make good use of the miniature fun fair.

Alternately, you could wander with your lemon Solero just a couple of minutes past Royal Street in the other direction, to find yourself, miraculously, on a city-centre beach with a mile of golden sands that stretch along the gentle curvature of Coruña's western flank, together with a spacious balustraded promenade, a sort of spillover facility to accommodate all the city's shufflers. An old-fashioned tramcar trundles up and down the seafront and will take you right around the peninsula, skirting the old town and Sir John Moore's tomb, until you find yourself in the marina, stuffed with gleaming white yachts, their bobbing masts reflected in the glass-galleried facades of the elegant nineteenth-century buildings that look out to sea and which gave Coruña its nick-name: the Crystal City.

Okay, Nico, I admit it, you were born in a nice place.

Back on Royal Street, if you cut through to your left about halfway along you'll find Bonilla, not much to look at, but Coruña's premier *chocolatería*. For most of the day, but especially in the evening (which in Spain they call the afternoon), you'll find Bonilla full of the city's finest señoras, powdered, plucked, and wrapped in furs. Gold-heavy fingers creep out from beneath the sable to snaffle another deep-fried, sugar-dusted *churro*, dip it in their cup of thick, steaming-hot liquid chocolate, and pop it in their mouth. Ever since Columbus brought cocoa back from the Americas, taking chocolate has been seen as the favoured pastime of Spain's idle rich. And in the Crystal City they really know how to do chocolate.

But I am not here for chocolate. Today I have decided to put pigs on the back burner and do a bit of historical research. So, at the ungodly hour of quarter to twelve (noon), which according to the Spanish timetable is midmorning, I take a little crooked alleyway that leads off Royal Street, and find the great brown doors of the Widows. They are closed. I hop into the bar opposite, order some rabid tigers, and wait.

This alley is part of a network of streets full of taverns and bars serving tapas and *raciones*, and commonly known as Los Vinos. Between here and the sugary town hall almost nothing but eating and drinking goes on; considering that not much else goes on in Coruña anyway, you can imagine how concentrated the activity gets here in the 'wine streets'. Many of the places I intend to visit today have not changed at all since the early 1980s, when Susana and her teenaged friends began doing what every teenager in Coruña does quite a lot: going out for drinks and tapas. My mission today, then, is to retrace the tapas route of my wife's formative years, and in doing so to paint a food and drink picture of what growing up means in the curiously elegant yet undeniably greedy city that I have come to regard as my own.

My rabid tigers (*tigres rabiosos*), king-sized mussels in a spicy sauce, are the speciality in the bar where I am sitting. The Spanish tradition of bars special-ising in one sort of tapa, even a single tapa, is still strong. There's a bar just behind the town hall that serves matchstick-sized potato chips. It serves lots of other things, but it is the only place you can get a tapa of matchsticks. Ditto the rabid mussels. All these bars have names, but no one knows them. It's the matchstick bar, or the angry mussel bar.

Close by is Bombilla (the Lightbulb), a corner bar permanently colonised by the city's young carousers. Inside, there's room for about a dozen people, but upward of forty or fifty souls are normally crammed in, arms held high, stomachs pulled flat, sardine-squashed in their desperate quest for hot finger food. You don't even bother to fight your way to the front

of the queue here, but use a form of flag-less sema-
phore to communicate your order to the barmen,
only a matter of feet away, but separated from you
by an unconscionable mass of elbowing Coruñans,
who, having long ago abandoned all pretence at
courtesy, are actually using one another to navigate
the human throng, pulling themselves into visibility
by means of a technique that resembles horizontal
shoulder-mountaineering.

The Lightbulb serves large, stodgy tapas. Piles
of tortilla slabs reach high into the air, tepid and
unctuous, and the deep-fried béchamel croquettes
are as big as your fist. For many, the Lightbulb is
the essential stop-off on the city's tapas trail, and
has been for years. I called in just now, at the lax
early morning hour, and asked the boss man if
he'd answer a few questions (how many tons of
tortilla they serve, that sort of thing).

'Me? *No!*' he said with high-minded derision,
almost surprised by my audacity, as if I'd just
asked the pope if he could stand me a pack of
Durex Featherlite.

So I eat my mussels in the tiger bar and wait,
amusing myself by reading the framed eulogy high
up over the bar:

HIS MAJESTY THE MUSSEL

This acephalous mollusc contains almost
the entire alphabet of vitamins and proteins,
as well as iodine, iron and phosphorous.

Cleopatra (seductress of statesmen) and Poppea (wife of Nero) both consumed it in abundance so as to be beautiful . . .

At twelve noon a lady in a long denim dress staggers out of the great doors opposite with a potted plant about as big as her, then goes back inside for another. The plants, which stand at each side of the imposing, anonymous doorway, are the only indication that through the doorway the best cheese and *chicharrones* in town await, as well as everyone's favourite widows.

Sisa and Mari Carmen (not the bladder-pudding Mari Carmen) are sisters, and have been working this place all their adult lives. Their father opened up in 1936, and as was the tradition with *tascas* (spit-'n'-sawdust taverns) it never had a name. People started calling it La Traida ('The Water Supply') because the water company had its offices opposite. There was never a sign, and in any case these days most people call it Las Viudas ('The Widows'), in reference to the current owners, although there is some doubt about this. And it's not the kind of thing you can just ask a lady, especially not *these* ladies.

Until about a century ago the building was a women's prison. There are no ground-floor windows, and only a few small ones above. Inside, the floor is ancient stone, and there are three tables with little stools, plus half a dozen barrels to lean on.

Sisa and Mari Carmen are both about ready for retirement, Sisa tells me, but why retire? Four decades they've been here, lunch and evenings, all week, and they still enjoy it. The two of them have their own unforgettable style. Mari Carmen, rather severe-looking if you don't know her, struts a little, immaculate blonde hair cropped short, head held high. She passes among the crowds, filling people's small, awkward ceramic wine cups (of which more, below) from a jug, giving you a schoolmarmish, almost indulgent nod as she goes. She has a great line in designer wear that is definitely not spit-'n'-sawdust; today she's in close-cut fawn jeans and a Paul Smith top. Her sister, Sisa, is a little more soft-focus, dark-haired and with a dimpled smile and playful eyes behind purple-framed glasses. Perhaps 'soft-focus' is not quite right. I saw her the other day in town wearing a wickedly shiny black cape; she looked like Catwoman's fairy godmother. The sisters, all told, are about the snazziest tavern owners you're ever likely to meet.

As is common in this type of tavern, the wine is white, straight from the barrel, and the barrel straight from the country. No vintage, no messing. You drink it in little ceramic cups called *cuncas*. These cups have no handles and are shallow, rather like the flattened-out cup you might use for a duck egg. By tradition they are filled to the brim, which makes it all but impossible to bring them to one's mouth without traditionally spilling any. Wine containers with vertical or at least relatively vertical sides are not good enough for Galicians; that would not be complicated enough. Something more troublesome is required, and what amounts to a small plate for your beverage is perfect. *Design me an intrinsically impractical wine cup*, you might say, and I would give you a *cunca*.

I order some soft, country cheese. It comes from Sobrado, about an hour's drive south and at the heart of Galicia's cheese-making area. I get some *chicharrones* too. And a beer. I can't stomach country wine for breakfast. This morning Sisa is full of stories about Turkey, the sisters' latest vacation destination. They go travelling several times each year, always with the same crowd: a group of twenty-one women, plus one attached husband. They've been to New York, Cuba, Buenos Aires, Brazil, Mexico, and Thailand. They're thinking about China for next year. One of the other ladies of the group, who Sisa tells me owns a ladies' lingerie shop in the barrio, does all the organising. For trips closer to home they charter a bus, stock it well with Galician cheese and wine, and off they go. Can you imagine being that solitary man? Twenty-one Galician women of a certain age cosseting and pampering you and encouraging you to eat?

The tavern itself has not been altered since 1936, other than the walls, which are covered in more recent posters and photographs of the city, with the wall behind the bar practically a shrine to Deportivo La Coruña, the city football club, of which Mari Carmen and Sisa are devoted fans. And please note that it is Deportivo *La* Coruña, and it will always be *La* Coruña. We'll get to the *La* soon, don't worry.

My cheese arrives. It has been cut into pieces, but this cheese exists right on the line between solid and liquid, so fresh you can hear it mooing. It has already started to morph, the gooey lumps spreading back into one another, as if drunk and overly affectionate. Sisa is now striding out across Europe: Italy, France, Austria, Germany, Slovenia, Switzerland . . . Then I see him! On the wall right above the cheese, a framed black-and-white photo: it's Creamy Vázquez! If you are a big lover of Coruña – as the sisters most decidedly are – you probably also love ex-mayor Vázquez, who might be Spanish ambassador to the Vatican at the moment, but whom many Coruñans consider worthy of beatification at the very least. As mayor he was ludicrously successful, winning six consecutive absolute majorities. He gave the city museums and art galleries, an oil refinery, parks and walkways, a professional symphony orchestra and concert hall, a university, and a conference centre, as well as attracting cruise liners to stop off here and disgorge their rich folk onto Royal Street. He also gave us tramcars.

So, here I am, staring at a photo of Creamy Vázquez, in a stone-floored tavern, eating cheese that came straight from the countryside this morning, and wine that comes direct from a barrel in the corner. But none of this exactly sums up Coruña, because in contrast to the Galician stereotype – modest, unpretentious, rural, quietly ironic – Coruña is almost the exact opposite – self-assured, vain, and almost hysterically metropolitan. Coruña is, I am afraid, rather disgracefully bourgeois. Now and then you hear one of its more deluded inhabitants refer to the place as Mini-Milan. And they're not being ironic. Coruña is not a place for irony; it's a place for Louis Vuitton.

It's also a place for *La*. Let me try to explain. The Galician language, which shares its roots with Portuguese, not Spanish, has a long history of being suppressed. During Franco's dictatorship, for example, it had no legal status, as the dictator sought to maintain a unified Spain by stifling regional differences. After his death in 1975, Spain moved through a period of transition toward a parliamentary democracy, and during this process the three 'historical nations' (Galicia, Catalonia, and the Basque Country) were granted extensive autonomy, though remaining within the Spanish state. At this point the Galician language was adopted as coofficial in Galicia.

Public institutions – from Galicia's new autonomous government down to village councils – began the shift from using Spanish to Galician. The new, coofficial language appeared on road signs, in hospitals and public offices, everywhere. This sometimes involved changing place-names. Orense, for example, became Ourense, the Galician spelling. In most cases people accepted these changes with a shrug, and ordered new letterhead. But here in the Crystal City, the change from La Coruña (Spanish) to A Coruña (Galician) was resisted. And no one resisted more than Mayor Vázquez, who resisted on municipal road signs, on plaques, on stationery and Post-it notes and souvenir pencils . . . It is not absolutely clear why he opposed this tiny change so virulently. He himself had been active in the movement toward greater autonomy for Galicia, and was also one of the first people during the Franco years to dare have a Galician-language wedding service.

Whatever the reasons, Vázquez made sure that the 'La' of La Coruña remained, for years and years. The whole thing got a little absurd. Legal challenges were seemingly endless, and the issue of the L dominated large amounts of council time and money, funds that Mayor Vázquez (a socialist) might perhaps have better spent on, oh, I don't know . . . the poor?

It wasn't just the mayor, either. Political graffitists took up the cause. Road signs were spray-corrected by Galician nationalists, from La Coruña to A Coruña, only for pro-Spanish aerosolists to reinsert the sacred L, on and on, until most signs these days just have a multicoloured splodge of paint where either a La or an A might once have been. This alphabetical turf war extended right along motor-ways, where signs were systematically daubed, no matter the danger involved. A third group of activists, the Galician Reintegrationists, who want the Galician language to be brought further in line

358

with Portuguese, started spraying forms such as 'A Corunha' and 'Crunha' (the Reintegrationists can't even agree on a spelling; that's how damn radical they are). La Coruña, A Coruña, A Corunha, Crunha . . . Take your pick. Personally, I just say Coruña. It makes for a quiet life.

Since Creamy Vázquez departed for Vatican City, in 2006, the issue of Coruña's *L* has been quietly dropped, no doubt saving the city administration a lot of money. One year later and the council booked the New York Dolls to play a (free) public concert as part of the city's Summer Festival, so it's nice to know that all the money they've saved is going to the old and infirm. The festival also includes an annual night-time fireworks display that reenacts the battle in which Drake the Pirate was repelled from the city by María the mule seller. I stood and watched in silence this year as my country was ridiculed in pink and green explosions.

Back in the Widows bar there's a constant stream of customers now, all known by name, all talking in insanely loud voices, all having an awkward cup or two of wine, perhaps a cigarette, then off on their business. In the evenings the clientele is more varied, but pre-lunch it's mainly older people from the barrio, and the atmosphere like that of a youth club for the over-fifties.

I lean on the bar and finish off my molten cheese, and start in on the *chicharrones*. Then, during a lull at the bar, I finally pluck up the courage, take a drink of beer, and ask Sisa, in a whisper: *Are you really widows?* She explodes with laughter, and obligingly repeats the question so that everybody around us can hear. I attempt to excuse the question, as the assembled customers at the bar guffaw with laughter. There's no need for an excuse. No one minds, least of all the two not-widows, who explain that they took over the bar when their father died, even while they were wearing mourning, and the name stuck: Las Viudas.

Thus I discover something about the bar that my wife, after more than a quarter of a century eating runny cheese and sardine *empanadas* there, never knew. I kiss Sisa on each cheek, promising to bring Nico to see them soon. She refuses to let me pay for my drink and food. I wander out into daylight, past the Lightbulb, on to my next rendezvous, with the Tailor.

Up ahead is a fashion shop called Zara, which sells 'designer-style' clothes at modest prices (i.e., knockoffs). Amancio Ortega, its owner, started work as a fourteen-year-old gopher in a Coruña shirt seller's. In 1975 he opened his first shop in the city, just up from the Widows tavern. Susana's mum took her there to buy T-shirts that very year. It was an old-style place, she recalls, with the products laid out in wooden trays, but the clothes were said to be good quality and not expensive. Thirty-three years later Ortega is still in the fashion business, but he now has over three thousand stores worldwide and a personal fortune in excess of $20 billion. He is worth more than George Soros and

Jeff Bezos combined; if you like your stats to swing a little, his fortune is greater than the combined worth of Steve Jobs, Donald Trump, George Lucas, Steven Spielberg, William Randolph Hearst III, and David Rockefeller. He has never appeared in the press, has never done an interview, and he does not wear a tie. Such is the mystique surrounding Ortega in Coruña that people boast of having had contact with him at second and third remove (i.e., your sister's boss once had dinner with his chauffeur). He has an apartment five blocks from ours, and not once have we been invited around.

O Viñedo ('The Vineyard') is my next stop. It's past one o'clock, but by Spanish standards it is still early for lunch. I catch the proprietor of this upscale tavern alone. He is known as el Sastre ('the Tailor'), and his *mesón* is one long room with hams hanging from the rafters, and seven barrels that serve as tables. At the back there are mirror-lined shelves decorated with chorizos and salamis, strings of onions and garlics, an *ibérico* ham in a state of semi-depletion, plus a nice dried pig's face centre stage, smiling. I am not allowed to take a photo of all this. I don't ask why.

El Sastre has never been a tailor, he tells me as he slices potatoes for what looks like a hundred tortillas, and the nickname is a mystery that even he cannot resolve. I ask him how long he's been open, but that appears to be as great a mystery to him as the nickname. I chat away, but the Tailor is a suspicious man. Only, I can't work out what he's suspicious of. It seems to involve a conspiracy between a journalist and/or neighbours who came in search of secret information of some sort, to which he makes gnomic reference as he speaks, sometimes accompanied by a knowing glance, a half wink, a counterconspiratorial nod in my direction.

The star dish in O Viñedo is roast ham with peppers. The ham is boiled for softening, then oven-roasted, producing outrageously tender and juicy meat. Even when the *mesón*'s barrels are full, and all leaning space around the walls taken, if a significant number of people are tucking into platters of roast ham, a curious calm pervades the place. Not quietness, naturally, this is Spain; but an air of relaxed, self-contained pleasure, as if the ham is giving everyone an invisible neck massage.

The (fried) potatoes that accompany the ham are from Coristanco, about thirty miles away and the potato mecca of Galicia; the roast peppers from the Bierzo region of neighbouring León. Galicians will regularly comment on the quality of potatoes, of peppers, whatever . . . They concern themselves with the taste, condition, and origin of the simplest ingredients. And when it comes to ingredients, they know what they're talking about. I sat in a *mesón* on one occasion, open-jawed as my sister-in-law, having ordered a plateful of fried Padrón peppers, called the waiter over and told him to take them away. Padrón peppers, you may recall, are small and green and trick you into believing they are inoffensive, before a spicy one blows your head off. The peppers we had been given were from Murcia in the south of Spain. She knew it. So did the waiter. Off he slouched, his peppers between his legs.

'That's all there is to it,' the Tailor agrees, still slicing potatoes. 'Good ingredients, cooked simply.'

An utterly Galician philosophy, and one which keeps his *mesón* full every evening.

On I go, trying to engage him in food conversation, but it's hard work.

'Do young people eat ham?' I ask.

What kind of a question is that? (Yes, apparently they do.) I persevere, with increasingly stupid lines of inquiry. I might as well be asking him the square root of 81. There really is nothing to say. He has great ham. Everyone loves it. I'm just making an idiot of myself. *How many humps on a dromedary?* He lets great big pauses build up between my fool questions and his shruggy responses. Galicians have a knack of pushing you into embarrassing corners in this way; it's as if the more unstoppable your bullshit, the more elastic the pauses they string around it all. *Just say less* is the key. If you need to practice, come talk to the Tailor.

By now it's about two in the afternoon, which is 'two in the morning' if you're speaking Spanish, still a whole hour ahead of 'midday,' which is at 3 p.m., long after all sensible countries have started thinking about the fact that it's nearly evening. I head over to As Boas Cepas ('The Good

Vines'), an old bar whose owner, Sisa told me, was called Jaime. It takes me a while to find, because although I know the bar itself, I didn't know it had a name. It does: in the window is a paper that says EL BAR DE RAMÓN. So, As Boas Cepas is 'Ramon's Bar,' which Jaime owns. In I go, for another awkward cup of wine.

The Good Vines dates from the early 1950s, and it too has remained unchanged since it opened. The white wine, once again from a barrel, is flowery and acidic. Like the Widows bar, it is served from a jug that Jaime (or Ramón) periodically refills from the barrel. But that's where the similarities end. There are no snazzy sisters here keeping things spic and span. As Boas Cepas is, indeed, a wonderful, in-your-face statement on the point-lessness of decor. Even back in the fifties they can't have made much of an effort with the place, and since then they've evidently made none, apart from the bar itself, which is painted bright yellow.

Almost the only bottles on the shelves are secondhand ones with homemade labels. There's another cluster of them on top of the fridge behind the bar, and some more on a table, hiding behind a couple of ten-litre boxes of red wine. All these bottles contain brightly coloured liquids – red, yellow, green, a variety of suspicious browns, some of which remind me of the murky oil in which Atilano's chorizos lurked back in Monteseiro. The colours, the labels . . . the scene is surreal; what with the decor deficit and the peculiar potions all around you, it's like stepping into Willy Wonka's garden shed.

Sipping and spilling my *cunca* of wine, I consider the names on the bottles: Caress, Love Bite, Ripper (as in Jack-the-), French . . . In these parts a 'French' is a service that professional ladies offer (and advertise in the local newspaper), although in this case it is a cocktail of liquors mixed on the premises: rum, vodka, gin, grenadine, triple sec, lime, and pineapple. If you survive your French, you can have a Cucumber, a Kamasutra, a Cock, a Klíktoris (sic), a G-spot, an Oral Sex, a Screw-me-well, a So-good-you'll-shit-yourself, or a glass of Knocks-God-out (firewater and sweet wine).

As Boas Cepas is an old-time bar for locals. But in the evenings (that's the night-time to you and I) it has a whole different vibe, the colourful cocktails attracting younger customers. The plan for your teenaged night out is simple: carb-up at the Lightbulb, perhaps some Widows cheese and an angry tiger, then some dangerous liquor mixes at Jaime's place; just at the point when a sane person might be thinking about going happily home to do some sleeping, the night can really begin. Because if Spain's daytime timetable is somewhat eccentric, going out at night is taken very literally; 'night' means night, all of it.

I stop off at a variety of other places over lunchtime, which in Spain runs conveniently on until about four-thirty, although shops don't reopen until about an hour after that, leaving a stretch of down-time in which visitors to these parts regularly suffer feelings of disorientation: it's not night, it's not day, it's not for working, yet on the other hand, it doesn't look as if anyone's taking a siesta.

Finally, and by this stage somewhat unfocusedly, I pop into Otero bar, a long, high-ceilinged, well-illuminated place. It's relatively quiet, but within a few hours it will be noisy again, full of office and shop workers, old folk, loudmouthed adolescents, gangs of middle-aged ladies in bold-hued trouser suits and big hair, kids loping about while their parents have a beer, babies in designer prams getting their fix of potted slop from the Argentinean help. Spain doesn't demarcate the different spheres of social living much, which makes the country a bit like a giant kindergarten with a bar in it and a permanent tapas menu fixed to the wall. And please, do smoke in this play area if you wish.

Otero is the kind of place where people come with their kids. In fact, you can go almost anywhere with your kids in Spain, especially in low-key, laid-back Galicia, safe in the knowledge that no one will mind if they scream, or get in the way, or take a nuclear dump in their diaper. It's really very difficult to do anything wrong here if you have a child with you. Unless you inadvertently subject him to a draught, in which case they'll throw you in jail. Your little mites will quickly get used to coming to Otero bar, just as Susana did, and they'll just keep on coming, through adolescence and into adulthood, eventually calling in with a pram and a baby of their own.

I think this sums up Coruña rather well: traditional even in its taste for tapas joints, a city full of *de toda la vida* (literally 'all of life') bars, places you've been coming to since forever, and which give structure to lunchtime and evening socialising. Traditions don't die here, they get handed down like family heirlooms. When it comes to going out to eat, Coruñans are like sheep with transgenerational memories. Everywhere I have mentioned – the matchstick bar, the Widows' cheese cellar, the Tailor's ham tavern, Jaime's cocktail den, bar Otero – are all places that Susana first knew as a child, brought here by parents or uncles out for a stroll and a Sunday lunchtime aperitif, or as a teenager, out with her friends in the 'evening' (night).

As for me, no one handed me down these traditions; I married into them. But I intend to hand them down. So you see, I had another reason for today's bar crawl: I wanted to check out the route that Nico will take in about fifteen years' time. Call in any of these places about a decade and a half from now, and look around for a blonde lad helping the other kids with their English homework: he's ours.

I sip on my last beer of the afternoon, and wonder whether I have come any closer to understanding how my adoptive city fits into the broader picture of Galicia. The question of the *La* in La Coruña has always bemused me, although it shouldn't really come as a shock to see the Galician love of doubt reflected in place-names. The very word 'Galicia' is controversial: the current president says *Galicia* (pronounced ga-LI-thi-ya) whereas his vice president prefers *Galiza* (ga-LI-tha). One place, two names; another victory for clarity and common sense.

The more interesting question, however, is the one about *Spanish-ness*. From all that we've seen over the course of our journey this year, the places and people don't *seem* very Spanish. Galicia is different, what with the wet, Atlantic weather and its reserved, mutedly ironic humour. Then there's the *butter line*. You can divide Europe broadly into two: the cold, hardy north, where animal fat (butter and lard) has always been the staple cooking grease, and the sun-drenched south, where olive oil dominates. Much of Spain is Southern European in character, *olive oil* territory. Galicia is pure pig fat. On top of all this, Galicians play the bagpipes, like the Scots, Irish, Cumbrians, and Bretons, all up there in Butterland.

Then again, what is Spain? What is Spanishness? A woman in a bright red dress clicking the castanets? The poet Miguel Hernández gave expression to the difficulty of trying to sum up this bewildering, diverse country in the poem 'Winds of the village carry me,' a sort of adjectival tour of

Spain in which the Basques become *fortified rock*, the Andalusians are depicted with tear-drenched guitars, and so on, a seemingly impossible patchwork of contrasting characters and temperaments from across the peninsula. Galicians? *Rain and calm*.

Spain is indeed quite a mix. And *Galicians of rain and calm* just about sums up the top left-hand corner.

As for bullfighting, that quintessentially Spanish form of sadobestiality, Coruña did have a *plaza de toros* once, but it was pulled down years ago to build apartments. There's still a short bullfighting festival each summer, held in a converted concert stadium (Creamy Vázquez's idea). I went to my first *corrida* last year, and watched as several taut-buttocked men in pink stockings flapped their capes at big, lumbering, confused animals, before killing them incompetently with swords and daggers. During one ovation, instead of throwing flowers at the triumphant matador, someone hurled an entire *empanada* pasty at him, Frisbee-style; from somewhere else in the crowd a leg of ham came hurtling down.

Only in Galicia.

MIOLADA MODERNA

Living deep in the heart of a city has its drawbacks, boxed up in an apartment five floors above the traffic. But there are advantages too. Our flat has a terrace right next to the kitchen. You can be hard at work cooking, the door flung wide open, the radio competing with the blare of a rampant rush hour down below, then slip outside for a cigarette or a glass of wine or a slice of ham you've just cut from your leg of *ibérico*. There you sit, hovering above the noise and surrounded by large pots of mint and basil, a mini-oasis that is both in the city and somehow out of it, a place for pause and reflection. As long as it's not raining.

I've come out here today with two cookbooks: Fergus Henderson's *The Whole Beast* and Álvaro Cunqueiro's *Cocina Gallega* ('Galician Cooking'). Buses rumble past below me, and somewhere in the mid-distance a blocked-in car gives sharp little toots of its horn. Meanwhile, I sip a glass of chilled Albariño and ponder the situation. It's eleven months since I began the quest to eat my way around a pig, and this is how the count stands:

shoulder ham
loin
neck and shoulder meat
ribs and vertebrae
bone marrow
side bacon
belly pork cheek
snout
ear
tongue
trotters
tail
whole head
blood
heart
kidney
bladder
ribs again (luxury)
ham

I'm not done. Will I ever be? No. There'll be no genitals. Male pigs are generally very well endowed, with penises up to eighteen inches in length, which, relative to body size, makes those pork swords among the most impressive in the animal kingdom. In Galicia's distant past, the pig's penis used to be stretch-dried and used as a donkey whip. There's no longer much call for donkey whips.

Carlos, our organic butcher, says there's no call for pig testicles either. No one eats them. And with an eighteen-incher, a substantial set of testicles would probably come as standard, so that's a goodly plate of meat going to waste.

Setting aside the pig's unmentionables, my list is still not complete. At the very least I need a recipe that contains brains and liver. So I open Cunqueiro's *Galician Cooking* and have a look. On page 120 is a recipe for *miolada*, a sort of brain curd made by stewing backbone and pig head until soft, then stirring in pig fat, bread soaked in milk, beaten eggs, and the brains. It is removed from the heat and left to set.

I have never heard of anybody cooking *miolada*. I think it's one of those recipes that was allowed to die quietly. Cunqueiro has been a useful companion over the course of this year, but I think I'll need to adapt his *miolada* for the modern palate. I turn to the master of 'nose to tail eating,' the British chef Fergus Henderson. The answer is simple: a fusion of Cunqueiro's brain curd with Henderson's sheep brain terrine, substituting pig for sheep. I will call it *miolada moderna*.

Carlos has a stall in Coruña's magnificent Plaza de Lugo food market, where Susana developed her vegetarian condition. There's a whole floor given over to meat, but the council functionaries who allocate the stalls must have looked at the words 'organic' and 'butcher', rubbed their chins as if some sophisticated play on words had been perpetrated, and decided he should be up on the fruit and veg floor.

Market managers notwithstanding, organic animal production is taking off here, what with Celtic pigs and the realisation that Galicia's countryside and its old breeds are the perfect springboard for an organic meat revival. Nonindustrialised animal production has its drawbacks, though: I ordered a blade shoulder joint a while back, only to be informed a few days later that the pig from which it was destined to come had given the slaughterman the slip and run off back into the woods. No one got their chops that weekend.

Today's supplies from Carlos are: a fresh half head of pig, liver, fatback, and streaky bacon. The brain from the half head won't be enough. *Sesos* (brains) are hard to get these days. Nobody wants them, and they are rarely removed to be sold. (Modern meat plants sometimes employ a technique that uses pressurised air to blast the brains out of the cranium, leaving 'brain mist' in the air.) I gave Pablo Valledor a ring the other day, and he put me in touch with an accommodating pork butcher in Santiago.

Armed with my bag of goodies from the market, I get home to find that the military campaign that constitutes our weekly grocery shopping is in full march. Six brown paper sacks block the entrance to the kitchen, just delivered by one of the organic food collectives that have sprung up recently. Interest in organic fruit and veg, like organic meat, has been relatively late arriving in Galicia. Unlike much of industrialised Europe, the rupture between local producers and local consumption has not been so absolute here, and small shops in the heart of the city still sell produce from local villages. If you have the time, you can visit local country fairs at the weekend and get the stuff direct from the people who grow it. You can also buy your *grelos* at the side of main roads, where women sit with piles of the stuff, and often a few jars of home-produced honey as well. Perhaps that's why the organic movement hasn't taken off so strongly here yet; it hasn't needed to.

However, the military-style food operation in our city-centre home demands efficiency and economies of scale, so in this case the mountain of veg comes to Mohammed. There's also a wooden crate of fabulous organic oranges that we get couriered up from the south of Spain. It sounds effete and uber-foodie, but at $24 a crate they don't cost very much more than shop-bought oranges, and as for the taste, you don't have to be married to a vegetarian to know that a ripe organic orange can be staggeringly flavourful; I never thought I would say this, but a really fabulous orange, in season, has to be among the most amazing eating experiences you can have. Then there's a consignment of oat milk from the local health shop. (You still drink cow's milk? *Really?*) On the table a dish towel shrouds what little is left of a leg of *ibérico* ham; there'll now be a couple of days of hacking at the hardened bits around the ankle, before we concede that there's nothing left but bone. Then another phone call south . . .

There's no point in me staying here this morning. Susana knows where I've been, and I am not welcome. Having overheard my phone call to Pablo, she has spent the intervening days trying to persuade me not to cook brains, claiming that they are the natural carriers of disease, and reminding me that Creutzfeldt-Jakob disease (the human form of Mad Cow Disease) killed over 160 people in the United Kingdom, and that it began as a result of feeding brains and spine to cattle. She didn't win the argument, but she is refusing to let me do it at home. She is also refusing to let me serve them to her parents on health grounds, although I'll be using their kitchen. So, I'm on my own with this one. If I have died of CJD by the time you read this, take comfort from the fact that I don't know what a chump I was.

Miolada Moderna in homage to Álvaro Cunqueiro and Fergus Henderson

Whiz some garlic in a blender. Add shallots and whiz again. Ditto pig liver. Combine with some pork fatback, lean veal, and lean pork (I used meat from the shoulder ham), all finely minced. Healthy pinches of: ground clove, cinnamon, nutmeg (freshly milled), black pepper. Slug of brandy. Salt, but only if your fatback (see above) or your bacon (see below) are not salted.

Meanwhile, carefully lower three or four pig brains into gently boiling water and cook for a few minutes. Remove with even more care, then refresh in chilled water. At this point, have a little nibble of your brains. They're very creamy, the consistency of set custard, and their taste is distantly fatty; an inoffensive taste, like tofu. Brains are also horribly full of cholesterol, so a modest layer in your terrine is probably enough if you want to persuade anyone else to join you for lunch.

Sometime previously (this is not a chronological recipe) take whatever part of the head meat you like best. I use the cheek and corresponding inner muscle. Chop into chunks, and set in a stewing pot with some fat (diced fatback, in this case). Fry briefly, then add a little water, cover, and cook over a lowish flame for an hour or so. Add more water and remove lid, and cook until the water has disappeared. This, in essence, is *chicharrones*, although Carlos tells me he doesn't use head meat for his *chicharrones* (which are delicious) because of the gristly fat nodules in it. Many other producers, I suspect, use plenty of face meat. So, if you want top-notch *chicharrones*, you need to go to the fruit and veg section of the market in Coruña.

Line a terrine dish with streaky bacon. Put a layer of the whizzed mixture at the bottom. Take your head meat and pull into shreds; mix with some of the whizzed-up mixture and layer it into the dish. Add a layer of sliced brains. Then put the remaining mixture on top. Wrap the ends of the bacon slices over the top. Cover with aluminium foil. Place in a deep cooking tray with water in it. Bake in moderate oven for two hours.

After it has cooled, put stiff cardboard on top of the terrine and weigh it down with something heavy. Leave in the fridge for a day or two.

Die a little death of pleasure as you taste your very own *miolada moderna*.

ENCOUNTERS WITH EMINENT GALICIANS III: DON MANUEL FRAGA IRIBARNE

G alicia has produced some interesting characters over the years, among them General Franco, one of Europe's longest-serving dictators; Camilo José Cela, novelist and winner of the Nobel Prize for Literature; and the Castro family. Those of Galician parentage include Julio Iglesias, Manu Chao, and Martin Sheen, and we can also throw in Jerry Garcia, who had a grandpa from Coruña. It's a mixed bag.

I've met all kinds of people over the course of my travels this year. Each one has in some way helped to broaden my understanding of Galicia and the Galician character. But today I've come all the way to Madrid to meet the most famous Galician alive: Senator Manuel Fraga Iribarne.

When I arrive, they're redecorating the Senate building. Senator Fraga has been lodged temporarily on the top floor, in an office so small that a middle-ranking manager in a provincial life insurance company would consider it an affront to his rank and standing.

It's just five days since Spain's general election, which the senator's party lost. As I wait nervously for him, my heart thumps so hard that it feels as though someone's practising quick-fire slam dunks in my chest (correction, *with* my chest). I'm at the centre of the country's political establishment, and about to have a coronary arrest as I prepare to meet the man who's been a part of that establishment longer than anyone else.

Then I hear his voice in the corridor, the unmistakable slurred patrician grumble of one of the oldest active politicians in the world, and a hero/bogeyman (delete as necessary) of epic proportions.

'What language would you like to do this in?' he says in perfect English as he extends a hand.

He is somewhat drawn-looking, but elegant and effortlessly courteous. As for speaking in English, I know that he was Spanish ambassador to the United Kingdom for a few years in the early 1970s, but that was a third of a century ago, and since then he's been kind of busy. I didn't expect him to have kept up his English-language skills. We plump for Spanish, and he offers to switch if things get difficult for me.

Every single person I have ever met in Galicia, left-wing, right-wing, educated or not, young or old, has an opinion on Fraga. His political career stretches from Franco's brutal military-Catholic

379

dictatorship to the exuberant, modern democracy that Spain has become. His contribution to Spanish politics is unique. And up in Galicia, his dominance of conservative politics makes *The Godfather* look like a romantic comedy.

I came to Galicia for the first time in January 1990. That was the year in which Manuel Fraga became president of the Galician regional government, at the age of sixty-eight. He was president until 2005, by which time his omnipresence in Galician politics had almost become a joke: *You heard the one about the politician whose grasp on power was firmer during democracy than under the dictator?* That's Fraga. He would have been president of Galicia to this day, but for the loss of a single parliamentary seat by his party in 2005, which finally forced this political behemoth out of the presidential office, although he had the Senate in Madrid as a backup.

Friends of ours responded to the news that I was going to see him with laughter-laced incredulity. Susana herself was kind of horrified-amused. She would never, ever vote for him. But Fraga has been an inescapable part of political life here since long before she was born, and he's hard to ignore. To many, he's a hate figure. But there are also those on the political right who go weak-kneed at the very sound of his name. He's a love figure too. Left or right, whatever your views, you would not be here in the Senate without at least some trepidation, without a certain awe.

We sit at opposite sides of his temporary desk.

He has a white handkerchief in the breast pocket of his jacket and a dark blue silk tie scrupulously knotted. The senator gives me his full attention, businesslike and serious. The sense of a man who has seen everything is palpable. From the 1950s onward he was part of the inner sanctum of Franco's regime, a regime that executed political prisoners and violently suppressed dissent. Yet just a few days ago, during Spain's general elections, he was out and about, kissing babies and pressing the flesh like a superannuated Jack Kennedy, trudging to political rallies in support of his party at the age of eighty-six.

I start the interview by explaining about my gastro-graphical tour of Galicia. He nods, his eyelids sagging almost closed as he listens, then lifting as he speaks. He says the project sounds interesting, and promises to send me a copy of his recently published memoirs. He has written upward of fifty books over the years, mainly on issues of policy, and that's just in his spare time. One book is about the British Cabinet, and he tells me it is considered one of his least bad books, which I think is a great statesman trying to be modest.

With that the formalities are over. They lasted a minute. Don Manuel is not known for his small talk.

'I think this will be about the least political interview you've ever done,' I quip, as an icebreaker.

'Everything comes back to politics in the end,' he says.

He's affable and intense. He neither intimidates nor relaxes you when he speaks, but rather creates the impression that he knows everything, that whatever uncertainty or doubt arises, he will clear things up for you succinctly. And when Don Manuel says something, he is not offering you his *take* on reality; he is laying out the truth.

We talk about food, Galician food.

'Of course,' he says, 'traditionally food in Galician village life was frugal. Boring and frugal. Then came the feast days, and it could get ridiculous, really. Thirty courses, excessive.'

These crazy rural feasts, I have heard, sometimes lasted days on end, sporadic bouts of gluttony in an otherwise stark existence. The tradition of outrageous, extreme eating has now disappeared (although you can still do yourself some serious damage at a Galician wedding if you go with the right attitude). But when you talk to people of Manuel Fraga's age, the memories are still strong. Food to Galicians was a symbol of celebration in tough times, a respite against hardship. And the more food, the greater the celebration.

'You know,' he says, grinning momentarily, 'I have the suspicion that sometimes they'd vomit between courses. Like the Romans used to.'

'The Romans had a special chamber for that, didn't they?' I advance.

'The Romans, perhaps. In Galicia they'd just do

it out in the yard. The human stomach only has room for so much.'

You can't argue with that. I certainly can't.

Manuel Fraga was born in Vilalba (famous for its capon festival) in the Galician province of Lugo, in 1922. A brilliant student, even as a boy his studies were coloured by politics. When his high school was taken over by republican forces during Spain's civil war, he moved to Coruña, then to Santiago, and finally to Madrid, where he graduated in law with the *premio extraordinario* ('extraordinary prize') at the prestigious Complutense University. He then got a second degree, in political and economic science, while also passing the competitive, nation-wide entrance exams for the parliamentary civil service (in first place), and soon after that similar exams for the diplomatic service (also in first place). Concurrently, he published his doctoral thesis, and at twenty-six was awarded a *cátedra* (the highest academic grade in a Spanish university) at the University of Valencia. Annoying, really.

In the early 1950s his abilities were recognised by Franco, and he was given several secretaryships within the administration, before being named minister of information and tourism in 1962, a post he held for most of that decade. It strikes me, as we talk about Roman vomiting protocol, that being a minister in Franco's regime meant wielding an absolute, uncontestable power, not unlike the kind of power that the Romans exerted over

383

their dominions. There was no free press and no political dissent. If you opposed the regime, you had several choices: emigrate, as many thousands did, keep your mouth shut, or participate in illegal, underground political organisations. For the unlucky ones, trial and imprisonment for political activism against the state, including execution, was not uncommon.

As minister for information in the sixties, Manuel Fraga was responsible for announcing these executions, and for justifying their legality.

I ask him what period in his career has given him most satisfaction.

'Being a minister,' he says without hesitation. 'That and being president of Galicia' [which came much later]. The ministry I was given in 1962 was the most difficult.' I think this is a great statesman implying that he did a good job in difficult circumstances.

Despite the violent and repressive nature of the administration of which he was a part, Fraga was known as favouring more political openness. He introduced a law on religious freedom, and another one relaxing press censorship (most important, abolishing the state screening of newspapers before publication). His most influential role, however, was probably in the area of tourism.

By 1962 Spain's economy had been opened up, and the country opted for a campaign to attract mass tourism to its shores. Fraga spearheaded this policy. Tourism would soon become the country's largest source of income, contributing to

Spain's 'economic miracle' of the sixties and early seventies (it ended with the oil crisis of 1973). In that period, Spain's economy went from being ridiculously backward by the standards of Western Europe, to a vibrant and modern one, laying the foundation for further economic growth in the 1980s and '90s. Apart from the crucial economic contribution that tourism made to the modernisation of Spain, Fraga's press reforms (as well as the influx of millions of tourists from democratic countries) probably did as much to open the country up as anything else that might feasibly have been achieved from within the regime. Mass tourism also brought the bikini and topless bathing to Spain, and I think we're all grateful to Don Manuel for that.

It was during his tenure as minister of tourism that the slogan *Spain is different!* was first used, a phrase that the Spanish still cry out in ironic frustration when anything goes wrong. The phrase promised a fresh, new destination for millions of holiday-makers from the rich industrial economies of Britain, Germany, and Holland, many of them having their first taste of foreign travel here, a country where life was still cheap and – as long as you did as you were told – cheerful. Yet also hidden in that phrase was a sly statement of political defiance – *Spain is different!* – a subtle reaffirmation of the regime, of the seemingly unshakeable grip that Franco had over the country, a dictatorship that (along with a similar dictatorship in neighbouring Portugal) was a blight on the otherwise democratic map of Western Europe. And all this during the swinging sixties, the era of the Beatles, the Summer of Love, of political rallies and demonstrations and student sit-ins across Western Europe and the USA. Meanwhile, in Franco's Spain public parks were patrolled by warders who made sure that no one was making too much noise and that young lovers were not kissing too ardently, and at night *serenos* (literally 'serenes', night watchmen) would pace the streets, carrying with them the keys to everyone's apartment buildings. *Spain is different!* Perhaps Fraga's knowledge of English was important here, because the more you think of that phrase, the more brilliantly double-edged you realise it was.

At this stage I want to move on and ask the senator about some of the other achievements of his career. One of these was the Spanish constitution, generally considered pretty good, and still in force today, having served the country longer than any previous attempt to define civil and political rights. But when your main area of expertise is the ability to recognise a Galician Celtic pig at twenty paces, what exactly do you ask a professor of constitutional law about the constitution that he wrote?

The year was 1977. Franco had been dead two years, and Spain was living through a tense and unpredictable period of political transition. The stakes could not have been higher. Seven men, including Fraga, sat down and drafted a brand-new constitution from scratch. Among these 'fathers of the constitution' were a communist, a socialist, a

Catalan nationalist, several conservative centrists, and Manuel Fraga, whose unexpectedly conciliatory approach is sometimes held up as one reason such a divergent group succeeded. Indeed, some members of Fraga's own nascent conservative party abandoned him at this stage, saying he'd gone all soft.

'What did you do on the first day?' is my inspired question about the writing of the Spanish constitution.

'We ate,' he says. 'We had dinner. That was important.'

Everything comes back to food in the end, Manuel, I want to say. But I don't.

I hope I am managing to convey the sheer difficulty of interviewing a man who has such an overreaching grasp of everything, who delivers his opinions like a Delphic oracle, and who famously does not suffer fools.

Shifting tack, I ask him about last week's election, in particular the performance of his own party, the conservative Popular Party. And it is *his* party. He founded it, led it through much of the 1980s, when it was the official parliamentary opposition to the socialist government of Felipe González, the period in which Spain's current democracy was consolidated. When you talk about modern conservative politics in Spain, you are effectively talking about Manuel Fraga, plus the rest.

'It's in fine shape,' he says, 'strong and solid for the future.'

The conservatives lost the general election five days ago. *Strong and solid for the future* . . . He stares me down with this answer, absolutely the only time throughout the interview when his directness even hints at something more combative. I guess he's a little touchy about the elections. His party lost the last ones too. In any case, what did I expect him to do? Light up a cigar, sit back in his seat, and say, *Yep, John, we screwed up. You've hit the nail on the head, son. We were rubbish.*

They *were* rubbish, by the way. Their campaign was a bit like watching your old uncle Ernie trying to chat up a waitress: outdated, somewhat embarrassing, and doomed to failure from the first word. Their main solace was that the victorious socialist party also ran a dreadful campaign, but managed to be more photogenic.

A couple of days after the election the conservative party bigwigs met to review the results. And there was Manuel Fraga, right at the centre of things. Like he always is. He was even at the centre of things during the tense transitional years following Franco's death, when, apart from writing the constitution, he was interior minister. *La calle es mia!* he claimed at one point – *The streets are mine!* – as he banned rallies and sought to keep a tight hold on public order.

These days he's showing his age a bit, but in the past he was a big, chubby, round-faced character, often scowling with seriousness, something for which he is known to this day. Yet there is a touch of the theatrical to him too. In 1966 an American bomber accidentally let several (unexploded) nuclear bombs fall on the beach and in the sea at Palomares, on Spain's Mediterranean coast. Panic followed, as fears of radioactivity grew. Accompanied by the U.S. ambassador and a large press corps, Fraga travelled to the site. The two men stood and surveyed the scene. Then, quite suddenly, the portly Minister Fraga dropped his pants, stripped down to a voluminous pair of bathing shorts, and jumped in the water for a swim. Not many ministers did that sort of thing when Franco was in charge.

And he's still at it. Last week, after a televised presidential debate in which the current president (the socialist José Luis Zapatero) made use of a white file containing graphs and charts, Fraga announced that he wanted a copy of the file, in case he ran out of toilet paper.

In 1989 Fraga vacated the leadership of the Spanish conservative party he had formed, a party that finally came to power seven years later under the leadership of the cringing functionary José María Aznar. Meanwhile, Fraga won a seat in the European parliament, and also contested the presidency of Galicia's regional government, winning by a land-slide. Never a dull moment with Don Manuel . . .

Our conversation continues. It's like a ridiculously mismatched game of tennis played across his Senate desk. I serve him a question, and the return is so quick and unplayable that before you've hitched up your shorts, the opponent has changed sides and is waiting for your next pathetic attempt.

We talk about his time as Spanish ambassador in London. I put it to him that it was perhaps difficult to represent a dictatorship at the heart of a proudly democratic and open society. He shrugs, and tells me an anecdote about his friend Lord Home (British prime minister, 1963–64), breaking into English for the punch line ('How is your wife?' someone asked Home. 'Compared to what?' he replied). I bet that had them rolling about in the corridors of power. There is no mention of how difficult being Franco's representative in 1970s London was. No mention, either, of the time that an anti-Franco demonstration took place outside the Spanish embassy, and Fraga let it be known that he was carrying two loaded pistols.

'I feel that I should mention Galician independence,' I say.

'Why?' he asks.

Independence for Galicia is an idea supported by only a minority. But among Galicia's nationalists (who are generally on the political left) a desire for greater separation from the Spanish state is strong. The movement is not as extreme as in the Basque Country, but the essential claims are the same: Spain is a colonial power that invaded these territories.

His jowls are already shaking, his head moving

from side to side. 'Why? What for? No. *De eso nada.*' 'Of this, nothing.'

His reply is not rude. It doesn't mean 'don't talk to me about this'. It means, quite simply, 'of this there is nothing to talk about'. Next question, please.

The next question is about the 'emigrant vote' in Galicia and whether it is justifiable. To freshen your memory: all Galicians who emigrated, plus their children and their grandchildren, have the same voting rights as any other Galician (including a vote in Spain's general elections). It matters not that these children and grandchildren live in Bogotá or Burkina Faso, where they will have nationality and voting rights in that country. Can you imagine if all the children and grandchildren of emigrants to the USA had similar voting rights? And if the Mexican and Italian elections just happened to fall on the same date? The streets would disappear beneath a carpet of discarded election pamphlets from Mexico's myriad political parties, the PRI, PAN, PdelT, PRD, PNA, PVEM, PC... trampled down by an army of Forza Italia agents busily handing out free salamis and voting papers to anyone whose surname ends in a vowel.

I put it to Don Manuel that the situation is a little strange.

'It's a very good thing!' he says. 'The emigrant vote is very good. Emigrants are important. They send money back, and they're part of the history of Galicia.'

There's that sagging of the eyelids again. It's as if they lift up when the truth is being disseminated, and roll back down when the information has been successfully delivered. And just to be on the safe side, he pins you with those dark eyes, just a sliver of them through nearly shut lids, but enough to let you know that you are being pinned.

Three possible responses occur to me:

1. Voters in distant lands, with foreign nationality and full voting rights in their own countries? It's a strange kind of 'representative democracy,' don't you think?
2. Hey, doesn't your own party usually benefit more than any other from the emigrant vote?
3. Okay.

I plump for number three.

Finally, toward the end of a long and utterly absorbing game of conversational tennis (6–0, 6–0 to the senator), we find some common ground. We are talking about Fidel Castro, with whom Fraga developed what must rank as one of the most unlikely political friendships in modern politics.

'Not really a friendship,' he corrects me. 'I tried to improve conditions for all the Galicians living in Cuba. That's all. We weren't friends.'

Nevertheless, he did invite Castro to Galicia in 1992, and also persuaded him to enlarge the Casa de Galicia (the Centre for Galicians) in Havana, using part of a building that had been expropriated during the revolution.

'I went over to Havana,' he tells me, 'and I stayed in the Cuban government's official guesthouse.'

I know all about that house! I want to say. *I know all about it! I know someone else who stayed there. For a year! I know Castro's cousin!*

But of course, I don't. You don't name-drop with Manuel Fraga. At least I got that right.

And thus it was that I met the senator, political ogre, chameleon, Methuselah . . . the most famous Galician alive. He started out as a rising star of Franco's regime, a regime that stifled and suppressed all forms of regionalism in favour of a unified Spain, banning all official use of the Galician language, and looking down on any expression of regional difference. Years later he wrote the constitution that granted his own native land of Galicia a high degree of autonomy, and years after that would be its president, speaking in Galician, arousing Galician sentiment, and stirring up regional pride wherever he went.

Franco's ex-minister of information rises slowly from his seat and takes a card from his wallet.

'If you need anything,' he says, passing the card across the desk, 'give me a ring.'

393

MANOLO AND THE BLOOD-IMP

December. Seven in the morning. The sky is pitch black, and I am driving through heavy rain. There seem to be more droplets per square inch than is possible, as if it's raining twice at the same time. And it's been coming down like this for three days straight. It's cold as hell, and it can only get colder. Gradually, as I make my way along a deserted motorway, shards of steel grey light filter through low-lying clouds, the kind of light that creeps in behind your eyes like a flat blade, exerting a cold, metallic pressure. I want to press 'delete', go home to bed, and wait for tomorrow.

Ever since the invitation arrived, we've had a dilemma: Should our son be allowed to witness violent death? It's the harrowing screams that worried us most. You can shield a toddler's eyes from the gore, from the physical rip and slash. But the cries of agony are difficult to muffle.

In the end we decided against it. Nico and his vegetarian mum will not be accompanying me on this long-awaited excursion. As the grey sky opens up, I drive, alone, toward the agricultural hinterland. It's a shame my Anglo-Galician son isn't coming with me, because today I'll be attending the most traditional event that rural Galicia has to offer. It's freezing. It's raining. And I'm off to a pig slaughter.

There are ten houses in the hamlet, of which five are currently inhabited. I drive past what might possibly be some or all of them. Up ahead a man emerges from a large farmhouse close to the road. He's tall, built like a wrestler, perhaps sixty years old, and stoops just a touch, as if he's saving his early morning stretch for later. His face has an all-over ruddiness, like a drinker's nose that's spread out as far as his ears.

'*Buenos días*,' I say. 'Good morning. Could you tell me where Esperanza lives?'

Esperanza is a colleague of Susana's. They work at one of Spain's state-run language colleges, and her parents are holding the pig slaughter today. I figure in a hamlet of ten houses first names are okay.

'She lives back there,' he says, pointing to the cluster of stone buildings I've just driven past.

'There's a pig kill today, isn't there?' I ask.

He nods, a flicker of amusement across his purple face. He stands and watches as I turn the car around and head back toward Esperanza's house.

I park, then realise I am no closer to knowing which house to go to. There are a lot of farm buildings huddled together. The entire settlement

395

is tiny, not unlike a miniature Santiago, ancient stone structures crammed cheek by jowl, and narrow stone-paved streets winding their way between. Among the dwellings are barns, from which the lowing of impatient cows can be heard. If a camera crew were to emerge from around a corner I would not be surprised, because this is exactly like a movie set, a place designed to be impeccably real, almost too real. I don't know how far back in time I have stepped, but I have to remind myself that this is not a Hollywood lot, but a place where people live.

Just outside the main nucleus is another farm, complete with an *horreo* (corn store), which in this part of Galicia are long and thin and built of stone, perched on granite stilts with half spheres of stone interposed to stop the rats from climbing up. They're a very recognisable part of village life, a vestige of the past, certainly, but still in use, and many of the better examples – which might be anything up to five hundred years old – are protected by law. The *horreo* I am now looking at has a small cross on one end of its roof, which is pretty much normal. Galicia is, after all, a Christian land. But Galicians can also claim a pre-Christian, pagan history, where folk myths merged with witchery and magic, and as a relic of this, *horreos* often have a pyramid or some other pre-Christian symbol of fertility on the other end. This one has an erect penis, thick and a little stubby, but standing proud, poking vertically up into the sky. Why they didn't just tell me to head toward the stone cock, I don't know.

Historically, killing the fattened hog would set a family up for the winter ahead. There would be fresh offal to eat, plus a mountain of meat to preserve in salt: hams and shoulder hams (*lacones*), the head, ears, tongue, tail, and feet, all the stuff I've eaten in one form or another over the past twelve months. Then there'd be two sides of good, fatty bacon, and a great bundle of lard for cooking with. Bones for broth, and in the east of Galicia the ribs, vertebrae, and tail would be crushed and stuffed into bowels for *botelo*. Blood for sweet pancakes, or for *morcillas*, thick blood sausages sweetened with sultanas and pine nuts. Meat from the ribs and loin (and just about anywhere else) could be eaten fresh, or turned into masses of chorizos, the great meaty stock-pile in any old Galician farmhouse; lungs, heart, and any other oddments could be combined with off-cuts for *longanizas*. Finally, there's the fine-grained, salami-like *salchichón*, if you have any off-cuts left. Meanwhile, the brains might be used for *miolada* curd, although these days you can make *miolada moderna* instead. The squeal would be discarded, unless they were really hungry.

The small holding belongs to Esperanza's parents, and is to be Slaughter HQ this morning. It is now several weeks since Saint Martin's Day (November 11), which marks the onset of the killing season, and here the ritual is being kept up. Four animals from the farm are to bite it, with some neighbours pitching in with a couple more head of hog to make it a party. These half dozen beasts are for home consumption. Farms around here tend to focus on producing milk to sell to the large dairies, and all else that is reared or grown or made – pigs, chickens, sheep, rabbits, cheese, wine, firewater, plus more fruit and veg than you can shake a stick at – is for private use. Give or take the odd bit of salt and a satellite dish, they can produce just about all that they need.

You can tell when a place is really old because those living there have no idea when their ancestors moved in. I ask about the age of the original farm, and no one has a clue. A guess puts the old stone structure at three hundred years, but it might not be the original one; some of the stonework in the hamlet looks way older than that. As elsewhere, rural dwellings here were designed to accommodate animals on the ground floor and the people upstairs. Over the last few generations, however, the animals have gradually been turfed out, which means that houses now have twice as much human living space as they once had. Esperanza's family lives in a small palace.

'Come in. Have you had breakfast?' says a lady who turns out to be a neighbour, and just happens to be at the door when I knock.

It's about nine in the morning, and the kitchen

is already full of people, a noisy kind of bustle everywhere. Two ladies in regulation blue pinafores are peeling potatoes over a bucket. The bucket is full, but one of the ladies says there aren't enough, and goes off to fetch more. Other people, meanwhile, seem to be staggering through the no-man's-land between getting up and waking up. I don't know who is emerging from the bedrooms upstairs and who is coming in through the front door. There seems to be no obvious distinction, and everyone acts as if they've been here a million times before.

On the table is a big *roscón*, a sugary, bready kind of cake shaped like a car tyre with glazed cherries and angelica on top. It is normally eaten at Epiphany and Easter, but I guess every tradition can be relaxed, especially when you have a lot of folk over for breakfast. I am handed a plate with three thick slices. Esperanza appears, and gets me some coffee. It's the first decent breakfast I've had since I started travelling around for this book last January.

The chatter is constant. Three children are being fussed over by a clutch of women who are simultaneously peeling garlic and doing a variety of other kitchen jobs, all based around the massive wood-burning range at the centre of the room. Just as we saw in Atilano's house in Monteseiro, and also in the kitchen of José's Galician-style hacienda in Liñares de Vilafurides, the range is encased on three sides by a cupboard-like structure. You can cook there, read the paper, or just huddle in close, warmed by the heat from the range, as the children are doing this morning.

From time to time people open the little iron door of the range and peep inside, then slip in a stick of wood. Several babies are brought in and passed around for kissing. A lady who must be well into her nineties, and dressed in the statutory black, is guided to a stool by the range. Everyone is talking. When someone new arrives, they talk too. They talk even as they enter. People talk back to them, the polyphony of conversation turning ever denser and more difficult to follow, especially for a foreigner. In any case, it is not clear who, besides me, is doing any listening.

There is an air of festivity here, something happy and familiar. If there are five households in the hamlet, then most of those people must be in the kitchen with us. Men in overalls begin to arrive. I am introduced left and right. No one seems surprised that I am here, but they all sound pleased to see me, and talk to me as though they've known me for years. The women joke about whether I understand Galician. I use my time-honoured but never very funny joke: *If I don't understand, I pretend.* They laugh kindly, and promise to speak in Spanish. I tell them not to. They do anyway.

Then Manolo arrives. Unassuming, almost mute. His gait is still a little heavy, a touch ponderous. But it's the tread of a very strong man.

The ruddy face I saw back on the road is now all smiles. He's in blue overalls, and he's carrying a nine-inch knife. I don't have to ask who's going to be doing the killing today.

The question of whether to bring our young son this morning has already been resolved. But there is a second problem. Prior to this day I have never seen an animal die. Not even a chicken. Not a mouse. Not so much as a goldfish. I have to descend three whole animal classes before I find anything I've actually seen in the act of perishing. And it's a spider, if you're interested. I once stamped on a spider so big and scary that its legs were like buffalo wings.

So: please don't let them have names. If today's pigs have pet names, I don't think I can watch. I might have eaten smashed ribs in a bag in Os Ancares, trotters in Santalla, belly in Santiago, snout in Lalín, face in Laza, tail in Ourense . . . but I had not met the animal from which these things came. It's going to be difficult enough witnessing my first killing. If one of the porkers is called Pepe, that's it, I'm away. Who knows, I might just join the ranks of Galicia's vegetarians, which will be most convenient, since we will both be living in the same apartment.

I step outside for a nerve-steadying cigarette. There's a saying in Spanish: *A cada cerdo le llega su San Martín* – 'Every hog has its Saint Martin's Day'. Suddenly, there's a shriek. To my left, at the cobbled entrance to the phallic farm next door, no more than twenty yards away, a pig appears, upside down, dangling by its right hind leg from a rope which is tied to the raised arm of a tractor. They are a-killin' there today too, using the modern innovation of a tractor for convenience: in the past the pig would be killed on a low bench or on the ground, with all available hands holding it down.

My stomach tightens. Should I retreat? By chance, Manolo and Esperanza's father emerge from the kitchen door and see that a pig next door is about to be killed.

'You came to see this?' they ask me, jokingly.

'Well,' I say, with smiling bravado, 'I eat it, so I ought to see it die!'

They laugh, puzzled, I think, at my succinct yet rather pointless motivation for being here, and wander off in preparation for the demise of their own six animals, who are but minutes away from their own encounter with Saint Martin.

I eat it, so I ought to see it die. All week I have been saying the same phrase, and still I have not managed to convince myself. The porker next door, meanwhile, seems to know what's coming, and his screams turn nauseating. I stay where I am, shuddering as the sounds echo off the damp stone around me. The pig, disoriented, begins to thrash about. Several men crowd around, tying ropes to its forelegs and snout and managing to bring it under control. For a second or two it hangs there. The knife goes in quickly, piercing the throat, then up into the heart. Blood gushes out, steaming and frothy, a strikingly bright fuchsia. Moments later the heart's frantic pumping turns the gush into a series of sudden mechanical bursts. The animal droops a little, its thrashing diminished, as the cobbled lane runs shocking pink. It makes a little shudder. Then the knife again. Less blood this time, and as the last of it trickles out in looping, syrupy threads that stretch right down to the ground, the pig quivers, its snout dripping, plastered red and frothy, its tongue hanging loose. It gives one massive lunge, thumping hard against the front of the tractor with the full weight of its body. Then it is dead. It took perhaps a minute.

Even as I stand and watch the tractor reverse away, taking the lifeless animal with it, and leaving the ground an eerie colour, a small herd of black and white Friesians rumbles past. I pull in close to the wall. They mooch along gracefully, minding their own business.

Our own pig slaughter gets under way. I am now somewhat emboldened, having lost my death virginity in furtive glances next door. I join the crowd of half a dozen men and a tractor. And it is only the men. It is drizzling. Manolo is in charge. Whereas both before and after the slaughter he gives the impression of being the big-hearted village joker, he's now the *matarife* (slaughterman). For the duration of the killing, people do exactly as he says. Which is very little. A word here and there, a twist of the hand, no hint of the former grin on his face. If an animal really must be killed with a big knife, then I think Manolo probably does it as quickly and efficiently as possible. There is something cruel to the proceedings, obviously. One or two men in attendance tell me that they don't much like the sound of the pig dying. In fact, almost everyone here owns up to some sense of regret over the course of the day. But it is an annual tradition, and without the slaughter the hamlet loses a crucial element in its centuries-old calendar, something like Thanksgiving and Harvest Festival rolled into one, a tradition wrought in live (then dead) flesh.

One must say a word more about tradition, though. I get talking to Jaume, a pig farmer who lives nearby. There really is no need for the animal to be alive and kicking as it perishes, he says; it can be stunned first. Modern pig farms don't even stun, they kill instantly with a special retracting pistol. Stunning the animal to avoid suffering is no longer just an option, either. After years of protests from animal welfare groups, stunning is now a legal requirement. In theory. All this unanaesthetised throat slitting is more than simple tradition, then, it's a ritual, a *sacrificio* (sacrifice), technically an illegal one. Standing there in the drizzle and dodging the spurts of warm blood, one feels that the animal's brief, awful death in some way consecrates the village; it represents, you might say, the very lifeblood of the place.

And it's worth remembering that these hogs have lived a far happier, freer life than any intensively reared industrial pig. Which would you rather have, a swift, gruesome death or a long, gruesome life?

The job is done without fuss. The pigs are brought out one at a time, swinging from the tractor, and Manolo dispatches them just about as quickly as he can. The tractor is an innovation. I begin to imagine how incredibly strenuous all this would have been in the old days, just a handful of men, some rope, and a very frightened three-hundred-pound hog. A friend of mine used to have the job of holding one of the writhing animal's legs as the slaughter took place, and this was when he was an eight-year-old boy. Some traditions have been allowed to die.

Manolo has a sidekick. Compared to the *matarife*'s solid mass, he's no more than an imp, somewhat younger than me, with pale, slightly crazy eyes and a cigarette permanently hanging from his lip. The imp's job, apart from acting as a sprightly, anorexic shadow to Manolo, is to do what for some reason they didn't bother to do next door: collect the blood. He stands, holding a plastic bucket beneath the animal's neck, and does his best to get the stuff as it gushes out. In his other hand is a well-worn stick with a bulbous handle. He stirs continuously, because without doing so the warm blood will clot as it cools, becoming useless for the sweet blood pancakes they'll all be eating tomorrow. Several ladies have now joined us, and they take turns with the stick as Manolo and the blood-imp prepare for the next pig. This, incidentally, is what I had seen on that deserted road early this year in Os Ancares: a woman stirring a bucket of hot blood after a pig kill.

As all this happens I take photos. What on earth I am going to do with so many photos of slaughtered pigs I don't know. I am ridiculously out of place, and the photos just underline the fact. Everyone else here has been doing this since they were children. Today's tractor driver has brought his son, who must be all of three years old, and perches behind his dad, looking down impassively as the animal kicks and screams. Nevertheless, I still think you had a lucky escape, Nico.

The most interesting part of a pig slaughter is not the death, but what happens afterward. Most of us, given the necessity, and a shotgun, could probably kill a pig. But what then? A dead pig is an awkward, unwieldy lump, and the process of dealing with the body begins by covering him in a blanket of straw and setting him on fire to scorch off the bristles and sterilise the skin. The first one to burn today is still twitching just a touch when the flames shoot up, but it's the last gasp of his nervous system, I am told; he is brain-dead. A diminutive man in his sixties, who tells me jokes in chuckling Galician all day and never stops laughing, says that once he was at a kill when they set fire to a pig that was still breathing. He finds this very funny. The flames rise high into the air, and I hear the guttural shriek of another pig outside. I go out to watch, as if it is only by witnessing each and every animal die that I can prove my manhood, that the folks here are going to be impressed that I have notched up all six.

Ninety long minutes later and the morning's corpses are all laid out on wooden palettes in the barn. It adjoins the back of the farmhouse, and in normal circumstances chickens run free, no doubt signed-up members of the Screen Actors Guild (Feathered Vertebrate Division), although today they are in their cages next to a large haystack at the back. Overhead, massive beams run the entire length of the barn, held up in the middle with stone pillars. The pigs will eventually be hung from these beams to be dismembered. But first there's the small matter of their insides. Several men have been at work burning the carcasses and then scrubbing away the bristles and the singed skin. But no one has opened the pigs up: this too is Manolo's job.

With the slaughter knife the big man now slits the animals open very delicately from neck to groin. Steam billows out. It smells like fatty bacon, but also acrid, a bit like hot vomit. The top part of the throat is cut free and torn away, and then, with infinite care and a deftness that I had not associated with Manolo's great big hands, the entire digestive tract is slowly coaxed loose with the tip of the knife, while attention is taken not to puncture the membranes of the intestine. The anus is carved out, the bowels are securely tied, and the area is washed thoroughly.

The hog is then hung, head downward, from a beam, before the beast's sternum is cleft with an axe, opening him up good and proper. The digestive tract is now on display, a heavy mass of yellow-grey intestines that seems to occupy almost the whole of the animal's insides. I peer at the glistening mass before me and try without much success to identify the various organs within. Someone stands behind the hog and holds open its flanks, and Manolo cuts out the heart, slitting it open so that it bleeds clean (and making it more difficult to stuff) then tossing it into a bucket. A few stringy, fatty bits are torn free and slung to the farm's Alsatian dog, who sits patiently to one side wearing a gigantic grin. A very big lump of pure white fat is then yanked free of the belly and deposited in a different bucket. Apart from that, though, the innards remain substantially intact. They look like a well-plumped quilt that's been dipped in blood-speckled honey. And they are plumped up with food – undigested, semi-digested, fully digested food. A huge, slithery sack of shit. With a little heaving from the big man, the whole lot tumbles down into a fifteen-gallon bucket, where it wobbles, still steaming, then settles, a jelly monster with the life sucked suddenly from it.

The pig is among the closest relatives of the

human being, and as I stare down at the bucket it occurs to me that I am not so very different in dimensions from this porker. If you were to cut me open, I would look and smell remarkably similar to this. I am nothing but a steaming sack of shit wrapped in bacon and blubber. Know thyself, said Aristotle.

Two of the village's ladies now appear. It takes both of them to carry the bucket away between them. The shit sack is theirs. By tradition. The innards are carried to another old barn, with a great, plastic-covered table at its centre, and are deposited on the table. Half a dozen ladies immediately get to work, sorting the stuff into large intestine, small intestine, stomach bag, and separating the various organs that nestle within.

'Can I come in?' I ask, hovering at the door, because this seems to be a very womanly office. They confirm the fact – by tradition a village's women have always done this, they tell me – but I am allowed inside to watch. The stench is pretty overpowering, as they take lengths of small intestine and, with long debarked twigs, coax out the half-digested food. I realise that whereas I certainly wouldn't want to be a pig in this village, I wouldn't much want to be a woman, either. These skins will be used to make various kinds of sausages over the next few days. A pancreas is tossed toward me. One of the few parts to be thrown away, I am informed.

'Well, my cousin eats it,' says another woman.

There is some discussion of eating the pancreas. Szechuan pepper and eleven hours *sous-vide*! I manage not to say.

I look around. The barn is dark, and to the meagre light of a single overhead bulb is added the glow from a fire in the corner, crackling quietly, low down in the floor-level *lareira*. Behind it, the wall is blackened right to the ceiling. The barn is also used as a smokehouse for chorizos and other sausages, and next to the *lareira* there must be enough wood for a thousand fires, stacked neatly. Above us, dangling from the rafters, are several dozen paper packages, about the size of loaves of bread. The big lump of white belly fat that Manolo tossed into a bucket will eventually get salted, wrapped up tight, and hung here for storage. Pig lard is the staple cooking fat in Galician cooking, and lends a taste to *caldo* and many other dishes that simply cannot be achieved with anything else. You can still buy it in butchers' shops everywhere, the telltale spiral pattern of its cross section indicating that the fat has not been rendered; it is simply the whole fat layer from the animal's belly, rolled. Rural breakfasts used to consist of a chunk of bread spread with pig lard and sprinkled with salt. The more robust would chase it down with some firewater before setting out for work in the fields. Go tell that to your cardiovascular physician. He'll have a heart attack.

Having separated the small intestines from their contents, the ladies throw them into a bucket, along with the still-bulging large intestines and stomach, which have been carefully tied up at both ends in foot-long pieces (to stop their contents from spilling everywhere), and their covering of abdominal membrane peeled away. I assume these are to be thrown away. Should I say something? This must be a mistake. The precious, delicate sausage skins are going to get thrown out along with the big bulging bags of shit . . .

Esperanza now arrives. She and her cousin carry off the mysterious load, and I am invited to follow them to observe the next stage in the process. It involves stooping over a tap behind the cow stalls and washing everything in the bucket, because it will all get used for something or other: nothing at all will be thrown out. The stomach (like us, pigs only have one) is sliced open and five or six pints of curdled brown slop rush out. The bag is then scraped clean with a knife and washed pretty hard, to be used in dishes like *callos*, chickpea and tripe stew. The small intestines, which resemble miniature ladies' stockings, are filled with water several times by means of a conjurer's trick that uses the force of the running water to send them inside out then outside in again. That night I lay awake for hours thinking about it, but cannot work out how it was done.

The larger pieces of intestine are sliced into foot-long sections, and poor Esperanza, wearing rubber gloves, has the task of manually removing the tightly packed shit from them, squeezing and cajoling it out, then washing the empty skins, all to be used for sausage of one kind or another.

Esperanza is a Galician linguist, and is also director of the language college where both she and Susana work. Despite having moved to the city, she is proud of the traditions that her family maintains. I guess this depiction of her, with a length of warm bowel in her hands, is not very glamorous. But it is an important one, because cleaning the intestines is a significant job, and one which was traditionally done by the younger generation. In times past, the farm's children would clean the intestines in a nearby river or brook. Bearing in mind that this is a winter event, when daytime temperatures in Galicia's interior might well be down to freezing, it would certainly harden the little darlings up. What are your toughest memories of childhood? Not getting that second Barbie doll? I think I am finally beginning to understand the formative role of the country-side in the Galician character.

I return to the singeing-gutting barn and hang around as pig after pig gets the whole outside-inside service. More men arrive, one of whom is allowed for the sake of efficiency to cut open one or two of the pigs with his own knife. Although he is young, he clearly holds a privileged position here today. He is the next generation's Manolo.

The others busy themselves with more menial tasks, and everyone seems to know just what he can and cannot do, according to a hierarchy that

412

I don't understand. One gent, a late arriver in pristine overalls, makes a beeline for the lungs, as if he and he alone were born to the task of washing them. Perhaps he wants them for a few dozen links of *longaniza* sausage he's got planned.

Everyone, apart from Manolo, talks as the various jobs get done. There is an atmosphere of a cheery routine, which is not surprising, because the average age of the men here is well over fifty, and they've been doing the same thing every year for at least half a century.

Gradually things wind down. Six splayed pigs hang ready for butchering. I now have a dilemma, because no one has mentioned lunch. Of course, the assumption is that I'll stay. But my annoying British reserve kicks in and I need a formal invite (it doesn't have to be printed). I amble back up to the farmhouse, somewhat abashed. Awkward and embarrassed, I peep inside the intestine-cleaning barn, which is now empty of women and instead is filling up with the men, who stoke the open fire and drink white wine that one of them brought from his own barrels this morning.

There is not much light in the barn, and it is a while before I notice that one of the older men is holding a toasting fork out above the flames of the fire in the corner. My eyes betray me. Before I can say *yes, please,* a slice has been cut from an old, pre-*matanza* side of streaky bacon and is being toasted for me. The bacon came from a large wooden salting cupboard, although I don't think it'll be going back. Even now the cupboard is filling up with today's early yield: the lard bundles are already there, plus two plump kidneys, shining like polished pebbles. Over by the fire a huge circular loaf of bread is conveniently lying around, and after a minute in the flames my sizzling slice of *panceta* is wrapped inside a hunk of bread and I tuck in. The taste of the animal is powerful, pungent, and savoury; the layers of fat are transparent, the rind crispy, blackened in parts.

As I munch, others procure *panceta* for themselves, not least Manolo, who arrives and immediately puts back a good bit of bread along with his wine, and seems more animated now that the work is done. There are perhaps six or eight men warming themselves by the fire and chatting, in Galician. There is also one lady, whom I earlier saw leading a small flock of sheep home from pasture, right past the slaughter. I listen, country wine in one hand, hot pig hors d'oeuvre in the other, and watch their faces through the half-light of the fire's flames. They are, quite literally, chewing the fat, enjoying each other's company, immersed in a ritual that is as much a part of this place as the stone houses themselves. It strikes me that I am witnessing a scene from a life which has undergone little significant change since before the French Revolution, since before the Enlightenment, before industrialisation swept across broad swathes of Europe, missing Galicia entirely. I am looking at a way of life that, though geographically close to my own, I have never seen before.

And I have been invited to share something of it, just for the day, no great formalities, no endless questions. Just a bacon sandwich, a glass of wine, and a spot by the fire.

After toasted *panceta*, we wander back over to the farmhouse. Three different people, sensing that I am looking a bit lost and unsure of myself, usher me toward a large dining room. The room contains a dining table with places for everyone, around twenty of us, the kind of space you get when you turf out the animals and redecorate. I sit next to Manolo, who is down at one end with some of the other older men, the Blood-Imp, and Jaume the pig farmer. The meal that follows a pig kill is just as important as the kill itself, and when Galicians do a celebratory lunch, there are no half measures. For weeks now people in Coruña have been asking me whether I'm going to stay for lunch after the *matanza*. They really eat in the villages, people say, with admiration, as if country folk are human ruminants with several extra stomachs. Well, I reply, I like to think of myself as something of an eater too. Lunch in the village holds no fear for me.

We begin with *empanadas*, flat, circular pasties. There are three varieties: cockle, of which I eat a small piece out of good manners, cockle pasty not being my favourite; mushroom, which I eat out of curiosity (it is superb); and minced veal and onion, which I eat two big slices of out of gluttony. I saw the veal *empanada* when it arrived,

415

about half an hour ago. They almost had to take the door off to get it into the house, and it was without doubt the biggest pie I had ever seen, perhaps three feet in diameter.

It is glorious. To my right is Jaume, and I now explain to him my theory about Galician *empanada*, that it gets progressively better as you head southward and eastward. According to this theory, in my hometown of Coruña (northwest), the pasty ought to be pretty bad; and the sad truth is that in Coruña I have never tasted *empanada* anywhere near as good as the one we are now eating. We are only in the centre of Galicia, though, and this doesn't add much weight to my theory.

Jaume nods and says I might have a point, although he doesn't sound convinced. I take yet another slice, a two-hander. And only now do I realise how modest everyone else's pasty eating is. Grown men are actually passing up a second piece. To my left Manolo is positively sparrow-like, nibbling at a bit of crust. I've done it again, stocked up too well on the first course. So be it. I am a fool. Put it on my gravestone.

After the *empanada* come piles of boiled greens, potatoes, and carrots. We charge our plates and await the platters of cold pork that follow: *lacón*, ear, some carved hock, I think. Traditionally, you might well be eating the fresh cuts and offal of the newly slaughtered animals at this point. But today they've cooked some pork in advance. It makes things a little less congested in the kitchen.

We tuck in. What we are eating is, in essence, a kind of time-delayed *cocido*. Just as soon as there is any room on people's plates, several serving dishes of boiled veal make their entry. Veal always adds a refined note to a *cocido*. It is softer textured, and you can use it to balance the saltiness of the *lacón*. Again we set to. Bowls of chickpeas and chorizos then make an appearance. The chorizos are homemade, less fatty than bought ones, packed tight and a deep red colour. I taste the chorizos and wince with delight.

The pork platters make repeated trips among us, along with more greens, more veal, more chickpeas and chorizo. Then they are left in the middle for anyone considering fourths or fifths. There are plastic lemonade bottles containing local white wine, and jugs of a red too. Esperanza's family, meanwhile, fuss around us as if we were royalty. There is beer for those who want it and even a pitcher of water, which one of the younger men across from me helps himself to, earning a certain amount of derision from down at our end of the table: you shouldn't really plan to be driving anywhere after a *matanza*. On we go. More greens, more pork. More wine. The men's voices are booming, as the stories get wilder, the conversation more animated.

By the time we are finishing off the pork and greens I am feeling pretty pleased with myself. I erred with the pasties, perhaps, but I have been well in control of the pork. As if to congratulate myself I drain my glass of white and take a small amount of red, which packs a bit of a punch, and I need to mix it with lemonade. Sipping my Galician *sangría*, I survey the table and congratulate myself. I have done well. My torso is not straining too much. I am satisfied. What arrives next is, then, a little disconcerting: the main course. Ominously deep dishes of fried potatoes begin to circulate among us, and a large quantity of roast veal is carried in. There are big bowls of salad too.

The roast veal is, I suppose, just for variation. Everyone fills their plate again, and I take a sizeable chunk, simply because it looks so good. It is, though, madness; technically I'm full. I carve small slices and pop each one between my slow-moving jaws with a growing fear that I might not actually be capable of swallowing. The salad offers something in the way of light relief, but I have a long way to go. The red wine is not helping. I add more lemonade. Then a platter of fried whole capsicums is passed around. I decline. Jaume, to my right, looks puzzled. Don't you like them? he asks, taking one for himself and passing them on.

I have struck lucky with Jaume. He is not Galician but from Catalonia, right on the other side of the Iberian Peninsula. He moved here when he married Esperanza's cousin. Having come to one of the most rural parts of Galicia, and having also built his own pig farm, he offers an interesting perspective on life. He's here to help, to join the celebration; throughout the day he has also helped me to understand things, sensing perhaps the natural reticence of a fellow outsider, and supplying me with just the kind of explanations that I need.

But Jaume is not an outsider, exactly. In terms of pig farming he is the very future of rural Galicia. He has a thousand piglets in an automated farm that he runs on his own, with only a computer for company. I ask him whether the old men to my left – Manolo and his cronies, now wolfing down their veal – are the last generation that will bother with the *matanza*. Possibly, he says, or perhaps the penultimate, indicating the other end of the table, where a handful of men in their thirties are now rolling up their sleeves and getting to grips with bottles of whisky and firewater. Among them is the young guy who assisted in cutting open the hogs. He will take over from Manolo one day, but will there be any house pigs for him to kill?

The younger men might carry on for another generation. But, as part of a way of life, I think it will come to an end. The process is, let's face it, an awful lot of work, and for how long are women going to be willing to clean a pig's intestines? Because I can't see the men taking over that particular job. It's not really an issue about food production, either. 'Slow food', the Europe-wide movement that promotes small-scale, artisanal forms of regional food production, tends to focus

419

on maintaining or resurrecting production techniques and celebrating the culture that underlies them. Pablo Valledor's Celtic pig program in Fonsagrada is a 'slow food' project in this sense. A *matanza*, though, is about the whole village, the extended network of a rural society that comes together at these key times of the year, but that exists the rest of the year as well. When that disappears, the basis for a whole tradition is lost.

Around the table today are two kinds of people. First, those for whom the pig slaughter is simply part of life, something they have known since childhood and that has never changed. Second are people such as Esperanza, those who grew up in this deeply rural environment, but who now hold down jobs in towns and cities, and whose relationship with the land is one of deep respect, and possibly nostalgia, but who are not bound to its daily rhythms, and whose lives no longer turn inextricably with the seasons. Many of those here today live away, and have come back for the *matanza*. When the next generation comes back, there'll be hardly anyone here.

There is a pause. Plates are taken away. Cheese and *membrillo* (quince preserve) appear, and I take what must be the smallest sliver of both that a knife has ever cut. Then come slabs of rich, dark brown chocolate cake. The cake catches me off guard, just as the food inside me is beginning to settle. I take a piece. It is robust but not heavy, just like it ought to be. I have a second

420

slice, followed by a piece of pineapple cake, when that makes the rounds. Esperanza is the expert cake maker (which makes her almost a goddess in these parts), and when she comes around with more cake, cajoling me toward another piece, I accept. After the cakes, large trays with puff-pastry fancies, small cream cakes, and assorted biscuits fresh from the local baker's shop are produced. I don't have any.

As coffee is being served, the gents at our end of the table begin to take a close interest in the issue of cleanliness. They use paper napkins to wipe every last crumb and fleck of food from the table. Bottles of firewater, whisky, and brandy now multiply around us, and a pack of cards appears. This is when the fun really starts. Perhaps they'll still be here when it's time to eat again. Perhaps they'll be here all evening, to stagger home late into the night, stuffed to the gills, the killing over for another year. I don't know. I have to drive back to Coruña. There's tomato and endive salad for dinner.

Before that, however, I have an appointment with the future.

Jaume's pig farm is up the hillside, overlooking a broad green valley spotted with farm build-ings. The only sound is the occasional clucking of the dozen or so hens from his menagerie, which comprises a duck, some rabbits, and the hens, a hobby that keeps him occupied up here when there's nothing else to do apart from babysit a thousand machine-fed piglets. In front of us are two long concrete sheds housing all the hogs, which he buys from breeders at a month old and fattens up for three more until they are sold for slaughter at four or five. Pigs, as I've mentioned before, are tremendous converters of energy, and before they reach half a year old they are ready for the chop, since these days the consumer demands very young pork. What Jaume does is make sure they get just the right food for maximum bulk. Or, more accurately, he makes sure the computer-controlled feed and temperature systems are working properly. Because our good friend the pig is a very low-maintenance animal, especially if you rear him in highly controlled conditions.

We take a look inside one of the sheds. About fifteen animals scamper about in each pen, flipping their rear ends in the air and snapping at each other's ears. They are normal white-leg pigs, destined for the industrial pork market. They look chirpy enough. Are these, then, the future of Galician pork? Within a generation, perhaps, the closest a Galician will get to a traditional pig slaughter is when they peel open a plastic packet of bacon and drop a couple of slices into the frying pan. It's already happening. When I was planning this book, I talked to a lot of people who remembered attending pig kills in the villages where they grew up, people my own age and even a little younger. But most of them told me that the *matanzas* had now stopped. With it, I guess, the blood pancakes also stop, and the homemade chorizos, the parcels of lard wrapped in paper, the toasted *panceta*. Then the women in blue aprons, the blood-imps, the knife-wielding slaughtermen . . . Not long after that people from the cities will buy up the old farms, install broadband, and use them as weekend homes.

We leave the computer-fattened pigs and make our way to the menagerie. Jaume offers me a rabbit. After a year spent in the company of pork, the thought of that white, lean, tender meat is almost comforting. Unfortunately, the bunny is still alive. It is white and fluffy. It is probably called Pepe.

I decline. I'm done.

ENDPIECE

The three of us are having lunch in a restaurant a couple of blocks from our apartment. It serves traditional Galician food, nothing fancy. For years we avoided it because the menu looked boring. Then, one day, we gave it a try, and now we go as often as we can.

It's the kind of place where well-to-do pensioners turn up for lunch, ambling in at their usual time without booking and sitting at the same table. Quiet, modest, and with a homemade *empanada* that really does taste as if it's from the extreme southeast of Galicia.

Christmas is approaching, and we can reflect on what has been a busy year. Nico is now chattering nonstop in both English and Spanish, and has developed a healthy enthusiasm for ham, although he does prefer broccoli. For my part, I've just finished writing up the last chapter of this book. It's been an interesting twelve months, and I'm glad I did it now, because in a couple of years Nico will be off to school. *What does your dad do for a living?* his schoolmates will ask. *He eats pig.* It just wouldn't be fair to the kid.

'Well?' asks Susana, as the drinks arrive. 'Have you managed it?'

Over the course of a year, the challenge of eating every bit of the pig sometimes seemed to take a backseat to the sheer pleasure of seeing so much of Galicia. Only now can I reflect on just how much has been eaten. Everything but the squeal? Perhaps not, but that little pig diagram in my notebook is covered in scribbles and shading. I ate until I could eat no more, from sausage festivals, ant-throwing bacchanals, pork stew bonanzas, to hippie communes. I found paradise in Negueira, and in Coruña I retraced the tapas-guzzling steps of my wife's adolescence. I visited some pretty amazing buildings, from Iron Age *pallozas* to country houses unchanged in two centuries, discussed vomit with a president, met Fidel Castro's favourite cousin, and watched a saintly pig called Antón as he slept. Finally, I had *panceta* grilled on an open fire after six of the amazing creatures I've been on the trail of all year were put to death with nothing more than a knife.

Yet through all this, what has struck me most is the kind, reserved nature of Galicians themselves, the people whom I met in remote villages and hamlets everywhere, calling on them unannounced and (probably) unwanted. People who invited me in, and listened patiently to my garbled explanations of why I was there. They no doubt thought I was a little mad. But I was seldom turned away. Many of them gave me food.

425

And there is no finer act of human kindness than that, wherever in the world you are.

So, I can now return to normal things. Today, as if to make the point, we have fried baby mackerel, followed by red bream, done in the oven and accompanied with large, waxy boiled potatoes drizzled with olive oil. Then a cider-baked apple.

Without doubt, this is my favourite restaurant in the world. If one can truly know happiness, then for me it is here, with these two people. And when Susana and I retire, this is where we'll have lunch, if it's still here, if it's still the same. In a quarter of a century, though, how much of Galicia will be the same?

This little-known corner of 'green Spain' has resisted change pretty well, especially the food. But there's an Indian restaurant now, Turkish kebabs, Chinese, Japanese, Macs, Subways, B-Kings. Yet something tells me that boiled pork shoulder ham and *grelos* are not going out of fashion here anytime soon, and that in a generation's time butcher shop windows will still be festooned with strings of dark red chorizos and the occasional dried pig face sporting comedy spectacles.

As the mackerel arrive, I glance again at the menu. 'I think I'll change my order,' I say. 'They've got fillet steak. By the way, I've got an idea for a new book.' 'Oh yes?' Susana says, her face blanching just a touch. 'Well, you know how much I like oxtail?'

¡Salud!

ACKNOWLEDGEMENTS

For information, advice, and ribs, thank you to: John McGlone, Olga Salazar, Ramón Cava, Paul Preston, and my mother-in-law's chiropodist; Florentino Varela, Fuco Peréz, Don Pepe of Casa Casao, Carmen and Manolo at the Piornedo Hotel, and the amazing Pepe Solla; Manuel Maldonado, *jamonero* extraordinaire, the enchanting Doña Marisol of Doiras, and Don José of Casa Meleiro, Láncara.

Special thanks to those eminent Galicians I had the privilege of meeting: Doña Victoria López Castro, Don Manuel Fraga Iribarne, and Antón of Espasante, although in fact he was an idle pig, and in any case he's dead now. Regards to the entire village of Laza, including the ants, to the two Mari Carmens in Cerdedo (thanks for the bladders!), and to Manolo and his fabulous pressed pig head in Ourense; to Sisa and Mari Carmen, the globe-trotting not-widows of Coruña, and to the tailor of O Viñedo.

An especially large dose of gratitude to Pablo Valledor for all his help along the way; to Atilano and Candido Fernandez for their generous welcome that morning in Monteseiro, and to José Rancaño Fernández and family for their equally warm hospitality. Best wishes to Speed, Neka, Guillermiña and the others up in Vilar and beyond, to Joselín at Three Mountains, and to Aurora, José, Monica, and Felix in Santalla; to Esperanza, Jauma, Manolo, and everyone at the *matanza*, thank you for inviting me to your yearly bloodbath.

Thanks to Liz Darhansoff and Michele Mortimer for patience and constant feedback, and to Courtney Hodell for being in charge and making the book such fun to edit. *Graciñas* to Mercedes Rey for all the *estofados*, and to Antonio Zas for all the chess, most of which he won. Thanks to Merce for occasionally asking me which films I've seen, and to María and Paco for being María and Paco. For encouragement, ideas, proofreading, plus many shades of wisdom and understanding, thank you very much indeed, Ramón Varela.

Finally, all love to Susana. It's over now. Let us eat veg together.